Libya since 1969

Libya since 1969
Qadhafi's Revolution Revisited

Edited by Dirk Vandewalle

palgrave
macmillan

LIBYA SINCE 1969

First published in hardcover in 2008 by PALGRAVE MACMILLAN® in the United States—a division of St. Martin's Press LLC, 175 Fifth Avenue, New York, NY 10010.

Where this book is distributed in the UK, Europe and the rest of the world, this is by Palgrave Macmillan, a division of Macmillan Publishers Limited, registered in England, company number 785998, of Houndmills, Basingstoke, Hampshire RG21 6XS.

Palgrave Macmillan is the global academic imprint of the above companies and has companies and representatives throughout the world.

Palgrave® and Macmillan® are registered trademarks in the United States, the United Kingdom, Europe and other countries.

ISBN: 978-0-230-33750-3

Library of Congress Cataloging-in-Publication Data is available from the Library of Congress.

A catalogue record of the book is available from the British Library.

Design by Scribe, Inc.

First PALGRAVE MACMILLAN paperback edition: November 2011

10 9 8 7 6 5 4 3 2 1

Printed in the United States of America.

Contents

About the Authors

Dirk Vandewalle, editor of the book, is Associate Professor of Government at Dartmouth College. He is the author of *A History of Modern Libya* (Cambridge University Press, 2006), and *Libya Since Independence: Oil and State-Building* (Ithaca: Cornell University Press, 1998), and editor of *Libya 1969–1994* (St. Martin's Press, 1995) and *North Africa: Development and Reform in a Changing Global Economy* (St. Martin's Press, 1996). In addition, he has written extensively on North Africa and, currently, on the Arab Gulf States. He has been the recipient of two Fulbright research awards, most recently for research in the Gulf Cooperation Countries (2005–6).

John P. Entelis is Professor of Government and Director of the Middle East Studies Program at Fordham University. He has been awarded several Fulbright fellowships, including a U.S. Department of Education Fulbright-Hays Doctoral Dissertation Abroad Fellowship to conduct research in Lebanon (1968–69), a Senior Fulbright Professorship at the University of Algiers in 1977–78 and at the University of Tunis in 1985, and a Fulbright Regional Research Award to Morocco, Algeria, and Tunisia in 1989. He has directed three National Endowment for the Humanities summer institutes and seminars. He is the author and co-author of numerous scholarly publications on the comparative and international politics of the Middle East and North Africa, and has written numerous book chapters, articles, and book reviews that have appeared in the leading scholarly journals in the field of political science, international relations, Middle Eastern affairs, and North African studies. He is the editor-in-chief of the *Journal of North African Studies* and Secretary of the American Institute for Maghrib Studies (AIMS).

Ronald Bruce St John served on the International Advisory Board of *The Journal of Libyan Studies* and The Atlantic Council Working Group on Libya. His publications on Libya include *The Historical Dictionary of Libya* (Lanham, MD: Scarecrow Press, 2006, 1998, 1991), *Libya and the United States: Two Centuries of Strife* (Philadelphia: University of Pennsylvania Press, 2002), and *Qadhafi's World Design: Libyan Foreign Policy, 1969–1987* (London: Saqi Books, 1987). He authored essays on Libya in the most recent editions of the *Encyclopedia of the Modern World* (New York: Oxford University Press, 2008), *Biographical Encyclopedia of the Modern Middle East* (Farmington Hills, MI: Thomson Gale, 2007), *Africa Contemporary Record* (New York: Holmes & Meier, 2006, 2004), *Worldmark Encyclopedia of Religious Practices* (Farmington Hills, MI: Thomson Gale, 2004), and *Encyclopedia of the Modern Middle East and North Africa* (New York: Macmillan Reference, 2004).

Amal S. M. Obeidi is Assistant Professor of Comparative Politics in the Department of Political Science, Faculty of Economics, University of Garyounis-Benghazi-Libya. In 1997, she obtained a PhD in Middle Eastern Politics from the University of Durham, United Kingdom. For two years, she served as Dean of Faculty of Economics at the University of Garyounis, Libya. She was recently awarded a Chevening Fellowship on Participation of Women at University College in London. Her publications include *Political Culture in Libya*; *Identity in Libya*; *Libyan Security Policy Between Existence and Feasibility: An Exploratory Study*; *Political Socialisation of Arab Women*; *The Development of Women's Movement in Libyan Society Between Empowerment and Activation: A Documentation Study*. She specializes in gender issues, public policies, human rights, civil society, and security issues.

Alison Pargeter is a Research Fellow at Kings College, London. She has been conducting research on North Africa for several years, with a particular focus on Libya. She has undertaken numerous research projects on Libya that included extensive fieldwork in Tripoli and Benghazi. Her other main research focus is on issues related to political Islam and Islamic radicalism, especially among migrant communities in Europe. In this respect, she has conducted major research projects on North African immigrants and political violence, and on the role of the Muslim Brotherhood in Europe and the Middle East.

Jon B. Alterman is a Senior Fellow and Director of the Middle East Program at the Center for Strategic and International Studies in Washington, D.C. Prior to joining CSIS, he served as a member of the Policy Planning Staff at the U.S. Department of State, and as a special assistant to the assistant secretary of state for Near Eastern affairs. Before entering government, he was a scholar at the U.S. Institute of Peace and at the Washington Institute for Near East Policy. From 1993 to 1997, Alterman was an award-winning teacher at Harvard University, where he received his PhD in history. He is a former international affairs fellow at the Council on Foreign Relations.

Hanspeter Mattes is currently the Deputy Director of the German Institute for Middle East Studies in Hamburg, Germany. After completing his dissertation—"The Political Development In Revolutionary Libya"—at the University of Heidelberg in 1982, he became a research fellow at the German Institute for Middle East Studies, responsible for the Maghreb countries. He has been in charge of several research projects focusing on political and socioeconomic developments in the Maghreb countries, with a special focus on Libya. In addition, he has been a consultant on North Africa and Libya for several German ministries, including the German Ministry of Defense. He normally spends up to two months each year in North Africa and Libya.

Ethan D. Chorin is Foreign Service Officer within the United States Department of State. He served as the country's first Commercial and Economic Attache to Libya since 1980. While stationed in Tripoli, he completed the Department of Commerce/Department of State Commercial Guide to Libya. In addition, he is the editor and translator of a volume of Libyan short stories that will be published by Saqi/SOAS in London.

George Joffé is formerly the Deputy Director of the *Royal Institute of International Affairs* (Chatham House) in London, and is now attached to London and Cambridge universities. He is currently engaged in academic activities, independent consultancy, and journalism. His journalistic activities have included both print journalism and radio and television work on Middle Eastern and North African topics for the past twenty years. As a consultant, he deals with the political, economic, and social affairs of the Middle East and North Africa, with special reference to Morocco, Algeria, Libya, Israel-Palestine, and Iraq. He has written widely on topics connected with the contemporary history, economics, society, and current affairs of the Middle East and North Africa, and is currently engaged in writing a study of the contemporary crisis in Algeria and a book on the Qadhafi regime in Libya. He lectures at London University's *Kings College*, where he is a visiting professor in the Department of Geography. He has been a visiting fellow at the *Centre for International Studies* in the *Department of International Relations* at the London School of Economics and Political Science, and is currently a research fellow and affiliated lecturer at the *Centre for International Studies* at Cambridge University, where he teaches the Middle East option on the MPhil course.

Foreword

Jon B. Alterman

Secrets are different from mysteries. Secrets are knowable. Mysteries stubbornly defy explanation, even when all that can be known about them has been discovered.

For much of the last forty years, outsiders have treated Libya as a mystery. To most observers, Libyans' actions have seemed utterly unpredictable and have defied conventional explanation. The government in particular, under the leadership of Moammar Qadhafi has veered between conflict and cooperation, and its statements have ranged from bitter vituperation to cloying sycophancy.

Libya's "rehabilitation" in the early years of this century, following its admission of responsibility for assorted bombings in the 1980s, its payment of compensation for those bombings, and the dismantlement of its covert weapons programs, has not wholly ended the Libyan mysteries. In November 2007, Libya suddenly decreed that tourists lacking certified Arabic translations of their passports could not enter the country and turned away a cruise ship with more than one thousand tourists who had been given no time to prepare. In September 2009, Gaddafi's speech to the United Nations was six times longer than his allotted 15 minutes. In it, he suggested that the U.N. Security Council should be renamed the "Terror Council" and appeared to tear up the U.N. charter while at the podium. Businessmen who have sought to work in Libya talk of the unpredictable work of securing visas and clearing shipments through customs. A luxury hotel recently under construction in Tripoli advertised no completion date because there were simply too many variables beyond the hotel's control.

For the last forty years, Libya's mysteries have overwhelmed its secrets. Few outsiders have had much sustained interaction with Libya and those who have done so have engaged only with a small slice of Libyan society.

Oil and gas trade sustained the country, but it also enabled millions of Libyans to survive off the foreign exchange that only a tiny number of Libyans helped generate. For most Libyans, and for most foreigners seeking contact with Libyans, the avenues for contact were small.

Libya was not, however, completely cut off. Especially in the last decade, the increasing availability of satellite television and other information sources gave Libyans exposure to the world beyond their borders. Libyan expatriates could communicate more easily with their countrymen, giving Libyans a clearer view of the world outside, and the outside world a clearer view of what was happening in Libya. Over time, it became harder for Libya to maintain some of its uniqueness, and when governments in neighboring Tunisia and Egypt collapsed early in 2011, many of Libya's people went to the streets.

It is tempting to see the Arab uprisings of 2011 as a single wave, crashing against the rocks of more than four decades of rigid authoritarianism. Yet the movements in each country have different causes, and the conditions in each country are dramatically different.

There is no country quite as different as Libya, in part because of the idiosyncratic legacies of more than forty years of Moammar Qadhafi's rule, and in part because Libya's isolation protected Libyans from some of the homogenizing effects of greater Arab integration in recent decades. Whereas tourism and investment brought together Gulf Arabs, Levantines, and North Africans time and time again, Libya remained stubbornly apart.

This volume is especially valuable, then, because it provides unparalleled insight into the context in which Libyan change will take place. Political Islam in Libya has its own contours and history in Libya. They are analyzed here, if few other places. The governmental system in Libya created committees upon committees—so much representation, in fact, that the system was merely a cover for despotism. When newspapers report that anti-Qadhafi rebels in eastern Libya have created committees to undertake the work of building the state, the reader of this book will understand the legacy of such committees and will be able to assess their prospects. Libya has its mysteries, to be sure, but there are simple secrets Libya's four decade–long isolation from the world helped engender. The volume here helps uncover those secrets, through the labors of brave and indefatigable academics who have pursued work in Libya over recent decades despite the difficulties inherent in it.

This volume, therefore, is not merely of historical interest. It uncovers the secrets of a country that is poorly understood and gives the reader unparalleled insight into where Libyan society has been and where it is likely to go in the coming years. At the same time, this book is no guide to

Libya's future. It is hard to imagine that Libya's future won't be very different from its recent past. It is equally hard to imagine that the weight of Libya's recent past will hang over the country for decades to come.

Mysteries remain, to be sure, but underneath all the mythologies and stubborn contradictions are people struggling to make sense of their lives. This book helps us understand how they have done that and how they may try to do so in the future.

Jon B. Alterman
May 2011

Introduction

Dirk Vandewalle

The uprising against the Qadhafi regime in February 2011 came in the wake of similar revolts in neighboring Tunisia and Algeria. Although few observers expected the rebels in the eastern part of the country capable of withstanding a sustained assault by the Qadhafi loyalists, the conflict soon turned into a war of attrition and, eventually, into a drawn-out civil war. Sustained by United Nations Security Resolution 1973 and supported by NATO forces that implemented a no-fly zone over the country, the rebels' Transitional National Council slowly—despite great logistical difficulties—extended its reach westward. While much was written about Qadhafi and Libya as the civil war unfolded, many of the aspects that have fueled the Libyan revolution since 1969 remain to a large extent terra incognita to most outsiders.

The civil war in Libya came almost a decade after the country had declared its Weapons of Mass Destruction in December 2003. Since that time, the regime had engaged in a process of reintegration into the international community and had made attempts to reform the country's economy. As several of the contributors to this volume have argued in their previous publications, history left a heavy legacy on the three provinces of Cyrenaica, Tripolitania, and Fazzan that became incorporated into the kingdom of Libya in 1951—a legacy that will undoubtedly come to haunt the successors of Colonel Qadhafi. From Ottoman backwater to Italian colony (1911–43), and from a conservative monarchy (1951–69) to a revolutionary military regime, Libyan citizens stood passively on the sidelines throughout history as foreign and local rulers and interests shaped their country. Certainly the discovery of oil has constituted the most important of those interests. It allowed both the monarchy and the Qadhafi regime after 1969 to avoid constructing many of the institutions of a modern state—keeping the administrative and regulatory capacity of the central government minimal while granting few political opportunities for local citizens to participate in building or governing their country. It is no exaggeration to state that even today, after more than half a century of independence, the notion of citizenship remains problematic to many Libyans: for despite his rhetoric to the contrary, their current ruler continues to view them more or less as his personal subjects, and he has done much to undermine confidence in the more impersonal institutions of a modern state. Indeed, to that extent, the Qadhafi regime shows a remarkable continuity with the monarchy that preceded it and has created a political system that will face considerable challenges in the future.

It is these two overarching themes—the shadow of the past and the shadow of the future—that provide the two bookend chapters to this volume. In the first chapter, the editor analyzes the political and economic goals and achievements of Libya's military regime from 1969 until 2003 when the country agreed to give up its Weapons of Mass Destruction. The first level of analysis looks at the persistent antagonism the Qadhafi regime has displayed toward the West since 1969, and delineates how this continuously fostered sense of antagonism has provided the regime with a level of legitimacy that only lost its coherence in the late 1990s. The second focus of the chapter is the impact that oil revenues have had within Libya, enabling the Qadhafi government to pursue highly idiosyncratic development plans—across the decades since 1969—that showed little regard for the country's real development needs. Some of these economic directives included, at one point, the nationalization of virtually all property and of all economic activity, including the country's retail sector. This willingness to sacrifice the chance at real development for the sake of ideological and political goals was legitimated in Qadhafi's *Green Book*, and the editor includes an analysis of the Libyan leader's philosophy to help explain the origin, the radicalism, and the extent of his political and economic experiments during the country's revolutionary phase.

As the first chapter makes clear, the use of anti-Westernism and of a highly charged symbolic rhetoric has, as in all self-proclaimed revolutionary regimes, been part and parcel of Qadhafi's Libya since 1969. It has provided a *leitmotiv* that many of the regime's neighbors, as well as the international community, have found difficult to understand or come to terms with. This was perhaps not so surprising, for in several important ways, the regime's rhetoric obscured the true nature of Libya's political system as it developed after 1969. One of the reasons is that Libya deliberately closed itself off during much of its revolutionary phase that lasted throughout the 1970s and the first half of the 1980s. Most accounts of the country, therefore, even by academics, were written from afar, often relying on secondary sources and on the more often than not contradictory statements made by Qadhafi himself.

But there was a second, perhaps more important, reason for the use of rhetoric: the fact that since the early 1970s there has been a firmly entrenched bifurcation between the revolutionary pretensions of the regime and the reality of the country's economic and political life. In Chapter 2, Hanspeter Mattes dissects this duality—what is referred to throughout this book as the formal versus the informal mechanisms of ruling. If the official expression of popular democracy in the *jamahiriyya* consists of the Popular Congress and the Popular Committee system, Mattes inquires, what do the real decision-making structures in Libya look like, and who have traditionally been the main decision-makers surrounding the leadership? Following from his analysis that focuses on individuals and structures of governing that most casual observers of Libya are, until today, largely unaware of, the author draws some conclusions that shed light on what a possible succession in Libya might look like when viewed from the formal versus informal power dichotomy inside the country.

In her chapter (Chapter 4), Amal Obeidi extends Mattes's analysis, and provides the first insider account of political elite formation in Libya since the 1969 revolution. Showing how the regime has carefully nurtured individuals or groups that can temporarily defend and project the interests of the country's top leadership—a group she refers to as a "temporary elite"—Obeidi's chapter emphasizes the fluidity and constant management of elites that has taken place in Libya since 1969. The chapter also provides more evidence that, even in highly authoritarian, seemingly immobile regimes like the *jamahiriyya*, the constant management of coalitions is a *sine qua non* for the survival of its leadership. In the process, the regime became increasingly narrow in structure, more hierarchical, and relied more and more on military and security personnel linked to Qadhafi's own tribe.

The progressive political narrowing of the Libyan regime was only one indication of the larger depoliticization Libya experienced since 1969. The *Green Book*, Qadhafi's ideological primer to his self-styled revolution, asserts that the country's citizens directly manage its political and economic life, but Libya, as the first few chapters reiterate, remains an exclusionary political system whose decision-making process has been restricted to a small cadre of advisors and confidantes, and where political decisions are similarly outside popular purview or devoid of any means of checks and balances. Similarly, and despite the regime's rhetoric that all power in the *jamahiriyya* belongs to the people, organized opposition has been expressly forbidden. Indeed, Qadhafi has often asked, rhetorically, if all power belongs to the people how can there be opposition outside the Popular Congress and Popular Committee system that represents all people? Clearly, however, not all Libyans were convinced by the regime's attempts at popular inclusiveness. For despite the often-draconian measures the regime adopted in the 1970s and 1980s to stifle dissent, one set of groups, centering their opposition on Islam, has repeatedly targeted the regime. Nevertheless, Islamic opposition seems to have played a relatively minor role in Libya's political life since 1969. Why this is so, and how the regime was capable of neutralizing it during the 1980s and 1990s are questions that have never been answered in a satisfactory manner. Pargeter, in her chapter (Chapter 3), focuses precisely on the fate of political Islam in Libya, and delineates the tactics the regime adopted to deal with what it considered an implacable enemy of the revolution. Often portraying the country's Islamist opposition as "stray dogs," and nothing but lackeys of the United States intent on overthrowing the regime, Qadhafi managed to contain its threat. Furthermore, the 9/11 attacks and the growing rapprochement with the West afforded the regime a chance to portray its internal struggle against *jihadism* as part and parcel of a wider war on terror. As Pargeter argues, however, this does not mean that the regime can simply ignore potential opposition based on Islamic sentiment. A regime whose basis of legitimacy has always been narrow needs to remain vigilant against any organized Islamist sentiment at home, even if it supports Islamist initiatives in its current sub-Saharan policies.

The contradictions that Mattes, Obeidi, and Pargeter observe between Qadhafi's rhetoric and the practice of politics inside the *jamahiriyya* are not limited, however, to Libya's internal politics. In their chapters, John Entelis (Chapter 7) and George Joffé (Chapter 8) show how the contradictions of the regime extend to its regional and international policies as well. From the start of the revolution in 1969 until his conversion to pan-African unity in the 1990s, Qadhafi claimed to represent the future of pan-Arabism and Arab nationalism in the Middle East. Yet, Libya remained forever too inconsequential a player on the regional political scene to pursue and implement such ambitions, and the Libyan leader's exhortations for Arab unity were routinely dismissed with derision and scorn in the Arab world and the West alike. Perhaps nowhere, as Entelis argues, have Libya's political presence and tactics been as pernicious since 1969 as in its relations with fellow Maghribi countries. Attempting to cloak himself in Gamal Abdul Nasser's mantle of Arab nationalism in the wake of the Egyptian president's death in 1970, Qadhafi had little time for smaller, North African initiatives that aimed at increasing political and economic unity within the Maghreb. By ignoring his neighbors' calls for greater integration—symbolized by the signing of the Arab Maghreb Union in 1989—Qadhafi effectively halted any progress toward greater cooperation with Tunisia, Algeria, and Morocco.

In his chapter, George Joffé turns his attention to the larger constraints of Libya's foreign policy, providing not only an overview of the regime's international orientation, but also questioning whether Libya's foreign policy, in the wake of its recent reintegration into the international community, will result in a more pragmatic pursuit of the country's interests? As Joffé demonstrates, Libyan foreign policy, mirroring internal political directives, remains a highly personalized affair. Arguing that Libyan foreign policy has traditionally been a mixture of ideological radicalism and different forms of pragmatism, he analyzes how Libya's rapprochement with the West has changed this mixture in favor of pragmatism—and wonders whether it represents a real conversion to pragmatism or just another form of the kind of "opportunist pragmatism" the regime has so skillfully employed in the past?

Chapters 5 and 6 then turn toward aspects of the Libyan economy. Clearly, oil revenues in Libya after 1969 created the permissive environment that allowed the Qadhafi regime to engage in its idiosyncratic mixture of internal and external political, economic, and ideological experiments that left the country isolated and exhausted by the mid-1990s. Badly needing both international investments to reinvigorate an ageing oil infrastructure and greater oil production, the regime was hemmed in by a set of United States and United Nations sanctions that proved economically and politically costly at home. The lifting of the sanctions and the reintegration of Libya into the international economy, as well as the reestablishment of diplomatic relations with the United States, provided Libya with a chance to capitalize, once more, on its abundant oil and natural gas riches. After two sets of stillborn attempts at economic liberalization in 1987 and 1991, however, observers wondered whether this latest wave of reform would finally lead to an economy liberated from the tight strictures imposed by the Qadhafi regime for essentially ideological reasons. In Chapter 5, Ronald Bruce St John focuses on the current wave of reforms, taking into consideration some of these legacies of the past. Distinguishing between efforts in the oil and non-oil sectors, he carefully analyzes the prospects for real reform across the different sectors of Libya's economy, drawing on a wide range of current and previously published materials. After almost four decades of intense state intervention in the Libyan economy—most often for reasons of patronage linked to regime survival—the most pertinent question about Libya's current reforms focuses on whether or not the country's oil economy is institutionally prepared for the dramatic changes real economic liberalization would entail—and whether the country's political system can be changed sufficiently to make the technical, institutional requirements of change possible.

For better or worse, and despite the rocky relations between the two countries since the 1970s, both Libya and the United States have always considered themselves as special partners in development. The expansion and growth of the Libyan oil industry was, in large part, tied to the presence of U.S. companies whose removal during the period of sanctions put a temporary halt to the special relationship many Libyan policymakers waxed about nostalgically as Libya became increasingly isolated in the 1980s and 1990s. Ethan Chorin (Chapter 6) describes this perception of exceptionality, and speculates on how some aspects of the previous special relationship may be resurrected as Libya's new wave of reforms is being implemented. He points out that the obstacles to economic liberalization and to reestablishing commercial relations with the United States could yet provide major stumbling blocks for the larger diplomatic, political, and economic relations between the two countries by pinpointing the different sensibilities and vulnerabilities each side has as they engage each other once more. So far Chorin's judgment seems supported by the cooling of relations, and the persistence of a lingering unease in Washington since the reestablishment of diplomatic relations.

What does all of this future, particularly in the aftermath of the still ongoing civil war? In the final substantive chapter (Chapter 9), the editor summarizes the often contradictory tendencies of the regime illuminated in the different chapters, and turns his analysis toward three major questions: What explained Qadhafi's decision to seek a reconciliation with the West? Was this attempt at reconciliation simply another unilateral decision by the Libyan leader—desperate to escape the country's diplomatic isolation and its increasingly unbearable economic hardships—or do the events of December 2003 indicate a changing pattern of governance in Libya that is bringing new elites to the fore, including the Libyan leader's own son? Looking at the period between December 2003 and the spring of 2011, the editor argues that Libya's attempts at economic reform were eventually jeopardized by the country's "revolutionary sector." By 2011, the country had managed to become once more an attractive place for international investment, and some measures of greater economic efficiency had been put into place. But what was ultimately needed to truly change the country's economy—political reform—remained off-limits. It is perhaps ironic that systematic economic reforms could at least in part have blunted the uprising that took place starting in February 17, 2011.

For all the attention that has been lavished on Libya and its leader since 1969, many aspects of the country's internal mechanisms of control, of the precise meaning and functioning of its political system, and of the bifurcation between formal and informal means of rule have not been clearly understood. It is, perhaps, not surprising that the actions of the country's leader often seemed illogical and irrational—authoritarian oil exporters have an extraordinary leeway in pursuing often ill-advised ventures, and possess an extraordinary tenacity when confronted by seemingly insurmountable obstacles. In Libya, the ability for outsiders to make sense of events was made more difficult by limited access and by the sheer confusion and contradictory nature of the regime's own directives. Much of the reporting during the country's civil war reflected in part this difficulty to explain to the world a political experiment that seemingly only made sense within its own almost hidden logic. Hopefully this second edition, by a number of long-term observers of Libya and of Qadhafi, will bring some more light to a political experiment that after 42 years now seems on the verge of destruction.

I

Libya's Revolution in Perspective

1969–2000

Dirk Vandewalle

The September 1, 1969 coup in Libya that brought Libya's young military officers to power put an end to the Sanusi kingdom—at the time universally considered as anachronistic. But while the general expectation in the West and much of the Middle East had been that a number of senior military leaders would take over in the North African country, the coup leaders turned out to be overwhelmingly young officers and captains with no links to the monarchy or to senior military figures. Although the first few days brought the unavoidable confusion over who constituted its leadership, from the first official communiqués onward, it was clear that Libya's new rulers were inspired by Arab nationalism and by a resentment of the West's role in regional politics. They also seemed determined to chart a new political course for Libya within the Arab world and within the world at large.

A week after the actual coup took place, the name of the regime's commander in chief, Mu'ammar al-Qadhafi, was revealed. He was identified as the chairman of a fourteen-member Revolutionary Command Council (RCC) that was put in charge of the revolution. It would take another four months—until January 1970—before the names of the RCC members were made public. They included Colonel Mu'ammar al-Qadhafi, Major Abd as-Salam Jallud, Major Bashir Hawadi, Captain Mukhtar Abdallah Gerwy, Captain Abd al-Munim Tahir al-Huni, Captain Mustapha al-Kharubi, Captain al-Khuwaylidi al-Hamidi, Captain Muhammad Nejm,

Captain Ali Awad Hamza, Captain Abu Bakr Yunus Jabr, and Captain Omar Abdallah al-Muhayshi.[1]

The new Libyan leaders clearly represented a break with the country's past. Their populist and revolutionary rhetoric was no coincidence. Their socioeconomic and political backgrounds stood in sharp contrast to those who had provided leadership during the monarchy. Virtually all of them came from the country's middle class, and from less prestigious tribes and families than those who had been affiliated with the royalist Sanusi government. Most came from rural backgrounds, and they were all young; all except two had graduated from the military academy in Benghazi in 1963, barely six years before the actual coup. Some of them were still captains at the time, including Mu'ammar al-Qadhafi. These Free Officers, as they were collectively known, had all attended the Military Academy largely because, under the restrictive policies of the monarchy, they had not been able to qualify for a university education that required a special certificate.

If their backgrounds set the Free Officers apart from those that had managed the monarchy, their ideological program differentiated them even more. Clearly guided by Qadhafi, who possessed an unlimited admiration for Egyptian President Nasser, Libya's new leaders clearly articulated their own vision for Libya in words and images that resonated strongly within the ongoing Arab nationalist language swirling around the region at the time. Qadhafi, like other young Arab nationalists who had followed the ideological debates and struggles within Arab nationalism, viewed Egypt's Nasser as a dedicated Arab revolutionary who could return to the Arab world much of the grandeur and the power it had once possessed. That Nasser cloaked much of his vision in language that took the West to task only added to his appeal for the new Libyan leaders who viewed the presence of British and American military bases as an unacceptable compromise made by a corrupt monarchy, conveniently ignoring that negotiations regarding the United States' withdrawal from Wheelus airbase had already started during the last years of the monarchy.

The arrival of Libya's new leaders raised a number of tantalizing questions about how they would deal with the dilemmas the monarchy had left unresolved. Would the young military officers use their power to counter the process of political and bureaucratic benign neglect that had marked the country since independence? Would they be able and willing to construct the new political community they envisioned, while simultaneously, and for the first time, bring a greater sense of participation by incorporating the country's citizens who had been sidelined during the monarchy? What would the impact of these efforts be on the structures of the country's traditional society, and on the elaborate patterns of patronage that dominated Libya's public life? And, finally, how would Libya deal with the West, at once seen as an enemy and as indispensable in running the country's oil-based economy?

It was not until December 16, 1970, that the regime's first clear political agenda emerged.[2] It included a call for the removal of foreign bases and troops from Libyan territory, for neutrality, for national unity, and—mirroring the monarchy's actions in 1952—for the suppression of all political parties. Much of the program was carefully interspersed with references to Islam, an attempt by the new regime to establish its own religious credentials in opposition to the old *ulama* once associated with the Sanusi leadership. But there was no clear outline of how the new regime's ambitious internal and international goals were to be accomplished at first. This oversight, and Qadhafi's penchant for projecting political energy (and, eventually, much of the country's riches) at the regional rather than the national level, would eventually open up fissures within the regime. Meanwhile, in 1970, the RCC proceeded with an attempt to destroy the lingering power of the monarchy's economic and political elites. In purging the old regime elites, the RCC was forced, in practice, to act much more gingerly than its rhetoric suggested, simply because the new regime did not possess the requisite skilled manpower to overnight staff all the bureaucratic, diplomatic, and oil-related positions. Despite this, by October 1970, all the country's ministries—except for the Ministry of Oil, where the regime simply did not have the expertise to replace existing personnel—were run directly by RCC members. At the same time, the Libyan army started to emerge as a major employment outlet for a young generation of Libyans.

With its position seemingly solidified, the regime turned toward mobilization of the population in earnest. On January 14, 1971, Qadhafi announced at Zawiya that the country would move toward popular rule: Popular Congresses would appoint representatives to the country's parliament, and would directly elect the country's president. RCC members fanned out across the country's territory to encourage people to participate. Despite their efforts, however, the country's first version of popular rule was quickly abandoned. Aware of the existing political apathy, the leadership then turned toward a more controlled system of mobilization. It announced the creation of the Arab Socialist Union (ASU) on June 12, 1971, following Nasser's earlier example in Egypt. Much like Egypt's ASU, the Libyan version was seen as a vanguard party that would not only mobilize the masses for political participation, but would also help to consolidate the revolution.

In retrospect, the ASU never enjoyed the confidence of the RCC or of Qadhafi himself. Although it lingered on a while longer, it never assumed any real power. Much like the earlier attempt at establishing Popular Congresses, the ASU had not been able to sufficiently mobilize Libyans. Instead of producing a new revolutionary leadership, as Qadhafi had hoped, it recruited many of the country's middle-class citizens and modernizing young bureaucrats, all of whom remained politically neutral. Tribal, personal, and regional solidarities still marked Libya, particularly in the rural areas. By 1973, as the regime took stock of its two experiments in popular mobilization, a sense of failure prevailed. Qadhafi then opted for a more radical strategy: removing all political barriers or intermediaries that stood between the country's leadership and the people.

On April 16, 1973, the anniversary of the Prophet Muhammad's death, Qadhafi launched at Zuwara what he described as a Popular Revolution. Rather than mobilizing Libya's citizens from above—as the ASU had attempted—the new strategy would rely on bottom-up mobilization. In reality, and despite the veneer of what became known as Popular Rule or People's Power, the RCC remained firmly in control. Indeed, the Popular Revolution marked the beginning of what would become an enduring feature of Libyan political life that lasted until today: a growing bifurcation between the formal and informal instruments of political control and power in the country (see Chapter 2). The Zuwara announcement, more than anything, had been an indication of Qadhafi's frustration at the political apathy within the country. The real revolution, he argued, was obscured and frustrated by elements within Libyan society that wanted to obstruct the country's progress. The only solution, he proposed, was to let "people govern themselves by themselves." The speech, thus, also marked an intensification of Qadhafi's populist rhetoric, and foreshadowed the three elements that would come to dominate the more spectacular revolutionary directives after 1973 and into the 1980s: the dismantling of a host of political and economic institutions that could provide coherence to the country, the destruction of representative political institutions, and the emergence of what would eventually become known as the Third Universal Theory as the country's ideological guideline.

The 1973 Popular Revolution was meant to create a locally based, youthful leadership drawn from the lower middle and lower classes that would have a substantially different socialization and education than that of the country's traditional elites. The revolution's success in achieving this aim also meant that many of the country's new bureaucratic cadres were highly inexperienced. The regime's inclination, furthermore, to create a growing number of government agencies whose activities were not coordinated created even greater confusion. This was further exacerbated by the fact that offices were often physically shifted around at short notice—a precursor of

Qadhafi's later attempts to shift ministries and institutions away from Tripoli. The combination of these factors produced a large amount of administrative and bureaucratic chaos in the country. By mid-1973, the country's bureaucratic structures, which the regime, along with the army, saw as an outlet for indoctrination, had nearly doubled in size.

Economic Management in the Early Years

During the first few months after the revolution, the country's new leadership—preoccupied with consolidating the revolution and aware of their inexperience in economic management—had proceeded cautiously with their economic programs. Their concerns initially focused on two readily visible economic and social problems within Libya: the fact that the country had become a dualistic economy where, beyond the oil sector, a number of other inefficient sectors still employed the majority of the Libyan population. Furthermore, oil production in 1970 had reached a record 3.7 million barrels per day—a figure which represented the entire capacity of the country's pipeline systems. It was a development the RCC considered detrimental to the long-term health of the oilfields. One year after the revolution, oil provided almost 99 percent of Libya's revenues, and constituted all of its exports.

Also, the young officers were worried that the oil sector employed only 1 percent of the country's active population, and that oil development had produced a number of undesirable social and economic ripple effects that could not easily be reconciled with the egalitarian tenets of the revolution. At the same time, the technocratic nature of the oil industry meant that Libya's new rulers had little choice but to continue relying on whatever expertise was present in the country, much of it consisting of expatriate personnel. By 1970, Libya had one of the world's most sophisticated oil infrastructures that constantly needed fine-tuning and upgrading. Under those circumstances, Qadhafi and his entourage realized that the nationalization of the Libyan oil industry was not an option at the time. By default, they turned to the country's oil pricing mechanism as the one aspect of the oil extracting and marketing process over which they had some control.

Libya's oil sector, however, exhibited some unique traits that could now be effectively exploited to the regime's bargaining advantage. The assignment of large tracts of oil exploration areas to small independent producers, in addition to the so-called Majors, during the monarchy now gave the military regime the opportunity to consistently press for higher profits for Libyan oil through a divide-and-rule strategy. The weak bargaining position of the Independents at the time—many relied on Libyan oil for a substantial portion of their revenues—facilitated the regime's strategy. For example, one of the country's two major independents, Occidental Petroleum, received 97 percent of its total production from Libya. Under those circumstances, the Independents were clearly more vulnerable to threats of cutbacks in production, or of expropriation, even if only implied, than the Majors for whom Libyan production constituted a small part of their global output.

The Independents, furthermore, had few incentives to join the Majors to cut production in 1970, a move undertaken globally to restore prices as an oil glut developed. As a result of the 1961 amendments to the country's petroleum law, the Independents in Libya had paid substantially less tax per barrel of oil than the Majors did.[3] This favored position now hurt the Independents, as the Majors refused to help them when the revolutionary regime demanded higher taxes. By systematically targeting the smaller companies—their situation made worse by an acute short-haul shortage in Europe at the time—the Qadhafi government cut back their production, forcing companies to acquiesce to the regime's demand for higher prices.

The government aggressively continued to pursue a policy of higher prices, greater ownership, and greater control over production. The frustration over the level of posted prices, determined by the oil companies, and left unaddressed during the monarchy's last few months in office, led the government to establish a committee in December 1969 to discuss the increase of posted prices with the oil companies. The same month, it reduced production allowances for individual companies, following and closely cooperating with Algerian authorities, who had started to take a series of increasingly aggressive measures aimed at the French oil interests in their country. When the small Independents in Libya—who produced more than half of the country's crude oil at the time—capitulated to the government's demands for higher posted prices, the rest of the industry had no choice but to fall into line. In January 1971, the government further ratcheted up both tax rates and posted prices.

When the companies attempted to develop a common strategy vis-à-vis the Libyan government—the so-called Libyan Producers Agreement of 1971—the regime's divide-and-rule tactic enabled it to withstand the companies' collective actions. Bypassing the arrangements made between oil companies and certain Organization of Petroleum Exporting Countries (OPEC) countries during the December 1970 Tehran Agreement, Libya lambasted OPEC for what it considered insufficient price increases and inadequate premiums for its short-haul advantage. Since the LNOC had managed to sell oil on its own—at prices substantially higher than the posted prices then available for Libyan crude—it pressed for even higher posted prices. The result of the negotiations—the Tripoli Agreement of March 20, 1971—raised the posted price for Libyan crude to $3.32 per barrel, a figure that included a Suez Canal Allowance, as well as a freight and low sulphur premium, and provisions for annual adjustments. By 1974, the price differential between Libyan and Persian Gulf crude was $4.12 per barrel—causing Libya to lose its cost advantage, and creating temporary difficulties for the country later that year. But the Libyan revolutionaries, in a series of audacious measures that added to their revolutionary élan, had proven themselves capable of inexorably ratcheting up their demands for greater revenues. In doing so, they laid the groundwork for the more intrusive demands they would make before, during, and after the oil crisis of 1973, which eventually led to a wave of nationalizations.

Although the increases between September 1969 and October 1973 were small, compared to what the quadrupling of oil prices would bring by the end of 1973, the actions of the Libyan government propelled the Qadhafi regime to a stature within the region that only its most ardent supporters had thought achievable. They also provided the Libyan leader with an unprecedented level of internal legitimacy. By the beginning of the 1973 October War, Libya had amassed reserves that would allow it to outlast a four-year economic embargo if necessary. In the wake of its victories against the oil companies, the government then turned toward strengthening the position of the LNOC, aiming to play a larger role in the actual management of the country's oil industry. The LNOC took under its management twenty-three concessions that had been abandoned by the oil companies during and after the oil price negotiations.

Outside the oil sector, however, economic realities looked distinctly less attractive. During the last decade of the monarchy, the share of oil in the country's GDP had jumped from 27 to 65 percent. By 1973, oil was the only commodity the country exported. Libya's population in 1969 was estimated at roughly two million people—almost a doubling since independence. Of those, a few hundred, at best, were employed within the oil sector. The country's other sectors were those of a more traditional economy, largely underdeveloped and marked by low investment, inefficiencies, and with a labor force that lacked the requisite skills for the kind of economic plans upon which the new revolutionary government would soon embark upon. As an example of the wrenching changes oil economies can engender, in 1969, agriculture and manufacturing contributed only 2.4 percent and 2 percent of the country's GDP, respectively.

In many ways, Libya had already become the dualistic economy characteristic of many oil states. Although per capita income at $2,168 in 1969 had improved dramatically from the subsistence level at the beginning of the monarchy, the increase was almost solely due to aid and, later, to hydro-carbon revenues.[4] When the first tentative and cautious directives for the country's economy emerged in March 1970, it was not surprising that they were marked by a suspicion of the role of the private sector, and aimed to bring substantial parts of the non-oil sectors under state control. The country's history of crony capitalism during the monarchy had sparked much anger among those who had led the coup, and they clearly consid-ered private entrepreneurship suspect. The private sector was, at least tem-porarily, retained, but the new decrees clearly stated that it could not impinge upon or contradict the economic policies of the government. It was also clear that retaining the private sector was a policy the regime intended to correct when they were in a position to do so.

Many of the achievements during the first four years of the Qadhafi government—in light of the existing circumstances and lack of political and social cohesion during the monarchy—had been relatively easy. The monarchy had enjoyed oil revenues for less than a decade, and the patterns of economic competition and differentiation that invariably lead to organ-ized and entrenched groups in oil exporters had not yet become visible in Libya when the coup took place. The relative ease with which the old elites could be replaced was heightened by the fact that the monarchy had retained few supporters that were willing to oppose the revolutionary regime. Much of this was, nevertheless, a remarkable achievement by the RCC in light of the difficult tasks they faced, not only in developing plans for the country's future, but also in persuading Libyans to participate in economic and political enterprises from which they had been systemati-cally excluded during the eighteen years of the monarchy.

But much harder tasks lay ahead. The transition toward the ASU, and then its abandonment, had been the first indication that political mobi-lization and indoctrination had not been as successful as the RCC had hoped. Libyans remained largely politically apathetic and showed little interest in the affairs of their country. To Qadhafi, who wanted to mobilize his citizens in support of his revolution so that the country could then become the vanguard of a larger regional movement, this was clearly unac-ceptable. His emergence as the charismatic leader of the revolution—which relied for its success on a skillful blend of traditional and modern ways to legitimate his rule—and the concentration of power at his dis-posal, had started to turn the Libyan revolution into a personal crusade.

With a growing lack of checks and balances on the power of its leader, or on his ability to use the country's resources in pursuit of his ideological zeal, it was highly problematic that the revolutionary regime showed little interest in systematically extending the power of the state. Beyond its nationalist and Arab nationalist language, the RCC had barely articulated a clear vision or program that could consolidate the country. The demise of the ASU as a political party, the repeated references to state institutions as antithetical to the implementation of the revolution, and the sustained use of populist rhetoric, all indicated Qadhafi's frustration with the slow pace of reform. The adoption of People's Power in 1973 had been the culmination of efforts to bypass the frictions that slowed down these reforms. As yet, however, the ideas behind its adoption did not contain the kind of programmatic unity and revolutionary fervor Qadhafi's ideological primer, the *Green Book*, would soon provide.

On the eve of the influx of massive oil revenues that would forever alter the direction and intensity of the country's revolution, Libya stood at an important crossroads. Qadhafi and the RCC seemed truly interested in mobilizing the population for the country's political and economic development, and in pursuing a viable, long-term economic strategy for the country. But they had also, virtually overnight, come into possession of the physical and economic resources that would allow them to shape both processes in an extraordinary fashion, devoid of checks and balances. By 1973, Libya's military leadership had, in many ways, already started to repeat the essentially distributive policies of the kingdom that proceeded it, in order to correct what it considered as a pattern of inequitable development during the monarchy. Whether they could, or would, go beyond this seemed much less certain. The Libyan revolutionaries had started to embark upon a course of increasingly dramatic and contradictory policies that simultaneously aimed at putting the state in charge of all economic activity, and tried to make it irrelevant as a focus for political identity. The contradiction between the two pursuits was seemingly lost on the Libyan leadership.

The Everlasting Revolution and the *Green Book*

Qadhafi's Zuwara speech had been an attempt to bring some programmatic unity to the different initiatives meant to overcome political apathy. But the two years following the Zuwara announcement had been marked by chaos and confusion inside the country. The creation of the popular committee system at Zuwara had been an attempt by Qadhafi to bypass the more regularized procedures of the ASU. The attempt, however, led to conflict within the RCC. At the November 1974 meeting of the ASU, a split between two factions emerged publicly for the first time. It pitted those who wanted a more orderly, planned course of action that included a carefully designed economic plan—a technocratic solution to the country's problems—against those who wanted to pursue a more activist policy that sacrificed some of the country's riches for the sake of Arab unity and other ideological pursuits. As the struggle continued throughout 1974 and into 1975, the fortunes of both sides waxed and waned.[5] Student unrest erupted in early 1975 and added to the tension, resulting in the RCC's announcement of compulsory military service. Despite the measure, the unrest continued and spread further, leading to the first large-scale arrests of students in April 1975.

Rumors of attempted coups surfaced in the Arab press throughout the summer and, at one point in July 1975, army units loyal to Qadhafi surrounded Tripoli. When the government was restructured in the wake of the ASU Congress, the technocrats seemed to have gained the upper hand: only four RCC members remained, while a number of newly created ministries were assigned to young intellectuals with no broad, nationalist credentials. But the ongoing debate within the RCC indicated the lingering disagreements over what some considered Qadhafi's growing personal power and over the rising costs of his pan-Arab pursuits, foreign adventures, and his aborted unity attempt with Egypt. There was also growing unease about the political interference of Qadhafi and his supporters in economic and development projects that some argued should be evaluated on purely technical merits.

The conflict between the two sides was highly ideological, focusing almost exclusively on the purposes to which Libya's oil wealth should be put and, in a related matter, about the role the state should play in the country's economic development. As the conflict intensified, both sides attempted to attract allies within the Libyan army to their side, leading to fears of another coup.[6] In August 1975, RCC members Bashir Hawadi and 'Umar al-Muhayshi launched a coup attempt against the regime. Muhayshi, who was Minister of Planning at the time, refused to give up funds that had been earmarked for local development projects, and fled with a number of his supporters to Tunis in the aftermath of the failed coup.

The event marked a political, economic and ideological breaking point in the politics of revolutionary Libya, lurching the country forward in an activist direction that would not be curtailed for more than a decade. The RCC, still the most powerful organization in Libya, was now reduced to five members: Mu'ammar al-Qadhafi, Abu-Bakr Yunus Jabar, al-Khuwaylidi al-Hamidi, Mustafa al-Kharubi, and Abd as-Salam Jallud. The way had been cleared for increasingly draconian measures to implement Qadhafi's vision of a stateless society. With no institutionalized opposition left, Qadhafi quickly moved to consolidate his own position, and the revolution inexorably became identified with his own personal vision. Throughout the remainder of 1975, civilian, military, professional, and technical personnel suspected of potential disloyalty were removed from the country's planning institutes and ministries. Those who argued for a greater prudence in the country's financial and economic affairs were systematically sidelined. Muhammad Mugharyif, the country's comptroller and later, after his own defection, one of the regime's most virulent and eloquent critics, was replaced. The coup attempt also marked the end of professional and technical criteria for military recruitment, and the beginning of a steady, but noticeable, influx of individual members of Qadhafi's tribe—and later of his family—into a number of sensitive security and army positions.

In the wake of the attempted coup, Qadhafi seized the opportunity to push forward his revolutionary agenda, soon to be finalized in three slim volumes of his *Green Book*, the ideological primer of the revolution. It contains a compilation of Qadhafi's utopian ideas on what Libya's social, political, and economic organization should look like. He refers to this new state as a *jamahiriyya*—a political community marked by consultation, rather than representation. In it, ordinary citizens own the country's resources, exercise authority, and directly manage the country's administration and its bureaucracy through a system of popular congresses and committees. Each volume contains common themes: a distrust of the hierarchical bureaucratic structures inherent in modern states, and Qadhafi's abhorrence for the presence of intermediaries who—via the impersonal structures of bureaucracies and administrative institutions—prevent individuals from directly managing their own lives. Qadhafi himself clearly viewed the *Green Book* as, above all, a manifesto for action. It was meant to intensify his earlier mobilization efforts that had been frustrated so far, he argued, because the country's political system could not express the true voice of the Libyan people (Part 1), because Libyans were not directly in charge of the economic resources of the country (Part 2), and because of the country's archaic social structures (Part 3).

The ideas are simple and, with their insistence on egalitarianism and lack of hierarchy, reflect a tribal ethos. The *Green Book*'s central tenet is that ordinary citizens can directly manage the bureaucratic and administrative institutions that shape their lives, and devise their own solutions to their economic and social problems. Hence, the *Green Book* contains the essential idea of statelessness, and of people managing their own affairs without state institutions. There is, as well, an emphasis on consultation and equality, and an explicitly voiced aversion to hierarchy and to the handing over of authority to state functionaries. There is, finally, a repeated insistence on "direct democracy" through which citizens will take control of the state. The new and cumbersome system of political governance—which included a total of almost one thousand representatives from throughout the country—was finally implemented on March 2, 1977. On that day, Qadhafi, at Sebha, announced that the "Era of the Masses" had arrived, and he renamed Libya *Al-Jamahiriyya al-arabiyya al-Libiyya al-sha'abiyya al-ishtirakiyya*—The Socialist People's Libyan Arab Jamahiriyya.[7]

Economic Development under the *Green Book*

The publication of the *Green Book*'s second and third volumes, *The Solution of the Economic Problem: Socialism* and *The Social Basis of the Third Universal Theory*, marked the extension of populist measures to the country's economy in a fashion that dramatically interfered with economic management after November 1977. With the help of the newly established Revolutionary Committees—whose creation had not been specified in the *Green Book*—the regime systematically implemented the ideas of the Libyan leader. The nationalization of all non-occupied dwellings began in 1976. The government reduced apartment purchase prices by 30 percent in late 1977. In May 1978, the GPC formally adopted a new real estate law that distributed confiscated real estate to mostly low-income earners.[8]

The impact of the directives regarding the abolishing of so-called wage-labor had an equally profound impact. Starting in earnest following his 1978 speech on the anniversary of the revolution, the first wave of business takeovers took place. Overnight, the country's merchants and small businessmen were reduced to passive onlookers in the country's economic life. These groups of small-scale business entrepreneurs, retailers, and private farmers had initially formed the backbone of support for the revolutionary government following September 1, 1969. Clearly, the regime now felt emboldened enough to move against their interests. By the end of 1980, the more important and larger industries were put in the hands of Basic Production Committees—selected groups of workers within each business or enterprise. Popular Committees replaced their administrators. Only the banking system and oil-related industries were, once more, saved from these popular takeovers.

The role of traders was abolished. Those that managed to survive until 1980 had already been subject to the Secretariat of Finance's selective and increasingly restrictive use of awarding or denying permits for business arrangements. In principle, the agricultural sector remained outside popular management. In practice, all available land in the countryside already belonged to the public sector from 1977 on, and survived only through heavy government subsidies. Individual farmers were only allowed to lease as much as they needed for their own requirements. By that time, the only land remaining in private hands was located along the coastal strip, owned by remnants of old landowning families or tribes. They would hold onto their land until 1980.

In his speech of September 1, 1980, Qadhafi emphasized that the country's entrepreneurs (an estimated 40,000 individuals) were nothing but parasites because their economic activities did not contribute to productive activity within the *jamahiriyya*. Private businesses closed throughout the country, often with the help of the revolutionary committees. Their function was taken over by a number of state supermarkets that soon dotted the country's landscape. Their construction effectively spelled the end of private commercial and retail transactions in Libya. Ten government agencies were responsible for the provision of all the country's import needs, ranging from oil technology to consumer goods.[9]

Ultimately, however, Qadhafi's entire *Green Book* experiment crucially depended for its implementation on the income from oil sales. Perhaps not surprising, therefore, the country's oil industry remained carefully shielded from the revolutionary fervor swirling around it. The October 1973 Arab-Israeli War, and the oil boom in its aftermath, found Libya halfway through the revolutionary regime's first development plan. A few months earlier, in July 1973, the regime had followed up its earlier suspension of awarding acreage to oil companies by introducing so-called exploration and production-sharing arrangements (EPSAs). Under these new arrangements—which had been pioneered in Indonesia and gradually adopted by other OPEC members—Libya's National Oil Company retained title to whatever acreage was exploited by international oil companies, and the latter, in effect, simply became contractors.

As a result of the 1973 oil crisis and the regime's hard bargaining, the country was awash with petrodollars by the end of 1974. Despite its growing power over oil companies' operations within the country, however, it remained highly vulnerable to the fickle conditions of the international oil market: by the end of 1974, the price of Libyan oil had dropped to slightly above $11. Some of the damage had been self-inflicted: in support of the Arab oil embargo, Libya voluntarily cut its production to the United States and the Caribbean refineries supplying the U.S. market to roughly 1.5 million barrels per day. It abandoned this boycott only in early 1975, almost a year after most producers had done so. The country's oil output dropped 26.4 percent in 1974, and its exports fell to 912,000 barrels per day by mid-February 1975, the lowest level in more than a decade. This forced the Libyan government to rely on a substantial part of its financial reserves for the daily running of its economy. The result was a short-term financial crisis in the summer of 1975, fueled, in part, by the continuing heavy outlays for military purchases and for foreign adventures that had provoked the

August coup. In 1975, Libya's balance-of-trade dropped from a surplus of $1.8 billion to a deficit of $.5 billion. The government requested financial aid from Saudi Arabia that was promptly denied. The rapid inflows of oil money, however, resolved the country's crisis soon thereafter, and Libya's planners once more faced the dilemma familiar to many oil exporters during the 1970s: how to distribute revenues they could not expect their economies to use efficiently.

Regarding the country's oil industry, the government seemingly paid little attention to the instability of the market throughout the 1970s, even though the country's dependence on oil revenues now amounted to 99.9 percent of total income. Despite new contracts for offshore production in 1979, the "spontaneous takeovers" of the economic sectors by the regime's militants—although still restricted to the non-oil and non-banking sectors—had a chilling effect on company-government relations, particularly with regard to European companies. The growing animosity with Libya forced several American companies—despite highly profitable contract terms—to start reconsidering their investments in the *jamahiriyya*. The government judged that, in the wake of the Iranian revolution, which more than doubled the price of Libyan crude between December 1978 and December 1979, actual divestment was unlikely. The 1978–79 price hikes pushed Libyan revenues to unprecedented levels, allowing the government to keep production levels untouched.

Technocrats at the LNOC, however, did not fail to notice that the real price of oil, even after discounting for indexation and inflation, had started to lag behind posted prices, indicating that a buyer's market was on the horizon. By 1979, government officials were sufficiently worried about possible depletion of its oil reserves that they moved aggressively toward new exploration contracts, known as EPSA II. Despite growing unease about the country's international reputation, and the fact that the terms of EPSA II were even less favorable to oil companies than those of its predecessor, interest proved high. As part of an attempt to make itself less vulnerable to outside pressure, the government also attracted East European companies to its upstream activities—a move that would consistently be resisted by the LNOC, who viewed these corporations as unreliable.

The involvement of the East European companies was an indication that, despite Libya's continuing ability to attract participants to its oil industry, its fortunes were slowly starting to wane. Already in 1978, the United States had started to place restrictions on trade with Libya because of its suspected involvement in terrorist activities. The withdrawal of some U.S. oil companies from the country in 1981 and the U.S. embargo against Libyan oil that started in 1982 were further indications of Libya's changing fortunes. In 1981, oil production tumbled from 1,700,000 barrels per day (bpd) in the first quarter to 600,000 bpd by the end of the year. Total production for 1981 was 40 percent below that of 1980. Of this reduction, roughly 500,000 bpd had routinely been delivered to the United States; the remainder of the cutback was due to phase-outs in production and the annulment of existing contracts by multinational companies. Furthermore, as a result of Libya's need to offer incentives to the remaining companies, the price of its oil had dropped by four to five dollars per barrel. Libya's balance-of-payments for 1981 showed a deficit of $4.8 billion, and the country's international reserves tumbled from $15.5 to $2.4 billion.

The combination of rapidly fluctuating income and popular management of the country's economy continued to take a heavy toll. The state's ability to function as an effective regulator suffered tremendously. By the early 1980s, Libya exhibited all the characteristics of a resource-rich, but badly managed, economy where efficiency and real concerns for development had yielded to the political imperatives of the regime. Small handouts were used to keep the population quiescent, and more substantial outlays were given to the regime's coalition of supporters, necessary to ensure the survival of the regime. The decline in the country's oil revenues, and the obvious need for serious economic reform after the country's oil boom provoked no serious corrective measures.

Between 1982 and 1986, the country's revenues tumbled from $21 billion to $5.4 billion annually. Despite this, and despite the growing need for economic reform, the half decade after the 1979 oil boom witnessed an unabated spending of the country's resources, and a continued resistance to economic reform. The revolutionary regime had managed to thoroughly transform Libya. Except for a few enterprises like the LNOC, the state's bureaucratic and administrative institutions had been put directly into the hands of the people through a system of political congresses and committees, and all private economic activity had been outlawed. Revolutionary Committees were in charge of supervising and implementing the economic directives.

But the early 1980s also marked the beginning of another period of uncertainty for the regime. In light of declining revenues, the regime had a number of options it could pursue. All involved more rational and efficient use of the country's revenues: reducing consumption at home, cutting back on development plans, and curtailing foreign adventures and military expenditures. None of these was particularly attractive since every measure meant cutting back on programs that, for political or ideological reasons, were linked to important constituencies of the regime and, as a result, had become part and parcel of the revolution.

Furthermore, diplomatic reasons made the regime cautious about borrowing on the international market, and Libya had little medium or long-term debt. Initially, the government used some temporary measures to overcome its emerging difficulties—most notably, shifting the economic hardships toward the expatriate labor in the country, increasing its reliance on East European and Soviet Union expertise, and limiting consumer imports. But the growing difficulties and increasing restrictions as a result of the country's confrontation with the West slowly, but steadily, decreased the number of economic options available to Libya.

Those options had also become more limited by the emerging realities within the Libyan economy since 1973: the massive, almost unregulated capital inflows; the removal of the country's technocrats from virtually all institutions except the NOC; the populist directives that stressed distribution at the expense of regulation; and the lackluster attention paid to efficiency and consistent planning. The turn toward popular rule—without built-in measures for transparency or accountability—and the ability to further circumvent popular rule when it suited the regime, meant that regulation and planning, much like the country's judicial and administrative institutions, fell victim to the ideological pursuits of the revolution during this long decade. What the kingdom had managed to accomplish through benign neglect, the revolutionary regime had achieved with a more deliberate, but equally disastrous, approach. Under both rulers, whatever formal mechanisms, rules, and checks existed to manage the country's economy for the benefit of all Libyan citizens, were easily avoided by relatively narrow cliques of supporters of each regime.

The quadrupling of oil prices in 1973–74 had created a greater need for financial and monetary management if serious inflation was to be avoided and sustained development pursued. The country's leadership needed to decide whether oil production should be limited and how to recycle oil revenues. This would have required the creation of much more elaborate and integrated information-gathering institutions for the country, as well as the implementation of a number of legal, disclosure, and accounting requirements that would have limited the political, revolutionary energy of the regime. Additionally, the rapid inflows of oil revenues vitiated any need for local, domestic savings, taxation, or other policies capable of curbing consumption throughout Libyan society.

Controlling the country's inflation would have necessitated a deliberate and sustained management of its revenue flows—which the regime was seemingly uninterested in doing. Much like the king before him, Libya's revolutionary leader primarily used economic resources to solve strategic political puzzles. The government abandoned serious attempts at planning, rather than carefully managing the country's economy, as a hedge against the difficulties of operating a volatile oil economy that needed access to external resources for its expansion, management, and survival. Its actions inevitably provoked a massive brain drain and left local and international investors weary of operating in an environment devoid of some essential legal guarantees. At the same time, and little noticed because of the country's non-transparent budgeting procedures, the regime invested heavily in military hardware throughout the decade.

At the end of the 1980–85 plan, economic management had suffered to such an extent that several of the country's ministries no longer produced annual reports that could accurately be relied upon for future use. In 1986, Libya's Central Bank temporarily suspended its yearly assessment of the country's economic performance. A dispute with neighboring countries in August and September 1985 that led to the expulsion of approximately 100,000 expatriate laborers—many involved in providing the day-to-day goods average Libyans needed—added to hardships inside the country.

By that time, the country's research institutions collected little primary information that would have allowed for more consistent and efficient planning. Many of the ministries' and research institutions' reports and planning papers became simple regurgitations of data provided by outside experts—data that often reflected the scenarios preferred by the regime without incorporating any real critical insights or suggestions. Except for the LNOC—that remained a privileged institution whose employees could collect data in an atmosphere untainted by revolutionary pursuits—most institutions in charge of gathering data needed for an efficient planning and management of the country's economy produced idealistic projections divorced from reality.

Revolutionary Authority and Informal Power Structures

As analyzed in greater detail by Mattes in Chapter 2, the creation of Revolutionary Authority in March 1979 marked the end of one aspect of the Libyan revolution and the beginning of another. On one hand, it constituted an admission that Libyan society was not reforming itself as quickly or as thoroughly as Qadhafi wanted. But it also marked the beginning of what has remained a dominant feature of Libyan politics until today: the persistence of a formal structure of government—centered around the popular congresses and committees—and an informal structure of power and authority. The latter includes a narrow circle of intimates around the Libyan leader (later formalized as the Forum of Companions of Qadhafi), supported and kept in place by a number of security sector institutions (most notably the country's layers of intelligence organizations) and the Revolutionary Committees.

The final sentence of the first part of the *Green Book*, perhaps inadvertently, more accurately encapsulated the reality of power in Libya, as Qadhafi cryptically noted that "realistically the stronger part in society is the one that rules." The fact that there were clear limitations on the competence and authority of the popular committees, and the fact that all of the country's security sector institutions—army, police, and intelligence— were outside the *jamahiriyya* system, indicated that, much like in the economic sphere (where the LNOC was excluded from popular rule), the ultimate control functions in the *jamahiriyya* remained tightly controlled at the top. Furthermore, the regime administered the country's budget without any real oversight by the GPC—budgets were normally approved pro forma, without discussion. Until today, Qadhafi continues to argue that he cannot be held responsible for economic or political setbacks since he no longer holds an official position. Every decision, once the *Green Book*'s directives had been adopted, was now the peoples' responsibility.

In reality, however, the people's authority had been challenged by the emergence of an institution whose existence had not been part of the ideological blueprint detailed in the *Green Book*: the country's Revolutionary Committees, created after November 1977.[10] Consisting of young, carefully selected individuals who are responsible directly to Qadhafi, they were seen as instruments for further mobilization and indoctrination. In particular, they were charged with encouraging greater popular participation in the Basic Peoples Congresses, where high levels of absenteeism persist even today. Clearly meant as an independent institution outside the control of the GPC—who, in principle, possessed all formal authority—their initial role, beyond indoctrination, remained undefined.

Qadhafi's pronouncement created, for the first time, a clear separation between those in power (in principle the BPCs and GPC) and those guiding the revolution. The distinction further consolidated Qadhafi's position since the Revolutionary Committees were entitled to replace BPC members judged unacceptable, thus allowing Qadhafi to have the people he preferred appointed. The Revolutionary Committees were, furthermore, directly responsible to Qadhafi, who coordinated their activities through a special Central Coordinating Committee for the Revolutionary Committees.

To further make the distinction between formal and revolutionary authority clear, Qadhafi resigned from the GPC—of which he had remained secretary-general—to commit himself fully to revolutionary activities.[11] The formal separation came at the GPC's second session on March 2, 1979. The remaining RCC members—Jallud, Yunus Jabr, al-Kharubi, and al-Hamidi—were also appointed to head the revolutionary authority structure, while all top positions within the formal authority structure became civilian. By the end of 1979, the Revolutionary Committees had fully insinuated themselves into the formal authority structure of the *jamahiriyya* and its public institutions: within the popular committees, the popular congresses, the Municipal People's General Committees (MPGC; these had been created as an additional layer of administration in 1979), as well as within the universities and the professional organizations. They quickly became—except for the remaining RCC members and an informal entourage around Qadhafi—the most powerful group in the country. At the January 1980 GPC meeting, the country's new civilian prime minister, Abd al-Ati al-Ubaydi, announced that "all People's Congresses, no matter what their level, as well as the Secretariat of the General People's Congress, and the secretaries of the Basic People's Congresses are under the permanent control of the revolution and the Revolutionary Committees."[12] Some members of the Committees' coordinating office at Bab al-Aziziyya became secretaries (ministers) within the formal authority structure.

When the *Green Book*'s second volume—on economic relations—was published, the committees were put in charge of supervising the implementation of its directives. They were further charged with rooting out corruption and the misappropriation of funds, charges that were often leveled against individuals—including remnants of the monarchy's elites—the regime considered undesirable. In October 1980, they took over the country's press, thereby concluding their first activist phase. Throughout the early 1980s, their functions expanded once more to officially include the right to propagate, guide, and control the revolution. Their final task was to defend the revolution at all costs, which included the power to pursue, hunt down, and physically liquidate (*al-tasfiya al-jasadiya*) "enemies of the revolution" abroad and at home. This led to a number of reprisals and assassinations abroad that would later contribute to the country's worsening relations with the West.

Perhaps the most worrisome development in the struggle between formal and revolutionary authority, however, centered on the infiltration of the country's legal system by the Revolutionary Committees, a process in which legitimacy was bestowed upon the use of violence.[13] In 1980, the Committees were formally assigned the right to create revolutionary courts—*mahkama thawriya*—based on the "law of the revolution"—*qanun al-thawra*. Since 1969, the revolutionary regime had attempted to devise a legal system that would underpin and enforce its social, political, and economic directives. Initially, the country's leadership had put forward the *sharia* as the only source of law applicable in Libya. With its clearly prescribed legal remedies and an emphasis on codification, however, it was hardly suited to the continual and changing nature of a regime that deliberately attempted to bypass formal and structured institutions. Several of the well-established principles of Islamic law regarding contracts and commerce, as well as the *sharia* protections of private property rights, for example, were inimical to the intentions of the government.

Already at Zuwara, Qadhafi had announced the suspension of all the country's laws then in force. The creation of the *jamahiriyya* in Sabha made the directives of the *Green Book* the guiding legal norms of Libyan society, norms that superseded the regime's first constitution of December 1969. In a number of major speeches throughout the 1970s, and then more formally during a prolonged and major debate with the country's *ulama* at the Moulay Muhammad Mosque on July 3, 1978, Qadhafi argued that Islamic legal rules could no longer be used as a guideline for economic and political relations in modern societies. He, furthermore, insisted that those who argued for their application were not entitled to do so.[14] At the same time, he also reiterated that the traditional guidelines for commerce and property rights in Muslim societies, based on the prophet Muhammad's actions and sayings, had no legal standing in modern societies. The elimination of the private practice of law in May 1980—a measure that included all other professional occupations as well—removed the last obstacle to the implementation of a virtually unsupervised revolutionary court system that could be used by the Qadhafi government to pursue its own policies.[15] Rather than relying on regular judges, the revolutionary courts were staffed by Revolutionary Committee members who were not bound by the country's penal code. Not surprising in light of the absence of legal safeguards, the revolutionary court system was left open to a large number of well-documented abuses, including several executions, throughout the 1980s and 1990s.

By 1980, the bifurcation between formal and revolutionary authority, as well as the manipulation of the *jamahiriyya*'s legal system, provided a clear indication of the narrowing power base within Libya. Although officially outside the formal framework of authority, Qadhafi virtually made all important policy decisions, channeling them, if necessary for purposes of legitimacy, through the GPC. In this, his small group of loyalists aided him in a fashion that much resembled the workings of the former royal *diwan*. As in all oil states where decision making is concentrated in a small circle of elites and a praetorian guard, this kind of rule depended on careful management of coalitions crucial to the Libyan leader's survival.

In Libya, this creation and re-creation of coalitions was inevitably accompanied throughout the 1980s by yet another *zahf* (wave, or march) of revolutionary activities and edicts that, hopefully, translated into support for the regime. The Revolutionary Committees were the most visible—but certainly not the last—of such attempts at (selective) mobilization and the retention of power at the top of the country's political system. By their unpredictability, Revolutionary Committees and revolutionary justice also ensured that groups and individuals were left politically unbalanced. The Revolutionary Committees—once meant to invigorate the revolution— quickly turned into one more instrument of control, meant to ensure the physical survival of the regime. For almost a decade, the regime would pay little attention to formal legal rules. The increasingly repressive revolutionary justice system that enforced the regime's directives would eventually be a major factor contributing to the growing tension within the *jamahiriyya*— and would lead to a number of restrictions on the Revolutionary Committees' powers.

Qadhafi, however, quickly developed reservations about the effectiveness of the Revolutionary Committees. In his September 1 speech following the downing of two Libyan planes by the United States in August 1981 over the Gulf of Sirte, he reiterated the need for further mobilization and called for the creation of a new type of vanguard, the so-called Guards of the Revolution.[16] In the same speech, he announced further popular takeovers, including those of overseas embassies, which were turned into People's Bureaus. The Guards of the Revolution, however, never became a viable organization. The rapid rise and partial curtailment of the Revolutionary Committees, in the span of a single decade, was symptomatic of the balancing act the Qadhafi government skillfully performed to remain in power. Their resurgence during the early 1990s to aid in combating Islamist opposition to the regime, particularly in Cyrenaica, shows how closely their fate was directly tied to Qadhafi.

Opposition, the Power of Symbols, and Apathy

Although Libya, with its small population, could never claim equal status with other revolutionary nations, Qadhafi considered what had happened in Libya after 1969 as one of the great twentieth-century revolutions for social liberation. In the *Green Book*, the Libyan leader portrays the Libyan revolution as an inevitable, historical process of social, economic, and political development—hence, the grandiloquent claim of the *jamahiriyya* being the alternative to capitalism and communism. In his speeches and exhortations since 1969, the Libyan leader has constantly invoked a sense of uniqueness, grounded in Arab history and tradition, in ways that resonated within Libyan culture and experience. But, eventually, the use of a combination of symbols, myths, and attempts to carefully exploit the charismatic qualities of the Libyan leader assumed an instrumental purpose as well: bridging the gap between the *Green Book*'s precise delineation of the country's formal political structures and the reality of an increasingly exclusionary political system.

When reading Qadhafi's speeches, one is struck immediately by the repeated and powerful references to shared traditions within the country and within the region, to notions of a common history that has pitted Libyans against the West, and to symbols that are uniquely Libyan and deeply embedded within local culture. The Libyan leader's speeches contain innumerable reiterations of words that reflect conditions in Arab society before state-building began in earnest: words like *turath* (heritage), *furusiyya* (chivalry), and *diafa* (hospitality). Dignity and the indignities suffered at the hand of the West have continually been used by Qadhafi to invoke a powerful sense of unity. History—and historical wrongs inflicted by the West on Libya—have been used from the beginning to create a sense of shared suffering and exploitation. The suspicion of outsiders was also richly nurtured as the Libyan government confronted first the oil companies and then the West more generally. Libyans were instructed to be vigilant against the West and to destroy those who would sell out the revolution for their own interests.

There is little doubt that Qadhafi's statements and actions tapped deeply into a rich source of resentment among Libyans against the West. Through the oil negotiations of 1970 and 1971, and the evacuation of the military bases, the regime provided many ordinary Libyans with their own sense of dignity, even though the monarchy had started negotiations for the latter. It was similarly important, therefore, that what had happened on September 1, 1969, be portrayed as a collective action: the Libyan people had rejected the kingdom and its corrupt pro-Western clique, and the military planners of the takeover had simply implemented their wishes. In order to convey this image, the regime needed to deflect attention from the fact that the events of September 1 had only involved a very small number of military personnel. Moreover, it needed to downplay the reality that the new leadership had very few clearly developed ideas beyond some rudimentary principles that could be condensed into anti-Westernism, Arab nationalism, and populism when it assumed power.

It was important, finally, not only in light of the existing *ulama*, but because of a wider popular appeal, to portray the revolution as consistent with the general precepts of Islam. The Qadhafi regime had inherited a legal system in which codified Western law enjoyed primacy over religious and customary law. Despite the fact that the *Green Book* elevated religion and custom to the status of the law of society, in practice, both were displaced as sources of law by secular policies. This break with Islamic law and Libyan custom, however, was never officially acknowledged. The *Green Book* continued to stress reliance on "a sacred law based on stable rules which are not subject to change," identified this sacred law with Islam and with the Qur'an, and Qadhafi claimed consistently that the revolution had reinstated true Islam.

The revolution of September 1, 1969, according to the regime, was meant to initiate a wholesale cleansing of perceived stains of Western culture, colonialism, and the monarchy (with its links to global capital) from the country's social fabric. A number of public and highly symbolic acts in the early years of the revolution were necessary to achieve this end, including the burning of Western books and musical instruments; the closing of nightclubs; the promotion of traditional Libyan dress; the conversion of churches into mosques; the adoption, in principle, of Islamic punishment; and the renaming of the Gregorian calendar. Oil was instrumental in achieving the regime's goals, confronting the West, and restoring to Libya and to the Arab world the cultural and political power they had once possessed. The confrontation with the West—and Libya's repeated efforts at creating alliances with other Arab countries—must thus be understood not only as a means of creating support at home, but also as fulfillment of the deeply-felt conviction that Qadhafi could indeed be the heir to Gamal Abdul Nasser within the region.

During the initial years of the revolution, one of the most powerful mechanisms for creating a following for the revolution was Qadhafi's own charisma. Informal, non-institutionalized, charismatic leadership fit perfectly within the kind of personalized politics that developed within the *jamahiriyya*. In contrast to a monarchy that had been dominated by an older bourgeoisie and an aging king, and lacking a desire to clearly define Libya's position within Arab politics, Qadhafi conveyed a sense of personal integrity and self-esteem. The overthrow of the Sanusi monarchy, a political system that had sidelined citizens since its creation, and had grown increasingly corrupt during the 1960s, initially added to the new leader's standing among the population. His hard bargaining tactics with the oil companies, and the eventual vindication of Libya's insistence on a greater share of oil profits, provided him with a stature far greater than that of those around him. His sense of righteousness and fearlessness, his willingness to take a clear position within intra-Arab politics, his sense of duty and of honor, his personal honesty—all these qualities put him in sharp contrast to what the country had experienced before. In a sense, Qadhafi was the revolution, *al-qa'id al'mu'allim*—the leader and teacher—as he became known in the *jamahiriyya*. His ability to insinuate himself—and the Libyan people simultaneously—into the troubled history of his country, by claiming that he followed in the footsteps of Umar al-Mukhtar and all those who had resisted the West, forged a sense of solidarity among Libyans.

Viewed against the backdrop of the monarchy that inevitably hovers in the background behind Qadhafi's exhortations, the Libyan leader seemingly possessed all the qualities Arab nationalism touted: militancy in opposing the West, youthfulness, and a high level of political energy. Above all, he possessed the will to pursue his own vision of what a political community should look like, despite numerous setbacks and (often self-inflicted) crises. But charisma is by its nature a fleeting political resource that needs constant rejuvenation and renewal to remain valid. Thus, successive waves of mobilization and consistently unbalanced politics were powerful mechanisms Qadhafi used to prevent the routinization of his charisma, no matter how seemingly incoherent or irrational these policies appeared to observers. As a charismatic leader, Qadhafi also insisted on direct contact with ordinary Libyans that allowed him to claim a link and legitimacy no other RCC member could match. From 1969 onward, he put great emphasis on personalized exchanges with the population, continuously meeting groups of Libyans within highly formulized settings, delivering speeches throughout the country, reinforcing the message of the revolution, and exhorting citizens in a way few recent rulers in the Middle East have attempted.

It was also clear, however, that, despite this careful manipulation of symbols, myths, and charisma, the revolution had created a number of enemies: monarchical elites who had been dispossessed or forced to flee the country; fellow revolutionaries, who like Muhayshi and Muqaryif, Qadhafi's former state comptroller and ambassador to India, took issue with the wasting of the country's resources; the *ulama* whose role had been severely restricted; and ordinary citizens who resented the unpredictability of the *Green Book*'s directives and the deep impact of the revolutionary measures on their lives. As the revolution unfolded and intensified, a multitude of Libyan opposition groups formed in the West and throughout the Middle East. Some of these regularly produced publications containing their own viewpoints. The best known opposition group was the *National Front for the Salvation of Libya* (NFSL), founded in 1981 by Muhammad Muqaryif. The NFSL also had a military wing, the *Salvation Forces* that, with French and U.S. support, conducted a number of military actions against Qadhafi in the 1980s.[17] Eventually, the different groups started to organize themselves more effectively, led in part by the leadership of the NFSL. However, their cooperation remained precarious and showed the deep divisions that, in turn, reflected the different aspirations and interests of each group.[18]

The fact that opposition failed to crystallize inside Libya can only be partially explained by the presence of the security sector institutions, the effectiveness of the use of symbols, the injunction against political groupings, and by Qadhafi's appeal to the population. The constant new waves of mobilization against any group that potentially threatened the regime also provided an important clue. The result of the regime's policies had, in addition to a level of apathy, also introduced a more insidious phenomenon: a depoliticization of the population and an atomization that took place as any type of organized activity was forbidden. This atomization was fostered by the fact that the state became virtually the sole economic provider under the directives of the *Green Book*. Under such circumstances, Libyans no longer possessed the kind of common economic interests that, in more productive economies, lead to common actions—and such common interests are, at any rate, not likely to be expressed during economic booms. As a result, conditions that might have facilitated the emergence of broad-based organizations to defend particular interests lost their salience—economic handouts and political silence became an ingrained part of politics.

In addition, when it became clear to Libyan citizens that the gap between formal and informal mechanisms of governing had become an insurmountable reality of politics in the *jamahiriyya*, most learned to cope with a political system they had no chance of reforming. Perhaps fitting in light of the regime's attempts to minimize the impact of the state on citizens' daily lives, the state had, indeed, beyond its economic largesse, become much less relevant for most citizens. But this decreased relevance also led to depoliticization, as previously described, something that the regime, at least rhetorically, had tried to avoid. This depoliticization was thus due to the fact that Libyans stopped making claims on a state they could not hope to reform. Indeed, in Libya, this process became so pronounced that even opposition groups operating outside the country were unable to develop a common plan for what the country's future should look like while Qadhafi remained in power.

The regime, nevertheless, did provide a number of symbolic outlets for citizens to vent their frustration. Qadhafi's oft-repeated remark that every popular congress to which individuals belong constitutes an opposition may seem trivial, but is nevertheless important. The congresses allowed individuals, without challenging the structure of the political system overall, to voice their complaints. Being officially outside the formal structure of authority, Qadhafi has often encouraged those criticisms, even in public settings, to extend his own plans and directives.

At the same time, Qadhafi's directives were meant to specifically prevent the emergence of any group that could potentially create an independent political base of support—whether as members of a tribe, a socioeconomic class, the Libyan military, a Popular or Revolutionary Committee, one of the country's multiple security organizations, or a class of intellectuals and students. The system of Popular Congresses and Committees was closely supervised in Tripoli, allowing the regime to create a security sector capable of preventing the emergence of any systematic articulation of political interests. Even the once most powerful members of that security system—the Revolutionary Committees—were never allowed to assume any autonomous power.

The absence of sustained and organized opposition until the country's fiscal crisis became acute in the late 1980s, however, testified once more to the resilience rulers in oil states like Libya possess in shaping, and holding in abeyance, demands for greater political input during boom periods—and, initially at least, during bust periods when reserves can be used to offset growing or persisting economic dislocations. By providing for Libyans' material and everyday needs, Qadhafi was able to prevent a coalescing of political interests based on purely economic criteria. It is this power, in addition to a preemption of the Islamic activism described previously and the skillful manipulation of charisma, myth, and revolutionary rhetoric, that were keys in maintaining his regime during the 1980s, even as its political and ideological fortunes diminished dramatically.

Confronting the West

Since 1969, Qadhafi's revolution has contained a strong element of anti-Western rhetoric that resonated strongly within the Middle East and North Africa, a region in the throes of Arab nationalism at the time. In Libya, the reaction against the West among the young revolutionaries was, in part, based on Libyans' historical memory of the Italian colonial period. But it also encompassed a much broader resentment against the role of the West, and particularly of the United States, within the region—a role Qadhafi would describe as imperialist and linked to an unwavering support for Israel. Following from this, the Libyan leader decried the exploitation of the country's resources by multinational companies that paid scant attention, he argued, to the needs of the country.

For most of the first decade after the coup, however, Libyan-U.S. relations remained characterized by caution and pragmatism on both sides. The United States, beyond its interests in the country's oil industry, was concerned about keeping the country outside the Soviet Union's orbit.

The Libyan government, despite the nationalization of some American and British oil interests in 1973, showed no inclination during its early years toward an open confrontation with the West. Its opposition remained a rhetorical tool used primarily for mobilization purposes inside Libya. Gradually, however, opposition to the West came to assume a larger role within the revolution during the 1970s and 1980s. When Gamal Abdul Nasser died in 1970, Qadhafi—much to the consternation, and often derision, of other Arab countries—thrust himself forward as the heir to the late Egyptian president's mission of creating a pan-Arab community that could blunt Western policies in the region. Qadhafi's politics within North Africa, however, systematically alienated most of his neighbors, leading to a protracted skirmish with Egypt in 1977—Qadhafi clearly viewing the Sadat regime as antithetical to the ideals of Nasser. In 1980, Saudi Arabia broke off diplomatic relations with the Libyan regime after a number of acrimonious exchanges over oil policies.[19]

That year, Libya's total development spending reached $10 billion per year. In 1981 alone, however, this still left $11 billion at the discretion of the government. Much of the money was spent, in part, on military purchases and international adventures. In 1981, Libya renewed its involvement in a dispute with Chad (dating from the monarchy) over the Aouzou strip. During the early 1980s, defense and military spending grew rapidly, even as development and regular administrative budgets were curtailed: defense, as part of the country's declared regular budget, climbed from $709 million to $1,149 million (16.7 percent and 23.6 percent, respectively) between 1982 and 1984.[20] Qadhafi's attempt to destabilize neighboring Tunisia led to a more open confrontation with France and the United States. In January 1981, the French government refused to implement a contract that had been signed between the oil parastatal Elf-Aquitaine and Lipetco, Libya's official investment company. France became more openly aligned against Libya following the latter's renewed invasion of Chad.

Libya's major confrontation, however, increasingly focused on the United States. The United States accused Libya of supporting terrorism, of engaging in subversion in sub-Saharan Africa and beyond, of boycotting the Middle East peace process and, eventually, of attempting to produce weapons of mass destruction. The assassination of Israeli athletes at the Munich 1972 Olympics and the 1973 killing of the U.S. ambassador to Sudan raised the first, albeit still unsubstantiated, questions about Libya's involvement with terrorist groups. These concerns were further heightened by the fact that the regime increasingly and openly expressed its support for radical Palestinian groups, and attempted to ship weapons to the Irish Republican Army. Several radical Palestinian movements—including the

Abu Nidal group, the Popular Front for the Liberation of Palestine-General Command, and Palestinian Islamic Jihad—had found a home in the jamahiriyya.[21] In 1989, Washington accused Libya of supporting roughly thirty international terrorist and revolutionary movements worldwide.

Libya's rhetoric against Israel remained intransigent as Qadhafi started to oppose U.S. efforts to resolve the Arab-Israeli conflict, culminating in the Libyan leader's public condemnation of the Camp David accords. Worried about these developments, and about the growing role of a Soviet presence in Libya, the Carter administration, in 1978, prohibited the sale of all military equipment to the jamahiriyya. By the end of the following year, Libya was put on the list of state sponsors of terrorism, which extended the ban to include most economic assistance to the country. On February 15, 1980, the United States closed its embassy in Tripoli.

In several ways, Libya's confrontation with the United States became a self-fulfilling prophecy as Qadhafi and successive U.S. presidents portrayed each other as outcasts in the international community. President Reagan's denunciation of Qadhafi as the "mad dog of the world" allowed the latter to deflect much of whatever internal criticism was gingerly voiced through the GPC, creating, as it did, the image of a highly unequal and hypocritical antagonism that the Libyan leader gladly exploited. President George H. W. Bush's later statement that "the politics and actions of the Government of Libya continue to pose an unusual and extraordinary threat to the national security and foreign policy of the United States"[22] only added to the David-versus-Goliath image Qadhafi was able to use for his own internal purposes

Clearly, however, the transfer of power in Washington from the Carter to the Reagan administration in January 1981 had marked a significant threshold for U.S.-Libyan relations. President Reagan, in part eager to demonstrate American strength in the region in the wake of the Soviet invasion of Afghanistan in 1979, viewed Libya as a highly visible and worthy target of his new policy of opposing regional adversaries. The United States moved with determination to further contain Libya. Arguing that the jamahiriyya was actively engaged in the destabilization of local regimes and in the promotion of international terrorism, in May 1981, the administration closed the Libyan People's Bureau (embassy) in Washington. The relations between the two countries continued to worsen when Washington accused Libya of attempting to assassinate U.S. officials. In August 1981, the confrontation took on a more ominous aspect when the United States's Sixth Fleet shot down two Libyan jet fighters over the Gulf of Sirte, which Libya claimed as its territorial waters, but which Washington viewed as an international waterway.

The dogfight and the way the dispute was addressed by both sides indicated the rapid deterioration of relations and the unwillingness of both sides to engage in constructive talks. In December 1981, U.S. citizens were prohibited from traveling to Libya, and President Reagan urged all Americans to leave the *jamahiriyya*. Soon afterward, in March 1982, all crude oil exports from Libya were embargoed, and exports of sophisticated oil and gas equipment prohibited. Meanwhile, on April 17, 1984, personnel at the Libyan People's Bureau in St. James Square in London shot and killed Yvonne Fletcher, a local policewoman who was on duty during an anti-Qadhafi demonstration taking place in the square. Reaction to the murder marked the beginning of more concerted efforts by the Europeans to isolate the country diplomatically—although, much to Washington's consternation, the European countries proved unwilling to move toward imposing economic sanctions. On the other hand, the U.S. boycott was further extended in November 1985 when President Reagan banned the import of refined petroleum products from Libya. A month later, terrorist attacks at the Rome and Vienna airports were linked to the Abu Nidal Organization, which, in turn, had close ties to Libya. As a result, in January 1986, President Reagan invoked the International Emergency Economic Powers Act that put a halt to all loans and credits to the *jamahiriyya*, prohibited all financial transactions of U.S. citizens with Libya, and froze Libyan foreign assets in the United States. In a message that showed how personalized the conflict between the two leaders had become, President Reagan clearly warned that the United States was willing to take further, and more decisive, steps if Qadhafi did not modify his behavior.[23] That next step—the bombing of Tripoli and Benghazi in April 1986—would prove a decisive turning point in the U.S.-Libyan confrontation, and would mark the beginning of a slow change and internal reappraisal of Libya's policies as well.

From the beginning of his tenure in office, Reagan attempted to destabilize the Qadhafi regime through covert actions, in addition to pinprick military confrontations over the Gulf of Sirte. Libyan opposition groups in the West and in Chad—where the administration supported the Chadian government of Hissen Habre in the war over the Aouzou strip—enjoyed U.S. support in an effort to further destabilize the regime. The covert efforts increased further after a June 1984 CIA assessment that asserted the overthrow of Qadhafi would be necessary to put a halt to Libyan aggression.[24]

The Libyan government skillfully exploited the confrontation with the West for its own purposes. In the wake of the Gulf of Sirte incident, in August 1981, Qadhafi attempted once more to mobilize Libyans in defense of the country, deftly using anti-American rhetoric for the purpose.[25] This time, the Libyan leader proposed a general militarization of the *jamahiriyya*—the creation of a popular militia that would gradually take over the functions of the regular army. Although Qadhafi had previously mentioned the idea on several occasions—and some arming of villages and indoctrination had started earlier under the guidance of ex-RCC member al-Hamidi—the 1981 attack provided the catalyst for this latest *zahf*.[26]

The skirmish also acted once more as a self-fulfilling prophecy for the regime. In addition to the surrounding countries that constituted Libya's "traditional enemies"—Egypt in the east, Tunisia in the west, Chad, aided by France, in the south—the country's leadership could now point to the United States as having crossed its self-proclaimed "line of death" in the Gulf of Sirte. The internal effects of the growing confrontation with the West were, at the time, seemingly of little importance. In many ways, the regime skillfully managed to exploit Libya's traditional distrust of outsiders. But the combination of diplomatic isolation—which made traveling outside Libya virtually impossible for its citizens—as well as the growing economic dislocations at home, had seemingly started to diminish Libyans' acceptance of their revolutionary leader's directives. In April 1986, when the United States bombed Benghazi and Tripoli, the attack was met by almost total apathy among the population: "One saw more demonstrators in Khartoum and Tunis than in Tripoli where the number of foreign journalists outnumbered Tripolitanians."[27] Several attempts by the regime to organize demonstrations in its wake were abandoned for lack of participants, and Qadhafi disappeared from the Libyan media for several weeks.

The worsening relationship with the United States, highly politicized by both sides for the sake of each country's political purposes, put increasing pressure on U.S. oil companies to review their investments in the *jamahiriyya* after the Reagan administration came to power. Exxon—represented in Libya by Esso Standard Libya, Inc. and Esso Sirte, Inc.—announced on November 4, 1981, that it would withdraw from operations in the country. Within a few months, on March 10, 1982, the U.S. government adopted a measure that prohibited the import of all Libyan oil into the country, and started to restrict the flow of U.S. goods to the *jamahiriyya*. In January 1983, Mobil followed suit and withdrew from operations after months of unsuccessful negotiations with LNOC officials.[28] By that time, several other companies had reviewed their own exposure in the country and, as in the case of the French parastatal Elf-Aquitaine, decided to at least temporarily halt the implementation of earlier signed contracts.

The Libyan government recognized the danger of a possible snowball effect and, throughout the 1981–84 years, consistently offered incentives to the remaining companies to maintain production. Occidental, one of the largest independent producers was offered a four-dollar price cut in

October 1981 in order to stimulate its production. The result was that prices of Libyan oil throughout 1983 remained substantially below the already low 1982 prices. The *jamahiriyya* was in the midst of an ambitious new development plan, and its planners had little choice but to offer incentives when the country's revenues were cut by one-third overnight as the United States implemented its boycott. Much of this financial crunch would be alleviated by the fact that European importers proved eager to take larger shares of Libyan production. But it meant that Libya, from July 1982 until the end of 1984, saw itself forced to consistently produce oil far in excess of the OPEC quota it had been assigned; during the first quarter of 1983, for example, it marketed 1.8 million bpd, an excess of 800,000 bpd.

United States' and Multilateral Sanctions

Between December 1979—when Libya had been put on the U.S. State Department's first list of state sponsors of terrorism—and the April 1986 U.S. bombing of Tripoli and Benghazi, several developments in the deteriorating relationship between the United States and the *jamahiriyya* had taken place. These included the closure of the U.S. embassy in Tripoli and of the People's Bureau in Washington, the embargo of crude oil, and then of refined petroleum products from Libya, and, finally, in January 1986, the comprehensive trade embargo against the *jamahiriyya*. Six years later, in April 1992, the United Nations, as well, would extend an economic embargo after Libya refused to turn over suspects involved in the December 1988 Pan Am 103 bombing over Lockerbie.

In order to understand the impact of both sets of economic sanctions, it is important to note that Libya's overall economic performance during these years steadily worsened. One aspect, certainly, was the decline of oil prices starting in the early 1980s, made worse by the dramatic plunge in 1986, when the Reagan administration imposed its first set of sanctions. With revenues from oil exports—which still made up 95 percent of the country's overall revenues—dramatically declining, and with the regime initially unwilling to cut back on military expenditures, the curbs on imports forced Libya to abandon a number of important projects that would have led to a greater diversification of the economy. The country drew down its international reserves, sought to conclude a number of barter deals rather than paying in cash for projects, and committed less money to making payments on its trade debts. A second point to consider is the impact of the economic directives of the *Green Book* during the regime's revolutionary decade, as described previously. While Libya may have outspent most other oil exporters in the region during the 1986–2001 period, its economic performance consistently lagged behind countries that were exposed to similar oil shocks. The turmoil surrounding the *Green Book*'s economic directives must be blamed, to a large extent, for that economic downturn.

In light of these two factors, the direct impact of the United States' unilateral sanctions between 1986 and 1992 was relatively small. Its importance was not so much in influencing Libyan economic decisions directly, but in heightening the country's vulnerability to the multilateral sanctions that were to follow in the 1990s: it also forced Libya to conclude deals with economic partners, particularly in the oil industry, it would normally have eschewed. Despite the fact that the United States had been the single largest importer of Libyan oil in 1981, the 1982 ban on imports of Libyan crude had been offset by the country's ability to sell to the European market, and by its ability to bring crude on the U.S. market via the spot market or as a refined product. Greater damage was done, however, by the impact of the U.S. ban on the country's investment pattern. Since the early 1980s, Libya had started to invest considerable amounts of money in downstream activities in Europe, acquiring a network of gasoline stations across Western and Eastern Europe, Egypt, and Malta, in addition to refineries for its oil. These investments had been made in part in anticipation of, and in part as a reaction to, the U.S. ban, in order to guarantee that the country would be able to find steady outlets for its oil. There was, in addition, a political dimension to these investments as well: Tripoli clearly considered that they would help to solidify closer relations with Europe. Once the U.S. ban had been expanded to all exports to the *jamahiriyya*, the impact on Libya became more onerous as the country faced the withholding of aviation technology, airplane parts, and other types of high technology for its oil industry. In 1983 alone, the United States had vetoed almost $600 million worth of large civil aircraft export licenses to the country. Libya proved able to secure most of these embargoed imports from other sources, but at a considerably higher cost.

Similarly, the 1986 freeze of all Libyan foreign assets in the United States was relatively benign since Libya had been careful not to make substantial investments in the country, and had shifted most of its liquid assets to other venues in anticipation of U.S. measures. Overall, it was estimated that less than 2 percent of Libya's total overseas investments of roughly $5 billion were affected.[29] United States' pressure on international lending agencies to avoid extending loans to Libya also proved, at best, a minor irritant since the *jamahiriyya* was either not eligible to borrow from the World Bank because of its relative wealth, or simply refused to do so. In part because of political considerations, but also because of a lack of sophistication in managing its financial fluctuations, Libyan policymakers, rather than increasing the country's foreign debt to offset balance of payments deficits simply ran down its foreign reserves, cut back on imports, temporarily suspended payment of trade debts, or swapped oil for imported goods. Hence, Libya's foreign debt remained quite small throughout the 1980s and into the 1990s. There was, however, an unavoidable demonstration effect to the U.S. sanctions and to the unorthodox methods Libya used to meet its financial obligations. Some Western export credit agencies refused to extend further government medium- and long-term credits to the country, and some banks, shipping companies, and assorted international companies reviewed their exposure to Libya, wary of the country's reputation for unpredictability and of the chaos brought about by the *Green Book*'s directives.

Until the imposition of the multilateral sanctions in April 1992, Libya's oil production and export levels remained in line with its OPEC quota. The LNOC assumed operation of the oilfields once run by U.S. companies as soon as Washington announced the sanctions. As a result, when U.S. companies were told in 1986 to curtail their operations in producing and marketing almost one-third of Libya's oil for the European market, the LNOC readily took over the responsibility. But most observers agreed that the Libyan oil sector was in urgent need of modernization, in part because some of the fields had been producing since the 1950s and needed new recovery technology.[30] U.S. technology, know-how, and equipment had been instrumental in building and maintaining the Libyan oil industry since the 1950s. The LNOC not only had difficulty acquiring the needed spare parts as the unilateral sanctions were put into place, but simply did not have the needed expertise and technological knowledge to maintain production at a steady level. In addition, many European firms proved reluctant to provide that expertise and manpower, despite a number of "gentlemen's agreements" between them and the U.S. government to watch over claims of American companies in the country.

Overall, the U.S. sanctions on Libya's oil sector by themselves had an almost negligible direct impact—Libya would unlikely have had the capability to produce substantially more oil during the 1980s, even if the sanctions had not existed. The regulations under the Iran Libya Sanctions Act (ILSA) of 1996 proved of marginal value in deterring investment. Investment patterns in Libya hardly changed after its passage, due, in large part, to the fact that the country—except for a major overhaul of some of its infrastructure—was not in need of substantial investments that would have superseded the $40 million limit imposed by ILSA. In addition, companies simply amended old contracts to accommodate new investments, and avoided signing new contracts that could have triggered ILSA regulations. But the combination of ILSA and previous sanctions did create an environment in which the long-term prospects for the country's oil industry became more closely circumscribed, and the earlier set of U.S. sanctions made the country's economy overall more sensitive (if not vulnerable) to additional pressures that would soon materialize in the form of multilateral sanctions. In many ways, the U.S. sanctions magnified the overall existing problems in Libya's oil sector, creating greater uncertainty in the process.

The seven-year period of multilateral sanctions (April 1992–April 1999) against Libya, combined with existing conditions within the country, proved much more damaging than the United States sanctions alone had been. Libya's economy grew only 0.8 percent a year during the period, and, at the same time, the country's per capita GDP fell from $7,311 to $5,896.[31] In 1998 alone, the country's export earnings had dropped to roughly $7 billion, the lowest since the oil price crash of 1986. The financial impact of the multilateral sanctions had, as in the case of the U.S. unilateral ones, been mitigated by shifting Libyan assets away from vulnerable locations. But, as a result, Libya's ability to earn income abroad hampered its ability to pay foreign companies. In the more restrictive economic climate of the 1990s this proved a much bigger irritant than it had been in the previous decade, forcing Libya to further limit trade, and making it more difficult to secure short-term credit at a time when oil prices further declined.

The trade restrictions under the multilateral sanctions proved much more difficult to deal with. Adjusting and shifting trade patterns, as Libya had done previously, no longer proved possible. The ban on imports particularly affected Libya's downstream oil operations and its aviation industry. Its inability to obtain equipment for the maintenance of its refineries forced Libya to search for substitute technology and parts (often, on the black market) that were often suboptimal, and were several times more expensive than normal international market prices. It also made it necessary for Libya to forego upgrading its refineries, making it impossible to produce more gasoline for domestic consumption. It also meant that Libya had to spend increasingly scarce foreign reserves for purchasing lighter fuels abroad, rather than being able to use its own best quality crude for producing more lucrative high-end fuels. The country's airline industry was also dramatically affected: with a halt in passenger traffic, a shortage of spare parts, and a deteriorating technical capability, the damage went far beyond the estimated financial loss of $900 million during the period.[32]

The uncertainty surrounding the sanctions proved, as always, to make matters worse. Subject to review by the Security Council every four months, the fear of additional, more stringent measures, as well as the continued pressure from the United States for such actions, proved a deterrent in several ways. The value of the Libyan dinar declined, and inflationary pressures were exacerbated by the fact that all commodities had to be brought into the country overland or by sea, and by the growing pressure of a burgeoning black market. The sanctions also forced Libya to maintain an unnecessarily high level of reserves, not knowing whether or not additional sanctions would be imposed. With domestic investment virtually halted, the government was forced to curtail several development projects, and the country suffered shortages of foreign exchange throughout the period of the multilateral sanctions. In addition, the continuing uncertainties, the lack of international flights into the country, the sheer inconvenience of gaining access to the country, and the lack of financial resources to devote to it forced Libya to further invest in several sectors, notably tourism, which had been earmarked for expansion.

As a result of the sanctions, international companies grew more reluctant to work in Libya, and the premium required for their services reflected the high price the country paid. As described in the next section, within the energy sector, Libya proved able to continue attracting largely Western and Eastern European investment, but, on some occasions, it had to rely on companies it would, except for the sanctions, have avoided. Several of these were small- to medium-sized companies with limited production capabilities or services that preferred to invest in projects with short-term payoffs rather than the more complex and long-term agreements the Libya government hoped to conclude in order to expand exploration beyond the Sirte basin. As the country's oil infrastructure aged, as the sanctions started to impinge on the ability of the country to get cutting edge technology, and as production leveled off, Libya's oil industry often relied on second-rate technologies, and proved able to attract only a few companies that had sufficient know-how for the kind of enhanced oil recovery techniques it needed.

The oilfields that had been taken over from U.S. companies by the LNOC slowly declined in production as Libya struggled to manage them with increasingly outdated U.S. equipment. Production from LNOC-operated fields declined, on average, 8 percent annually after the take-over. Finally, Libya also hoped to exploit its enormous, and largely unexploited, natural gas reserves, primarily for the European market, but also to substitute natural gas for oil on the domestic market. Although several companies expressed an interest, it was clear that interest among international companies remained limited as long as the sanctions were in place. In 1993, LNOC ultimately signed a large $5.5 billion joint venture for development of the Western Libyan Gas Project with one of its oldest customers, Italy's Agip-ENI. It involved an undersea pipeline—since constructed—to bring the gas, via Sicily, to Italy. Agip-ENI argued that, since the original contract had been signed in 1993, it was exempted from ILSA's regulations. The controversy surrounding the contract, however, ensured that further development of the country's enormous natural gas fields would remain suspended until more propitious times made international investments possible again.

The Limits of Revolutionary Fervor

In retrospect, it is quite clear that the April 1986 bombing of Tripoli and Benghazi, as well as the combination of U.S. and multilateral sanctions, created considerable difficulties for the Libyan leadership. It also, in some ways, came to represent a watershed for the country's international politics. The bombing, in particular, created a high level of consternation among the country's leadership. The country's defenses, in the face of the attacks, had proven feeble. Some Revolutionary Committee members had quietly abandoned their positions, and there were rumors of organized resistance in the eastern part of the country immediately after the attack. The response of the population to calls for massive anti-U.S. rallies by the Libyan leader were, at best, lackluster. The psychological shock that the United States would actually target Libyan cities—and, it was hinted at, the Libyan leader himself—left a deep despondency and an initially confused attempt to evaluate what the country's options were.

For weeks after the bombing, the Libyan leader did not appear on television. When he finally did so, he defiantly called for *tawsi' ath-thawra*—an extension of the revolution. But beneath the veneer of traditional rhetoric, this new wave of reforms represented nothing but a careful recalibration of the country's structures of control. Aware that the previous decade had witnessed the introduction of a number of nefarious measures—particularly the expansion of the unpredictable revolutionary authority system that had raised considerable concern and uncertainty among Libyan citizens—the "extension of the revolution," in reality, meant its opposite: a curtailing of its more disliked political and economic revolutionary measures. Qadhafi, in his speeches after April 1986, castigated Libyans, in his usual populist fashion, about their waste and lack of initiative, and decried the impact of some of the "revolutionary means of governing," and of the isolation the country found itself in. These concerns were taken up publicly at the February 1987 GPC meeting in Sabha.[33] The delegates at the meeting, as well, voiced a number of public concerns about economic management of the country, their specificity and sophistication indicating that the criticisms had been approved in advance by the regime.

Throughout 1987 and in 1988, Qadhafi publicly deplored the excesses of the country's security organizations and of the Revolutionary Committees. Particularly, the latter were singled out for their behavior. A special committee was appointed under the leadership of the country's Minister of Justice, responsible for investigating charges of corruption and of abuse of power by Revolutionary Committee members. By December 1988, the Revolutionary Committees started to lose power, as their presence in the intelligence, police, and security sector was curtailed. A Ministry of Mass Mobilization and Revolutionary Leadership was created under Ali Al-Sha'iri, one of the regime's most trusted members. His task was to control the Revolutionary Committee movement, and to bring its task more narrowly back from an overall guard dog of the regime to its original role as an ideological vanguard.[34] Simultaneously, the regime attempted to expand its political liberalization to a wider audience. In 1987, and throughout 1988, scores of political prisoners were released.

After the difficult years of the country's revolutionary decade, these small, but symbolically important, measures provided the regime with breathing room that had not existed before. It reached out, furthermore, to entice Libyan exiles back to the country, making promises of employment and of immunity from prosecution. Confiscated passports were returned to Libyan citizens, and their issuance was now entrusted to Popular Committees rather than to the security sector organizations. The Libyan leader also met with some opposition figures, hoping to bring them back to Libya as a show of support for the regime, but largely failed to do so.

In one of his most remarkable declarations since 1969, Qadhafi then adopted the *Al-Wathiqa al-Khadra al-Kubra lil-huquq al-insan fi 'asr al-Jamahir*—the Great Green Charter of Human Rights in the Era of the Masses—a document meant to provide greater personal rights to Libyans, and to halt the arbitrariness and unpredictability of the country's previous revolutionary decade.[35] Its Article 11, for example, recalled the earlier revolutionary directives on private property, and declared it "sacred and protected." There were further references to accountability for everyone, much in the same vein as the earlier criticism of the Revolutionary Committees.

Qadhafi's attempt to bring greater predictability and accountability must be viewed, therefore, within the larger context of the country's political life, and particularly within its formal and informal power structures. The Great Green Charter did not contain any stipulation that would have allowed political opposition, nor did it make the expression of such opposition in any public setting possible. As the Libyan leader continued to argue, Libya was a *jamahiriyya* ruled directly by its citizens. Hence, the rules of opposition and of free expression did not apply. In effect, the Great

Green Charter did not provide either the civil or political rights that are normally provided under international law nor, as one long-term observer noted, "the privileges of citizenship."[36] In the end, many of the Charter's stipulations and guarantees were eviscerated in the early 1990s as opposition to the regime intensified. The simultaneous reshuffle of the country's cabinet that followed the announcement of the Great Charter further heightened existing uncertainties. Two of its newly appointed ministers were long-time "Green Men"—dedicated revolutionaries. Their appointment indicated that the regime was not taking any chances. Furthermore, Qadhafi's reconfirmation at the March 1990 GPC Congress of the separation between formal and revolutionary authority was the final confirmation that, for all its promises, the Great Green Charter would never be allowed to affect or diminish the control functions of the regime.

The Limits of Economic Reform

The relaxation of some of the regime's revolutionary measures was matched in the economic arena by an attempt to reduce the hardships of the *Green Book*'s directives regarding the role of the state and of private enterprise in the *jamahiriyya*. While Qadhafi skillfully blended populist appeals with his usual blunt criticisms and exhortations for greater personal involvement, Ahmad Jalud at the GPC Secretariat meeting of July 18, 1987, dissected the structural origins of Libya's economic difficulties in a more technocratic fashion. He pinpointed the persisting mismanagement of the economy, the difficulties in establishing coherent acquisition programs for the country—in light of the growing impact of the economic boycott by the United States—high levels of inflation, and an inability to guarantee distribution of goods for both industrial and consumer purposes.[37]

Jalud's expose had captured the by now familiar dilemmas of development in oil states. Libya's first oil boom during the monarchy, as well as the oil booms of 1973 and 1979, had represented peculiar challenges to the country, such as how to efficiently use the sudden windfalls for purposes of general economic development. In the *jamahiriyya*, this process of spending and of foregoing regulation to manage the local economy had gone far beyond simple benign neglect, and had been exacerbated and purposefully extended by Qadhafi's insistence that state institutions were to be smashed. Even more than in other oil exporters of the region, the distribution of the country's revenues, and the virtually unlimited spending, even as economic clouds gathered on the horizon during the early 1980s, were meant to achieve political goals. The spending had implicitly imposed upon the country's citizens a social contract during the boom years that, in return for political quiescence, promised that the state would take care of citizens' daily economic needs.

The economic and political reforms in Libya after 1986 were, therefore, intrinsically linked—for real economic liberalization and reform would have meant the introduction of markets and competitive market processes that inevitably create conflicts between citizens about access to economic resources. Markets also invariably create disparities in income. Indeed, it was to avoid both phenomena—which Qadhafi viewed as detrimental to citizen interaction in a political community—that the *Green Book* had eschewed a reliance on market mechanisms. Economic liberalization efforts in Libya, therefore, represented a fourfold challenge to the regime: a need to create new institutions to better regulate and make economic transactions more transparent, to reform institutions whose primary goal often focused on simply distributing revenues gathered by the state, to introduce markets and competition for resources, and, finally, to contain whatever political fallout the three previous sets of measures might entail. Qadhafi clearly understood the implications of what a sustained economic liberalization effort would mean but, despite his reservations, embarked upon a liberalization of the country's economy: a first attempt between 1987 and 1990, followed by a second set of initiatives after 1990.

The first set of reforms centered on the introduction of *tashrukiyya* (self-management) enterprises that allowed for the creation of coopera- tives that workers could manage collectively. Simultaneously, the ban against the retail trade was lifted, allowing private shops to reopen. In September 1988, the state's monopoly on imports and exports was aban- doned, as well as subsidies on tea, flour, salt, and wheat. Farmers' markets— officially abandoned, but reluctantly tolerated, during the revolutionary decade—reappeared. Professionals were allowed to resume private prac- tices, even though the government maintained its role in setting fees.

The measures taken after 1990 were meant to reinforce and extend this earlier wave of reforms. Qadhafi now argued publicly for a clear distinction between the private sector and the state, in order to "take the burden off public institutions."[38] He suggested the closing of unprofitable state enter- prises, the imposition of higher fees for state-provided services like water and electricity, and a reduction in the number of state employees. A num- ber of state and commercial banks were created. Hoping to capture some of the capital flows that sustained the informal economy, special laws were passed to offer protection for reinvested capital. The second wave's final directives, in the spring and summer of 1993, focused on efforts to pro- mote tourism—hoping to capitalize on the country's desert and archaeo- logical sites—and to provide greater guarantees for foreign investment.

Convertibility of the Libyan dinar was taken up by the GPC in January 1994, but remained unaddressed for the time being.[39]

At the surface, the number and range of measures suggested in the adopted legislation would have made the Libyan economic liberalization one of the most dramatic in the region's history of economic reform during the 1980s and 1990s. It would also have dramatically recalibrated the position of the state within the economy and, by implication, altered the way in which the regime could use economic patronage for its own political goals and, ultimately, for its survival. In the end, the liberalization effort faltered. In effect, the attempted reforms could, perhaps, be best described as a subterfuge, where a hesitating, newly created private sector was allowed to provide and distribute what the state—through its inefficient distribution system of state supermarkets—could not deliver to Libyan citizens, leaving the state in charge of the distribution of welfare provisions. As a result, by the mid-1990s, Libya was filled, once more, with the kind of consumer goods and food supplies it had enjoyed before the revolutionary decade. The lack of confidence in the local economy, however, was demonstrated by the fact that, for most everyday purchases, the U.S. dollar had become the currency of choice.

The failure of the reforms furthermore revealed, in stark fashion, the deleterious impact of the long-term neglect of the economy, and of the impact of the revolutionary measures on the economy and on the country's political system. In addition, as one of the country's top policymakers admitted in retrospect, reform of the economy was unlikely to take place under the difficult circumstances that resulted from the sanctions.[40] In desperation, in 1997, the General People's Congress adopted Law No. 5 that allowed for foreign direct investment in the country. But it was a sign of the times that the measure generated virtually no response.

Libya's economic dirigisme, once imposed according to Qadhafi's *Green Book* precisely to avoid the economic differentiation and the intense struggles that regulating private sector activities entails in market economies, could no longer be sustained as a result of the economy's inefficiencies, the rampant corruption, and the growing impact of the multilateral sanctions. But the challenges to the country's economic and political mechanisms were enormous after decades of centralization and lack of regulation. The very purpose of the country's liberalization had been to introduce market mechanisms. This would have necessitated, on the part of the country's rulers, an attempt to create functioning regulatory and administrative institutions that could support a market economy. A sustained liberalization in Libya would, at least temporarily, have meant a greater involvement by the state in making an economic transition possible—to tax, to collect and disseminate information, to dispense law, and to define and enforce property rights. This "perfection of the state" very clearly remained unacceptable to Qadhafi, whose basic philosophical tenet still focused on the lessening of the state's impact on citizens' lives.

In addition, the dirigisme of the country's economy had, long ago, become an important mechanism of control for the Qadhafi government. Not surprisingly, therefore, local reactions to the country's attempts at reform and liberalization revealed the interests and power of different constituencies in Libya. The initial phase met with little resistance since the liberalization of trade and the end of import regulations benefited consumers and small entrepreneurs who were now free to import food and consumer goods from abroad. This first set of measures also did not affect the fortunes of those groups deemed vital to the Libyan leader's maintenance of power: the country's top technocrats within LNOC, and other privileged and protected state institutions, managers of state enterprises, the military, and those entrepreneurs with close links to the military. Indeed, the first phase strengthened their fortunes: they could now more easily gain access to credit, engage openly in import and export transactions, and use more readily available foreign currency for major capital goods imports.

The second wave, if implemented, would have hurt virtually all groups in the country. Real import regulations and free access for everyone to a liberalized banking system, for example, would have ended the economic riches provided to those who could obtain licenses. For the average Libyan, the second wave proved unwelcome as well. The loss of wage policies and subsidies that had kept their standard of living (at a relatively low level) would perhaps disappear. The idea, furthermore, of becoming entrepreneurs in a political system that had been marked for almost two decades by high levels of unpredictability produced little enthusiasm. The Qadhafi government had fostered this unpredictability, and had implicitly, through its distributive policies, fostered citizens' inclinations to avoid personal initiative and risk. In the end, no group in Libya considered the economic liberalization strategies in their interest—an ominous omen for the renewed liberalization efforts a decade later (see Chapter 9).

The End of the Revolution

By the year 2000, three decades after his 1969 military take-over, Qadhafi's attempts at statelessness and popular rule looked increasingly tarnished, if not in outright disarray. Neither the successive waves of mobilization, nor outside military action against the *jamahiriyya*, had managed to maintain or rekindle a measurable level of popular support. Despite the regime's attempts to portray itself as a victim of U.S. and international aggression, and to link the country's economic difficulties to the imposed sanctions, none resulted in a hoped-for surge of support and legitimacy for the regime. The Popular Committee and Congress system persisted as the country's sole political institution, but few Libyans had any illusions as to its actual power. As in most other oil states in the region, legitimacy in the *jamahiriyya* remained intricately linked to the regime's ability to provide a certain level of economic well-being to local citizens. As the sanctions took hold, inflation soared, and the delivery of goods often became erratic and unpredictable. The everyday lives of Libyans had become measurably more difficult. At the end of the 1990s, wages, often at a dismal 250–300 dinars per month, even for highly qualified personnel, had been frozen for almost two decades. Petty bureaucrats and professionals alike were moonlighting to make ends meet. The regime had allowed the reemergence of some retail trade in the cities, while the state supermarkets stood abandoned or were transformed into government offices. Despite these palliatives, however, the diplomatic isolation that made travel and education in the West more difficult—and, in the case of the United States, impossible—still imposed a heavy toll.

The "extension of the revolution" after the U.S. bombing in 1986, the two waves of economic liberalization, the Great Green Charter of Human Rights, the halting diplomatic attempts to bring Libya back into the international community, the temporary curtailment of the Revolutionary Committees: all were meant to rejuvenate support for the regime at a time it felt besieged. None of these, however, altered the country's basic political structures that concentrated power at the very top around Qadhafi, protected by a bevy of security apparatuses and informal groups. Although the economic liberalization and the curtailment of the Revolutionary Committee movement fleetingly tempered the confusion and the arbitrariness that had marked daily life in the *jamahiriyya* since the early 1970s, there were, as yet, no signs of any kind of political transparency, accountability, or the rule of law that could have consolidated both sets of reforms on a more permanent basis. In the end, the regime reaped what it had so deliberately sown: unwilling to remove the kinds of unpredictability that made Libyan citizens reluctant to participate either economically or politically in running the country, most had simply become bystanders in a system they had no chance of reforming. So profound was this depoliticization that even opposition groups operating outside Libya confessed their inability to affect events inside the *jamahiriyya* until the Qadhafi regime had been removed.[41]

It was ironic, therefore, that, despite the use of continuous revolutionary exhortations for self-reliance and activism, the *jamahiriyya* had become a county where virtually everything—from food to high technology items—was imported. Libyans absorbed all the benefits bestowed upon it by an oil economy, but politically stood cowered and silent. Opposition was, by the fact that Libyans, in principle, ruled themselves, impossible. This enduring contradiction between Qadhafi's incessant calls for activism, and the passivity the political system itself engendered, stood starkly revealed as Libya moved toward the new millennium.

The failure of the two waves of economic liberalization provided important indications of the intimate links between the politics and the economic development problems of the country. After three decades of centralization, of poor decision making, of outright neglect, and of making economic development subject to the whims of revolutionary pursuits, Libya had developed intricate patterns of patronage that, in effect, constituted major political, as well as economic, liabilities to serious reform. The state's ability to provide (decreasing levels of) welfare to the general population had—as long as the oil boom lasted—became part and parcel of the regime's populist rhetoric, and of its ability to handsomely reward its close supporters. Both sets of entitlements were under siege by the end of the 1990s.

Such is the resilience to reform in oil exporters like Libya, however, that it would take another two-and-a-half years before the spectacular announcement of Libya's renunciation of weapons of mass destruction in December 2003 opened up the road toward full-fledged international normalization, and toward badly needed economic reconstruction and possible reform. As the new millennium dawned, however, seasoned observers and participants alike realized that—whatever the outside pressures on Libya were, and for a number of internal reasons as well—Libya's revolution had run its course. Qadhafi himself, in a number of adroit speeches, tried to portray Libya's shifting policies—in such sharp contrast to his old rhetoric—as a new beginning: the "liberation stage" of his revolution had successfully ended, and a new page could now be turned. As the daily reading of a fragment of his *Green Book* on Libyan television proclaimed, the world was now ready for its own international version of the Enduring Revolution. The *jamahiriyya* should take up its historic role in facilitating its adoption everywhere.[42] Except among a handful of the regime's core supporters, the exhortation no longer had the power to even provoke serious debate.

Almost a decade later, in February 2011, Qadhafi's Libya would erupt into an uprising that would change Libya's political landscape forever. The period between December 2003 and the uprising in 2011, however, witnessed some of the most intense—and ultimately unsuccessful—attempts to reform the country's political and economic systems. The failure to reform arguably contributed to the events that transpired in the spring of 2011.

Notes

1. Ruth First, *Libya: The Elusive Revolution* (Harmondsworth, England: Penguin, 1974), 110–16.

2. Qadhafi, Mu'ammar al-, *As-Sijil al-qawmi bayanat wa ahadith al-aqid Mu'ammar al-Qadhdhafi* (Tripoli: Marakiz ath-thaqafiya al-qawmiya, 1969–70).

3. See Judith Gurney, *Libya: The Political Economy of Oil* (Oxford: Oxford University Press, 1996), 48–49 for details.

4. *Middle East Economic Digest*, August 31, 1979.

5. *Al-Fajr Al-Jadid*, September 12–13, 1974, September 13, 1974.

6. Hervé Bleuchot, *Chroniques et documents libyens, 1969–1980* (Paris: Editions du Centre National de la Recherche Scientifique, 1983), 86–89.

7. *As-Sijil Al-Qawmi (SQ)* 1976–77, 470–78.

8. *Al-Jarida Al-Rasmiyya*, May 8, 1978, 491.

9. Mimeo General People's Congress (GPC) Tripoli, December 12, 1989.

10. On the revolutionary committees, see Habib el-Hesnawi, *The Revolutionary Committees and Their Role in the Confirmation and Consolidation of the People's Authority* (Tripoli: Green Book Center, 1987); *Al-Lijan ath-thawriya* (in Arabic) (Tripoli: al-Markaz al-'alami li-dirasat wa-abhath al-kitab al-akhdar, 1985); and the relevant chapters in Hanspeter Mattes, *Die Volksrevolution in der Sozialistischen Libyschen Arabischen Volksgamahiriyya* (Heidelberg, Germany: Kivouvou Verlag, 1982).

11. *SQ* 1978–79, 21.

12. Cited in Mattes 1982, op. cit., 97.

13. *SQ* 1980–81, 567–81; see also Ahmad Ibrahim, *Revolutionary Organization* (Tripoli: Green Book Center, 1983). Ibrahim specifically condones violence as a tactic. He later became secretary (minister) for education and scientific research and remains (in 2007) Assistant Secretary of the General People's Congress.

14. Elizabeth Mayer, "In Search of sacred Law: The Meandering Course of Qadhafi's Legal Policy," in *Qadhafi's Libya, 1969 to 1994*, ed. Dirk Vandewalle (New York: St. Martin's, 1995), 114–15.

15. *JR*, May 29, 1981, 1124.

16. *SQ*, 1980–81, 1207.

17. For more information, consult Dirk Vandewalle, "The Failure of Liberalization in the Jamahiriyya," in *Qadhafi's Libya, 1969 to 1994*, ed. Dirk Vandewalle (New York: St. martin's, 1995).

18. For a flavor of the continuing infighting among the groups, see FBIS November 3, 1993, 21 and FBIS November 17, 1993, 26–27.

19. *Middle East Economic Digest*, March 11, 1980, 1.

20. *MEES*, April 15, 1985, B1–2.

21. For Libya's involvement in terrorism, see the annual volumes of the U.S. Department of State's *Patterns of Global Terrorism*.

22. Bush 1993, 3.

23. *Public Papers of Presidents: Ronald Reagan, 1986,* vol. 1, 18 (Washington: Government Printing Office, 1988).

24. "CIA Anti-Qaddafi Plan Backed: Reagan Authorizes Covert Operation to Undermine Libyan Regime," *Washington Post,* November 3, 1985, A1.

25. *Al-Zahf Al-Akhdar* August 22, 1981; *Annuaire de l'Afrique du Nord* 1981, 561.

26. See *Annuaire de l'Afrique du Nord (AAN)* 20 (1981), 558 for more details on the January 1981 Congress.

27. Alain Frachon, "Les défauts de l'armure du colonel," *Le Monde* April 30, 1986.

28. For more details, consult *MEES* 25, no. 41 (July 26, 1982), 3–4; 25, no. 42 (August 2, 1982), 3.

29. Economist Intelligence Unit (EIU), *Country Report: Libya,* First Quarter, 1986, 13. Also cited in O'Sullivan, 192.

30. See Gurney, 97.

31. EIU, *Country Profile: Libya 2001,* 25.

32. An estimate by the chairman of Libyan Arab Airlines. See EIU, *Country Report: Libya,* Third Quarter, 1997, 15. Also cited by O'Sullivan, 381, 89n.

33. *Al-Zahf Al-Akhdar,* February 15, 1987, February 17, 1987.

34. The most complete analysis of the fortunes of the Revolutionary Committees can be found in Hanspeter Mattes, "The Rise and Fall of the Revolutionary Committees," in *Qadhafi's Libya, 1969–1994,* ed. Dirk Vandewalle (New York: St. Martin's, 1995), 89–112.

35. See Ann Elizabeth Mayer, "In Search of Sacred Law: The Meandering Course of Qadhafi's Legal Policy," in *Qadhafi's Libya, 1969–1994, ed.* Dirk Vandewalle (New York: St. Martin's), 113–38 for a detailed analysis of the Great Green Charter's provisions and shortcomings from a legal viewpoint.

36. Moncef Djaziri, "Creating a New State: Libya's Political Institutions," in *Qadhafi's Libya, 1969–1994,* ed. Dirk Vandewalle (New York: St. Martin's), 197.

37. *Al-Fajr Al-Jadid,* July 20, 1987.

38. FBIS, September 2, 1992, and FBIS, September 1, 1988, for the earlier reforms.

39. MEED, September 18, 1992; FBIS, March 24, 1993; JR, March 27, 1993; FBIS, May 10, 1993; FBIS, July 13, 1993; FBIS, February 2, 1994.

40. Interview with Abu Zayed Dorda, Tripoli, January 17, 2005.

41. A comprehensive anthology of articles and statements published by the National Front for the Salvation of Libya can be found in *Libya Under Gaddafi And The NFSL Challenge* (National Front for the Salvation of Libya, 1992).

42. Among a plethora of articles and speeches, see Douglas Jehl, "Thirty Years Later, Is It Really Qadhafi?" *International Herald Tribune,* September 7, 1999.

2

Formal and Informal Authority in Libya since 1969

Hanspeter Mattes

In 2008, Libya's revolutionary regime will have existed for thirty-nine years. Its leader, Mu'ammar al-Qadhafi, has become the doyen of the Arab heads of state. The durability of the regime, despite numerous domestic and foreign political challenges and conflicts, has provided analysts much to ponder. Two areas of focus provide the structure to this chapter: (a) an analysis of the institutions, organizations, and political groups that have been used by the revolutionary regime to keep itself in power since 1969, and (b) an elaboration on the mechanisms the regime uses when faced with challenges and opposition. These mechanisms have ranged from outright repression and physical liquidation of opponents to the revitalization of tribal structures within the country's civilian and military sectors. All organizations used in the maintenance of the regime have been created by its leadership and are beholden only to it.

The political flexibility of these arrangements has resulted largely from the informal character of the Libyan state, whose institutions were only defined for a short period between 1969 and 1977 by the Provisional Constitutional Declaration of December 11, 1969. Since 1977, none of the country's central political personalities have been constitutionally defined. Their existence is based purely on their revolutionary legitimacy. Actors like the *Free Unionist Officers Movement*, the *Revolutionary Committees*, the *Forum of the Companions of Qadhafi*, or the *Social People's Leadership Committees* have internal statutes, but they were not created as the result of actual legislation. In addition, the existing legislative and executive organs of the state have no constitutional basis in the *jamahiriyya*. *The Declaration of Authority of the People* of March 1977, a document that has assumed the stature of basic law in Libya, clearly spells out the lines of authority in the third of its four articles: "The People's direct democracy is the basis of the political system in the Socialist People's Libyan Arab Jamahiriya, where the authority is in the hands of the People alone. The People exercise their authority through the People's Congresses, the People's Committees, and the Professional Unions." The regulations of the congresses, committees, and professional unions as well as the dates of their meetings are defined by law. Nevertheless, as described below, legislation in Libya most often mirrors the visions of the revolutionary leadership, and clearly indicates the dominance and supremacy of the revolutionary sector over the state's legislative and executive organisations.

The Libyan Political System and Its Main Protagonists

Mu'ammar al-Qadhafi was the engineer and driving force behind the *Free Unionist Officers Movement* that overthrew the Sanusi monarchy on September 1, 1969, and proclaimed the *Libyan Arab Republic*. From the very beginning, Qadhafi had definite ideas about the objectives of political action expressed in his often repeated slogans of "freedom, socialism, unity," but lacked notions of precise political structures. Although the young leadership soon adopted a Nasserist constitutional model on December 11, 1969, it was never made clear how precisely Libyan citizens would participate in political decisions. The model of a Nasserist single party came to dominate the county in the shape of the Libyan *Arab Socialist Union* (ASU), founded in June 1971. In April 1973, the political system was redesigned according to revolutionary principles, abandoning the Egyptian model—a move that had been announced by Qadhafi during his important Zuwara speech of April 15, 1973.[1] The speech had been a reaction to what he considered the unsatisfactory attempts of the single party structure to enforce the revolutionary socioeconomic edicts of the regime. At Zuwara, the Libyan leader announced his *People's Revolution*,[2] which would lead to the reshaping of the country's state structures according to the *Third Universal Theory* and the first part of the *Green Book*.[3]

These new state structures were constitutionally solidified in the Proclamation of People's Power[4] of March 2, 1977. The new structures represent what the Libyan leader called a form of direct democracy, and are expressed institutionally by People's Congresses (having a legislative function), and by People's Committees that possess executive functions. People's Congresses and People's Committees are fundamental aspects of the *Green Book* and, as such, are a core element of the Libyan leader's ideology.[5]

Since 1977, however, the central element of the Libyan political system has been the Revolutionary Committees, which were not mentioned in the *Green Book* or in the Proclamation of People's Power. The Revolutionary Committees under Qadhafi's personal leadership are responsible, along with other security departments, for protecting the revolutionary system. Even though the Committees have lost some of their profile, as domestic policies became more pragmatic in the last few years, they remain a privileged security organization within the Jamahiriya that can rapidly be reactivated, if needed.[6] This insistence on revolutionary methods of governing means, in effect, that, although the scope for political criticism by the people has increased while access to information (e.g., via satellite TV, Internet) has become relatively unrestricted, while the freedom to travel abroad now exists, and while pragmatic adjustment has been forced upon the regime by national and global political and economic constraints, Qadhafi continues to insist on *revolutionary leadership*[7] and on the historic mission of the September Revolution. The ideological positions taken by Qadhafi as leader of the revolution is officially regarded as irreversible.

State Institutions

The overthrow of the Sanusi monarchy inaugurated a number of institutional transformations that nevertheless contained a number of basic unchanging elements:

- The revolutionary legitimacy of the revolutionary leadership, i.e., the revolutionary leadership is neither elected nor can it be dismissed.
- The rejection of parties (except between June 1971 and December 1975, when the pan-Arab unity party, the *Arab Socialist Union*, was allowed to exist) and the rejection of party pluralism.
- The rejection of elections in the classical sense. Instead, representatives are elected by vote (Arabic: *tas`id*) by the masses (Jamahir) into the institutions of direct democracy.[8]

With this background in mind, the institutional development of the revolutionary regime can be divided into two main phases: a first phase, in which the Provisional Constitutional Proclamation, made by the *Revolutionary Command Council* on December 11, 1969, was valid; and a second phase, which began with the *Declaration of the Authority of the People* on March 2, 1977. The second phase, almost three decades old,[9] has not been without changes: one of the most significant was Qadhafi's introduction of the "Separation of Power and Revolution" on March 2, 1979.

Since then, the Libyan state has effectively consisted of two separate, often competing subsectors:

1. The *Revolutionary Sector*, consisting of the revolutionary leadership, including Qadhafi,[10] the members of the former Revolutionary Command Council that are still in office, and the Revolutionary Committees. The latter are an effective instrument for mobilizing the masses, for exercising political influence, and for maintaining control on behalf of the revolutionary leadership. The actions of the revolutionary sector are not, in any way, regulated by legal statutes.
2. The *Ruling Sector (Sector of People's Power)* is the core of Qadhafi's *jamahiriyya*, a model of direct democracy that is based on *People's Congresses* and *People's Committees*. Its functions are regulated by law, and are promulgated by the General People's Conference.

Since the "Declaration on the Authority of the People" and the "Declaration on the Separation of Rule and Revolution" in 1979, there have been no changes in this basic duality of the political system. There have only been alterations within the given framework: for example, the creation of new regional organizations (*sha`biyat*) from 1998 onward, and the implementation of general policies (concerning investment, and economic and educational reforms.)

The Legislative and Executive Organizations of the *Jamahiriyya*

Today's legislative organizations are the descendants of the *Arab Socialist Union*, reformed in 1975, and were first announced by Qadhafi in a speech he gave on March 27, 1975. The most important element of the transformation of the current political system was the dissolution of the *Arab Socialist Union* by the removal of its party character. From that time onward, the basic cells of the party were open to all Libyans, male and female, within a geographical area, and then reshaped into so-called *Basic People's Congresses*. Theoretically, all political decisions are to be discussed in these Basic People's Congresses. The *People's Committees* are supposed as the collective executive organ to be answerable to the *Basic People's Congresses*; its members are to be elected every three years by the Basic People's Congresses. All employees (e.g., teachers, engineers, doctors, farmers, and even students) were requested to join *Professional Congresses* and to express their views about national and international developments several times a year. The formal system of direct democracy in Libya is thus based on three foundations: the local *Basic People's Congresses*, the *local*

People's Committees, and the *Professional Organizations.* These organizations nominate representatives who possess a mandate to the national legislative body, the *General People's Congress.* It meets annually, forms the local resolutions into national resolutions (laws), and nominates the members of the national executive, *The General People's Committee,* often described as the "council of ministers."

This system was modified in October 1998, when twenty-six regional units, so-called *sha'biyat,* were created. The *sha'biyat* were positioned between the basic and national levels.[11] They have their own People's Congress[12] and People's Committee.[13] On the one hand, the *sha'biyat's* task is to improve the coordination of local interests; on the other hand, they are also meant to decentralize authority—in March 2000, they assumed several responsibilities that the national General People's Congress had previously assumed.

The Basic People's Congresses generally convene three times a year. Local concerns are discussed during two sittings, while the third focuses on national issues, including foreign affairs.[14] The decisions of the Basic People's Congresses concerning national issues usually provide the basis for the bills to be debated by the annual General People's Congress.[15] After the Arab Socialist Union had been reformed in 1975, the General People's Congress sat for the first time between January 5 and January 18, 1976, and their meeting has taken place every year since then. The People's Congress/People's Committee system of government has lasted thirty years now, reflecting a remarkable institutional stability. A critical look at this system reveals major weaknesses, however. *Technically* at least Libya is one of the few countries in the world to practice direct democracy. In reality, its form of direct democracy must be considered in light of the fact that no actions may be taken in Libya without the intervention of the country's revolutionary sector. The presence of the Revolutionary Committees reduces the freedom of direct democracy to that of an "occasional democracy" whose limits are temporally variable but nevertheless existent. Any breach of these limits is considered counter-revolutionary and faces sanctions. The system of direct democracy in Libya functions best when the agendas of the tri-annual sessions of the Basic People's Congresses do not touch upon political issues.

The agendas for the sessions are generated by the General Secretariat of the General People's Congress, and provide plentiful opportunity to manipulate the order of events or voting behavior. For example, some issues and items on the agenda can be suppressed,[16] or controversial issues that are being resisted by the locality can be repeatedly introduced until approval is granted. Free political opinion is not tolerated by the revolutionary leadership. Direct

democracy practiced in Libya thus suffers from the permanent intervention of the revolutionary sector, and reveals a weakness that this form of
participation generally has: the hyperactive participatory state (as desired
by Qadhafi) is confronted by the problem of permanence. It means that the
nonattendance of citizens in direct democratic organizations deforms the
state. Even in 1975, the Arab Socialist Union was heavily disadvantaged by
the absence of members at its sessions: in some districts, the rate of absence
was up to 75 percent. The rate of participation in the Basic People's
Congresses has never really improved. There is a lack of exact empirical
data necessary to document the percentage of members attending or not
attending sessions of the Basic People's Congresses, but personal experience supports the claim that only an active minority participates in the
Congress's regular and extraordinary sessions and passes the appropriate
resolutions.[17]

The democratic functioning of the Libyan system of congresses is burdened or conditioned by further factors. First, by the strong "social roots"
of the inhabitants, especially in rural areas where tribes and extended families still dominate. Any resistance against individual administrative measures has usually led to politically motivated reorganization of the
administration of the local decision-making unit by either dividing or
combining the administrative centers. The dominance of tribes and families helps make the People's Congress and Committee system more suscep-
tible to informal behavior when a management team is being formed (for
example, the leadership's secretariat in the Basic People's Congress), or
when members of the People's Committees are being appointed.[18] Second,
it takes a lot of effort to coordinate the basic structures and those at the
national level.[19] The congress system also requires an enormous amount of
traveling. When there are sessions of the *General People's Congress* or
General People's Committees, more than over one thousand delegates have
to travel from the 436 local units or the 22 *sha`biyat*. Third, the meetings
are burdened by Qadhafi's pretense concerning power and function. It is a
fact that Qadhafi's revolutionary legitimacy makes him, in practice, the
highest authority in the country, even if, as seen in the case of the extradition of the suspected Lockerbie bombers, he emphasizes, in almost playful
tones, that he has no official position and, therefore, no powers of decision
in Libya: "The system of the Jamahiriya is simple: People's Congresses and
People's Committees, nothing else. There is no (traditional) government,
no instrument of authority, no apparatus of this kind. The possibility for
one to exist was eradicated at the roots. All decisions, strategic or not, are
made by the People's Congresses alone. The center that makes all decisions
and plans for every eventuality are the People's Congresses."[20]

Reality, however, is a little different. It is reflected by the continuous presence of Qadhafi in the streets, where his image looks down from posters, and his statements can be read everywhere. Qadhafi, who, according to the *Declaration on the Authority of the People*, does not have a function and stands outside the ruling sectors, is the one who receives foreign heads of state,[21] ministers, and economic delegations; who speaks to the international media on behalf of Libya;[22] who initiates domestic policy discussions; and who makes unilateral decisions or decisions for the ruling sector. This centralization within the decision-making apparatus inevitably leads the lower levels of government to ignore the codified routes to decisions and to look to higher authorities for their approval before resolutions are passed.[23] In the tradition of the classical Bai`a (oath of allegiance) there is, in Libya, another variation of this conformity to the revolution: at almost all events, hagiographic telegrams are produced, which are then sent by the event's organizers to the Leader of the Revolution, Qadhafi. In the telegrams, Colonel Qadhafi's pioneering role in establishing the authority of the masses and other assorted praises are regularly on display.

Quasi, Non-Governmental Organizations

Within the *jamahiriyya*, individuals can only organize themselves within clearly defined limits. An application must be made to the Secretariat of Public Security (Interior Ministry) for permission to form an association. The legal basis for the authorization of associations is found in the Association Act No. 11 from 1970, which is still valid today. Associations whose aims do not conform to the aims of the September Revolution— such as associations that are regionalist, "separatist," or "party oriented"— are refused a license. As a result, very few associations have received authorization to do so: *The Libyan Red Crescent*, the *Boy Scouts*, women's associations, or the *Association to Combat Drug Consumption*. The latest association to be permitted was the *Gaddafi International Foundation for Charity Associations*,[24] an umbrella organization of seven charity associations, set up in 1999. The establishment of political associations (parties) was forbidden from the very beginning of the revolution. The revolutionary leadership merely continued a policy that had already existed since 1952 during the monarchy. By rejecting conventional parties, unions, or other organizations with political ambitions, Qadhafi wanted to overcome the "unjust" political order that had existed before the September Revolution. In addition, parties were seen as threatening because they fostered separatist tendencies that could endanger the unity of Libya, and because group interests do not have the welfare of the whole of Libya as their objective. One of Qadhafi's slogans since the beginning of the revolution has, therefore, been "*man tahazzaba khana*" ("Whoever forms a party, betrays"). One of the direct consequences of this was the formation of a party of *unity* (Arab Socialist Union 1971–75), and a ban on the creation of parties found in Law No. 71 of 1972. This law is still in force and prevents the institutionalization of political pluralism. A softening of this policy is not expected.[25]

In Libya, only organizations representing specific legal interests are permitted to function within the model of the *jamahiriyya*. They are professional and functional amalgamations that, along with the People's Congresses and People's Committees, retain an important role within the system of direct democracy. These include *The Women's Union, The Student's Union, The Judges' Association, The Lawyer's Union, The Doctors' Union, The Producers' Union (Trade Union), The Union of Farmers*, and *The Union of Libyan Writers and Literati*. Following a restructuring in 1976 and 1977, these organizations have been following exclusively revolutionary objectives. Since the establishment of the direct democratic system, they have been involved in debates and have sent representatives to the *General People's Congress*. Within the General Secretariat of the *General People's Congress*, they have their own secretary who is responsible for the needs of the professional congresses and the professional organizations.

Protagonists with Political Influence

Behind every revolution, there are individuals or small circles of leading figures that are the driving force in the preparation and implementation of the transfer of power. Around this decision-making center, there is usually a series of subordinate organizations and institutions with diminished responsibility and power to command. Within the latter, those occupying leading positions were often retained due to their at least public loyalty to the political/revolutionary leadership. In Libya, Mu'ammar al-Qadhafi is, without question, the absolute head of the state. Since the 1960s, he has collected officers of the same age or younger around himself in the *Free Unionist Officers Movement*. After the transfer of power in September 1969, the most important officers of the movement sat on the *Revolutionary Command Council*. As the political system underwent various stages of development and adjustment, so has this central body gone through a corresponding institutional transformation. The *Revolutionary Command Council* (September 1, 1969 until March 2, 1997) became the *General Secretariat of the General People's Congress* (March 2, 1977 until March 2, 1979), and then, finally, the *Revolutionary Leadership* on March 2, 1979, which it remains today. At the same time, it shrank in personnel after its members formed factions and clashed over the objectives and strategies of the revolution.[26]

The mostly civilian "companion fighters" of Qadhafi (former fellow pupils and students and long-standing loyal coworkers) have been meeting as the *Forum of the Companions of Qadhafi* since 1996 to give advice and to vote in an informal capacity. Below this core elite of a few dozen persons resides a series of organizations and institutions whose task, on the one hand, is to protect revolutionary power and anchor that power within society. Beside the classical state institutions (secret service, *Jamahiri* guards, and others), two different categories of institutions contribute to securing revolutionary power. The first contains the *Free Unionist Officers Movement*, the Revolutionary committees that have been increasing their power since 1977, and the so-called *Cleansing Committees*, which were created in 1994 to "combat corruption, fraud, and breaches in exchange control." The second category includes the most important organizations of the *Islamic Call Society* (for religious issues), *The Green Book Center* (for ideological issues), and the *Mathaba/World Center for the Struggle Against Reaction, Racism, and Imperialism* (for international "revolutionary cooperation").

Contributions to the protection of the revolutionary system are also made by loyal and politically active supporters of the regime. They are especially active within the "pillars of the political system" that were formed in 1973—i.e., within the legislative People's Congresses, the executive People's Committees, and the professional bodies, which include women's and student's organizations. Since the mid-1970s, these institutions have guaranteed loyal supporters of the regime considerable social advantages that under other conditions would be unavailable. This large group includes many women who, due to the educational system and the founding of the Military Academy for Women in Tripoli in February 1979,[27] have benefited from numerous professional opportunities. They form some of the most vehement supporters of the regime today. Currently, the most important (informal) actors with political influence, whose functions are not specified by law are as follow in the next several sections.

The Free Unionist Officers Movement

The *Free Unionist Officers Movement* is, according to Ronald Bruce St John, "the secret army organization which claimed credit for organizing and executing the coup which ousted the Idris regime on September 1, 1969."[28] It was founded in August 1964 after numerous colleagues of Qadhafi (many from his school days in Sabha and Misurata) had joined the military academy of Benghazi. The leadership of the Free Unionist Officers consists of the

Central Committee recruited from the twelve members of the academy's seventh year of military training. After the takeover, it established itself as the Revolutionary Command Council. Although the Free Unionist Officers Movement has continuously existed since 1969, and has an important historical role, it no longer plays an important *public* role. It is seldom mentioned today as it was in the preamble of the "Declaration on the Authority of the People" on March 2, 1977. Nevertheless, the Free Unionist Officers continue to play an important role. Its members still occupy central positions within the armed forces. They stabilize the system because they have their roots in the tribes and clans, whose interests they perceive and balance out.

It is impossible to say exactly how many officers remain in the Free Unionist Officers Movement today, especially since Qadhafi, in recent years, has repeatedly enlisted new, younger members. At the beginning of the 1970s, sixty to eighty Free Unionist Officers formed the backbone of the Revolutionary Command Council within the armed forces. The names of other members (in addition to the eleven officers who, along with Qadhafi, formed the Revolutionary Council) that were mentioned during the TV broadcast announcing and describing the transfer of power on "revolution night" on September 1, 1969, included First Lieutenant Muhammad Aun (today Brigadier General), Ahmad Abu Lifa, Muhammad al-Sadiq, and Abd al-Fattah Yunis.[29] Yusuf Dibri, "an intimate of Qadhafi since their student days at military college" (in Benghazi) was also mentioned. Not much is publicly known about the activities of the Free Unionist Officers, except that they meet with Qadhafi on a regular basis to vote on policies, and only a few vague details can be ascertained from time to time concerning personnel changes. It can still be assumed, however, that membership in the Free Unionist Officers and, thus, loyalty to the revolutionary order, plays an important role in the appointment of military and civilian political positions. The most current example of this concerns the appointment of Libya's governors. According to Law No. 2 of 1998, the regional administrative units (*sha`biyat*), newly created in Autumn 1998, are supposed to appoint the new governors. At this moment, sixteen current or former officers of the Free Unionist Officers, Qadhafi's nephew, Saiyid Muhammad Qadhaf al-Dam (Sirt region) among them, can be found at the head of the regionally most important *sha`biyat*. This is proof that Qadhafi's security considerations, and not legal stipulations, motivate the "election" of governors.

The Forum of Companions of Qadhafi

The *Forum of Companions of Qadhafi* has existed since 1996 and is a non-military supplement to the Free Officers Corps. According to Libyan sources, the *Forum of the Companions of Qadhafi*, led by General Secretary Ibrahim Bijad, the closest civilian companion of Qadhafi since his school days in southern Libyan Sabha, has "more than a hundred members."[30] The forum encompasses those persons to whom Qadhafi has had close relations for years, and whom he consults when making political decisions. The *Forum of the Companions of Qadhafi* provides a reservoir of personnel that Qadhafi can turn to when filling important civilian posts (executive, diplomatic corps, universities, research institutes, etc.). The members are primarily former school friends of Qadhafi, teachers, and other friends. For example, Ibrahm Bijad, Muhammad Khalil, and Muhammad Aqil are contacts from Qadhafi's time in Sabha; from his time in Misurata (1961–63), he knows Ali Salim and other "friends who helped him gain admission to Masrata High School" (Musa Kousa).[31] The Companions of Qadhafi, as the name suggests, are persons to whom he has a special relationship and, therefore, enjoy advantages when it comes to the filling of important positions. Muhammad Aqil, who hails from Fazzan, was first "Secretary of the People's Bureau" (Ambassador) in Bonn (1979–81) before becoming de facto head of the *Green Book Center* that was set up in February 1981. This center, whose headquarters are in Tripoli, is the central institution for the worldwide dissemination of Qadhafi's ideology. Muhammad Aqil's successor as head of the *Green Book Center* was the previously mentioned Ibrahim Bijad, who held the post from 1987 to 1994.

The members of the Free Unionist Officers Movement and the Forum of the Companions of Qadhafi are rewarded for their positions of trust as members of those two informal groups with posts that are essential for the stability and dominance of the revolutionary sector (over the ruling sector). Only the leading members of the Revolutionary Committees, whose main task it is to protect the revolutionary sector, have a similar function. When judging the stability of the regime in Libya, the Free Unionist Officers, the Forum of the Companions of Qadhafi, and the leading members of both organizations, deserve to be regarded intensively. Changes in the makeup of their personnel, and in their functions, enable us to draw conclusions concerning the potential stability or instability of the regime.

The Revolutionary Committees

The *Revolutionary Committees* were founded in the mid-1970s.[32] They were the institutional innovation that, more than any other in the last three decades, has inspired the political usurpation of power and conflict. The rise of the Revolutionary Committees and the corresponding increase in their political influence was closely tied to the ideological development of

Qadhafi's own thinking.[33] In November 1977, he published the second part of the *Green Book*. It instigated a so-called producers' revolution that, among other things, aimed to transfer private economic property to collective ownership, to do away with private trading, and to turn rented residential property into privately owned property. This new revolutionary stage triggered massive opposition from those dispossessed of their property. The Revolutionary Committees were supposed to help crush this opposition.

The Revolutionary Committees are directly answerable to the revolutionary leadership, and are obliged to enforce the political program of that leadership. They are not subject to the normal legal procedures, which are the task of the *People's Congresses* and the *General People's Congress*. The *General People's Congress* did not, therefore, have a voice in the founding or internal organization of the Revolutionary Committees. They fall within Qadhafi's power and gain their authority directly from the revolutionary leadership. In accordance with Qadhafi's dictum "al-lijan fi kulli makan" ("Committees Everywhere"), five to ten person revolutionary committees were set up within all Basic People's Congresses, People's Committees, professional unions, educational congresses, and state institutions. At the sixth annual conference of Revolutionary Committees in 1983,[34] the participants passed a statute where the internal rules of the committees were specified. The stipulations included, among others, the following:

- The location of the headquarters (mathaba),
- The necessary characteristics of members of the Revolutionary Committees (they must be followers of the *Third Universal Theory*; demonstrate a willingness to take part in further training seminars; and demonstrate a willingness to carry out *every* assignment given to them).

The conditions of membership include:

- A "dossier of revolutionary control," with details of counter-revolutionary incidents in the region for which the Revolutionary Committee is responsible;
- A daily set of minutes containing, for example, the opinions stated publicly in Basic People's Congresses and other institutions, and an index of the instructions issued by the superior Revolutionary Committees;
- The keeping of a so-called *Green Register* in which the activities and important announcements of every member are registered. Copies

of the *Green Register* are to be passed on to the Coordinating Office of the Revolutionary Committee in Tripoli.

According to the statute, the Revolutionary Committees are not to keep contact with one another, but are connected vertically with the *Coordinating Office of the Revolutionary Committees* in Tripoli, which reports directly to Qadhafi.

The Revolutionary Committees are furnished with the authority of the *Revolutionary Sector* and are employed as *pressure groups* to enforce Qadhafi's ideology. They circumvent the hierarchy of decision-making processes of almost all state institutions (with the exception of the oil sector and the armed forces). Originally, the members of the Revolutionary Committees, who wear civilian clothes, were designed to mobilize the masses and to reinforce the system of the rule of the people. However, from 1979 and 1980 onward, the task of "revolutionary control" began to dominate the country's political life, and the Revolutionary Committees' main task became the security of the regime. Two factors contributed to this change of function. First, the Revolutionary Committees were spread throughout the country and were mostly made up of dedicated followers of the ideology developed by Qadhafi since 1973. The Revolutionary Committees are divided into eight regional commandos and are directly subordinated to Qadhafi's office. The coordinator in charge, until his death in March 2007, has been Muhammad Amsaid al-Mahjub al-Qadhafi. The Chief Editor of the revolutionary magazine *Majallat al-zahf al-akhdar* (*"The Green March"*), Dr. Muhammad Khalfallah, estimated in May 2002 that the Revolutionary Committees had sixty thousand members. Second, the Revolutionary Committees were well armed and well equipped. To demonstrate their efficiency, in a confrontation with a commando from the *National Islamic Front for the Salvation of Libya* in May 1984, they managed to quickly erect roadblocks and to eliminate the commando group.

The main tasks of the Revolutionary Committees are defined at an annual conference. At the twenty-fifth conference on April 26, 2004, under the motto "Consolidation of People's Authority and the Confirmation of *Jamahiri* Values,"[35] Qadhafi, in his welcoming speech, extolled the "pioneering ideology of the Fateh revolution." According to the Libyan press agency JANA: "Qadhafi emphasised that it is only in the Jamahiriya that direct democracy exists. All Libyans, adult men and women, participate in planning internal and external policies, enact legislation, set budgets and decide on issues of war and peace."[36] Within a very short time (1978–80), Qadhafi endowed the Revolutionary Committees with substantial authority, which, in an emergency such as a threat to the regime, they continue to exercise even today. Among these areas of competence are the following security related tasks: police functions (arrest of counter-revolutionaries; interrogation centers); the job of "guaranteeing internal stability"; and the "elimination of enemies of the revolution" (currently suspended).[37] The responsibilities of the Revolutionary Committees within the area of justice include "revolutionary jurisdiction" (the establishment of Revolutionary Courts that led to numerous death sentences between 1980 and 1986).

Since 1987, the Libyan leadership has diluted its revolutionary policies for foreign and domestic reasons,[38] pushing the Revolutionary Committees into the background. The superior position of the Revolutionary Committees within the overall political system was not affected, however, as was evidenced by developments in the 1990s, when they were rapidly reactivated to guard against Islamic underground organizations in Cyrenaica (see Chapter 3 in this book). Since the mid-1990s, the Revolutionary Committees have been employed to combat black market activities, commodity speculation, and illegal currency trading, all of which were widespread at the time of the United Nations sanctions between 1992 and 1999. It was astounding, given their reputation for corruption, that the Revolutionary Committees were employed along with the so-called *Cleansing Committees* that were set up in 1994 to "clean up" corruption. That the regime resorted to using the Revolutionary Committees can be explained by the concentration of decision-making and control mechanisms within the relatively small circle of closely connected families and tribal factions.

The People's Social Leadership Committees

The People's Social Leadership Committees were first introduced as a new form of organization by Qadhafi in a speech at Darna on July 21, 1994. Between July 1994 and April 1996, these new committees were formed all over Libya. The local *People's Social Leadership Committees* are permanent committees formed from the heads of families and other important persons in each region. Their task is to establish social stability and control, that is, to prevent opposition by family members and by tribal members. In addition, they are responsible for the distribution of state subsidies and, recently, for the issuing of legal documents. The local *People's Social Leadership Committees*, which still have no formal legal standing, but draw their legitimacy from Qadhafi himself, were brought together in a national organization in March 1996. Each local committee sends a representative to this national organization.[39] Qadhafi inaugurated the national *People's Social Leadership Committee* on March 2, 1996. The national committee is directed by a *General Coordinator* who is in charge for six months at a time. The General Coordinators have all been, with the exception of the first holder of the post, Dr. Mohammad Ahmad al-Sharif (1996), high ranking members of the military. The general assemblies of the *People's Social Leadership Committees*, and the assemblies of their regional coordinators, have become favorite venues for Qadhafi to debate domestic political problems. For example, in 1997–98 at the General Assembly, Qadhafi talked about illegal drug dealing and corruption; at the end of 2000, he called for an end to attacks on (black African) foreigners, and, in 2001, he spoke about the reforms needed in the economy.

The Islamic Call Society (ICS)
and the World Islamic Call Society (WICS)

In order to assure its dominance, the Revolutionary Command Council emphasized not only the "Arab" nature of the September Revolution, but also its "Islamic" character. The individual measures used to reinforce the Islamic character of the revolution have included the ban on alcohol consumption, introduced in 1969; the exclusive use of the Hijra calendar; and the founding of the *Islamic Call Society (ICS)*. The ICS was founded in 1971 and made a legal organization in 1972. Its main task is to provide for worldwide proselytizing for Islam by building up Islamic centers, organizing conferences, sending missionaries, and through publishing activities (e.g., translations of the *Quran* into numerous languages). The main source of financing for the large ICS budget has been state subsidies from the so-called Jihad fund (a special tax instituted in 1972). The ICS is headed by a General Secretary,[40] and contains an administrative council and an annual assembly. In 1982, the ICS was altered institutionally: in keeping with Qadhafi's wish, representatives of Islamic parishes abroad were given a more active role to play. This institutionalization resulted in the transformation of the ICS into the *World Islamic Call Society (WICS)* and the creation of a thirty-six person *World Council of Islamic Mission* (led by General Secretary Muhammad Ahmad al-Sharif, who has a special role among Qadhafi's advisers). Al-Sharif is not only an adviser, but actually shapes foreign policy and organizes political activities (e.g., the dialogue between Christians and Muslims in Tripoli in February 1976). He has been responsible for the spread of Islamic missions in sub-Saharan Africa, and has played a major part in fulfilling Qadhafi's wish to see foreign policy directed more toward the African continent. Dr. Sharif organized the so-called Jihad trips that Qadhafi made to Niger and Nigeria in 1997 and Chad in 1998, and helped to turn them into successful religious and political events. Within Libya, Dr. Sharif has influence beyond the confines of The Islamic Call Society/World Islamic Call Society, and enjoys Qadhafi's full confidence. As a result, in March 1996, for six months, he became the first General Coordinator of the *People's Social Leadership Committees.*

The Tribes and Their Management
for the Protection of Influence

In Libya, the view was widespread that only a few clans and tribes controlled the whole country at the time of the Sanusi monarchy.[41] These families were accused of collaborating with the Italian colonialists, often to their own advantage; for agreeing to an arrangement with the British; and, finally, for serving British and American imperialism after independence. This judgment, shared by Revolutionary Command Council members, led to the discarding of the traditional concept of family power after the September 1969 revolution. Politics was no longer to be the preserve of *walad al-wujaha* ("sons of influential families"): new structures should emerge in which the masses (*jamahir*)—the "sons of the Bedouins, the desert, the villages, the wide land" (Proclamation of the Revolution on September 1, 1969)—would help to determine the political and socioeconomic development of the country.

The revolution subsequently took over the political dominance that families living in the coastal towns had previously possessed. The revolutionary leadership, with Qadhafi at its center, came mostly from tribes originating in the Sahara.[42] After September 1,1969, therefore, the revolutionary leadership supported greater regional diversification. Political participation was meant to be more evenly distributed. In addition to the regional diversification of the elite, its social profile was also to be transformed. The majority of decision makers today come from simple backgrounds—from former farming or semi-nomadic milieus, or from families that had migrated to the coastal areas as a result of the changes prompted by oil in the 1960s. Prior to the revolution, makers of political policy mostly came from families with traditionally higher standards of religious and literary education, such as the Sanusi, Baruni, Ghirbi, and Sharif. Today, both the members of the current elite and the revolutionary leadership have had military training (at the military academy in Benghazi and, sometimes, higher education in the United States and Great Britain). They are graduates of the *University of Libya*, which existed until 1972, or its successors, the universities of *al-Fatih* in Tripoli and *Qar Yunis* in Benghazi, or of courses at foreign institutes.

Since Libya is still very much a tribal society, it is important to analyze the influence of tribes on political developments under the revolutionary leadership. In order to do this, it is necessary to consider the relationship between individuals in the tribes. Relations within the tribes are determined by the tribal leaders (*shaykhs*) and family elders. In return for the absolute loyalty of tribal and family members, they provide material services (for example, the provision of jobs for family members, or the acquisition of development projects from the state that benefit the tribe) and social security. These internal tribal functions are still valid today,[43] and have two consequences for government policies in Libya:

1. Despite the partial changes made by the revolutionary leadership and the introduction of the people's congress system, decision making in Libyan society is still a very authoritarian process. "Heads or chiefs of social units, in consultation with some of the elders in these units, make the decisions. Kinship and unit solidarity provide the support of the rest of the unit members necessary to carry out those decisions."[44] The decision-making processes within the tribes and clans have, however, been disturbed since the end of the 1970s by the formation of the Revolutionary Committees. The decision-making processes of the Revolutionary Committees are not entirely determined by tribal or familial relationships but are more likely to be linked to the authority of the revolutionary sector they reside in. This does not mean that the tribal structure has disappeared. Since the beginning of the 1990s, Libyan society has, to some extent, turned to the tribes to protect the status quo and, in doing so, strengthened the traditional leaders. This development has been institutionalized in the *People's Social Leadership Committees.*

2. Whenever positions are to be filled in administrative committees or in political committees (the leadership committees of the Basic People Congresses), or when political directives are to be approved, decisions are often made along tribal lines. Even today, what Omar al-Fathaly said of the 1970s is still true: "The saying *weld qabeletna* ('the son of our tribe') will be the slogan of the supporters. *Weld bladna* ('the son of our village') will be the slogan when the range of competition is wider."[45] These traditional guidelines on decision making often push other criteria, such as training, ability' and efficiency, into the background when it comes to filling jobs.

The attitude of the Qadhafi regime toward the country's tribes and clans and their informal influence has modified itself several times in the last three decades, or has been adjusted to fit social developments. After assuming power in 1969, the Revolutionary Command Council followed a pan-Arab and Nasserist style of politics, at the center of which was the party of unity (Arab Socialist Union), institutionalized as the "Alliance of Active People's Forces" (workers, farmers, students, the military, intellectuals), and which distanced itself or actively fought "reactionary elements of the society" (including the tribes). In early summer 1971, during the mobilization campaign of the Revolutionary Command Council on occasion of the founding of the Arab Socialist Union, Qadhafi was particularly critical of the country's families' use of their influence for their own interests: "In the heat of his campaign for his 'Socialist Union' and 'People's Councils,' Gaddafi stressed the end of family rule and family influence in Libyan politics. He enumerated as example several families, some of whom were of considerable importance, and declared them and their likes to be of no political value whatsoever."[46]

The Revolutionary Command Council used several measures at its disposal to reduce the power of the tribes. In June 1970, the local bureaucracy was reorganized; the tribal sheiks were replaced by administrative officers; and the administrative boundaries were changed to make them different from the tribal boundaries. Tribal influence diminished still further when the administration was restructured, and after the People's Committees and People's Congresses were introduced in 1973 and 1975. Nevertheless, both immediately after the revolution and later, the tribes continued to informally play an important role. It was important for the regime first of all, to protect the revolution by creating new tribal alliances against the large tribes in Cyrenaica, which had supported the Sanusi monarchy and rejected the revolution. The alliance policy was so important to Qadhafi because he originated from an unimportant tribe, the Qaddadfa from the Sirt region. The background of the members of the *Free Unionist Officers Movement* and the *Revolutionary Command Council* made an alliance possible between the influential Maqarha tribe from Fazzan (whose representative was Abd as-Salam Jallud) and the Warfalla tribe that had settled in west-Tripolitania (represented by Muhaishi). It was clear that Qadhafi could never quite negate the tribes as a social phenomenon in his political ideology. In the first part of his *Green Book*, the tribes, along with parties, classes, or religious sects, were rejected as political activists because he considered them "dictatorial instruments of rule." In the third part of the *Green Book*, they were more positively regarded as a social network based on blood relations. This means that the tribes were respected from a social point of view, but the use of tribes for the benefit of the tribes was rejected: "When the tribes of a nation are in conflict and only watch out for their own interests the continuation of the nation is at risk" (*Green Book* Part III).

The ideologically motivated actions of the Revolutionary Command Council, which aimed to gradually subject society to the contents of the *Green Book*, sparked increasing opposition. Since the 1980s, in response to this, Qadhafi has relied more and more on his own Qaddadfa tribe when appointing personalities to leading positions. This has been especially true of leading positions within the security forces and the Revolutionary Committees, where the recruits have increasingly been chosen from among kinsmen that are seen as loyal, and not because of job specification or ability: "Within a decade of coming to power, and as his regime faces increasing political opposition, Qadhafi himself has fallen back on reliance on his own kinsmen. He had entrusted a cousin with his personal security, and two brothers, also his cousins, not only served as his personal envoys in sensitive foreign missions but also held important positions in domestic intelligence. Still another cousin was commander of the armed forces of the central region, which included the oil terminals and the disputed Gulf of Sidra."[47]

Safeguarding the Revolutionary System and the Role of the Qadadfa Tribe

In revolutionary Libya, there has been no ministry of defense, except in the period between September 8 and December 7, 1969.[48] It was disbanded after the minister of defense of that time, Colonel Adam al-Hawaz, was involved in an attempted putsch. That attempted putsch not only led to the immediate passing (on December 11, 1969) of the still effective *Law to Protect the Revolution*, but also to Qadhafi assuming the office of Prime Minister for himself. Thus, he united, in one person, the function of Chairman of the *Revolutionary Command Council*,[49] Chairman of the *Ministerial Council* (at least until he handed over this post to his deputy Abd as-Salam Jallud in July 1972), and *Commander in Chief of the Armed Forces*. Other members of the original twelve who had sat on the *Revolutionary Command Council*[50] have spent time as Commander in-Chief and as General Inspector, or have been governors of the country's military regions. Since the political reorganization of March 2, 1977, Colonel Qadhafi has been "Highest Commander-in-Chief of the Armed forces." The remaining members of the former Revolutionary Command Council have held various other posts. General Abu Bakr Yunis Jabir has been Commander-in-Chief of the Armed Forces, Lieutenant-General Mustafa al-Kharubi was Chief of Staff and Leader of Military Secret Service, and Khuwildi al-Humaidi worked as Representative for the

Implementation of the Concept of the Armed People before becoming Inspector General of the Armed Forces.[51]

Since the 1990s, al-Kharubi and al-Humaidi have assumed numerous political tasks (such as traveling as special representatives of Qadhafi and receiving foreign state representatives), and Major General Jabir has taken on the de facto role of defense secretary (minister). The most important colleague of Jabir is the Chief of Staff of the Libyan Army, the largest branch of the country's armed forces, Brigadier Ali Rifi al-Sharif.[52] Libya's military leadership comprises other persons besides these formal posts. It should be noted, however, that rank does not translate into actual influence. Tribal membership, loyalty to the Revolution, as expressed by membership of the *Free Unionist Officers' Movement* and tasks assigned to them, allow us to compile a list of persons who either directly belong to the military leadership or belong to the influential circles surrounding it. The members of the military leadership—and the government's other security organizations—that do not belong to the historical personalities of the September Revolution, such as Qadhafi, Jabir, Kharubi and Khuwildi do, can be divided into four groups, as follow.

(1) Blood Relatives of Qadhafi

In principle, this refers to Qadhafi's two nephews:

- *Brigadier Ahmed Qadhaf al-Dam*,[53] long-term commander of the Tubruk military region and, since 1995, Chief Commander of the Cyrenaica region (military regions of Tubruk, Benghazi, Kufra); at the moment, Special Representative of Qadhafi for Relations with Egypt, and
- *Brigadier Sayyid Muhammad Qadhaf al-Dam*, an officer with political control functions. He was Secretary of the People's Committee of the important *sha`biya* Sirt[54] from October 1998 until March 2004. Since March 2004, he has been General Coordinator of the *Social People's Leadership Committees* and, thus, according to Qadhafi, will be his successor as Head of State should he die.
- *Colonel Khalifa Hanaish.* For many years, he was Qadhafi's personal bodyguard and Commander of the *Presidential Guard*. In October 1993, he was responsible for quelling the Bani Walid uprising and, since the end of the 1990s, has been in charge of armaments procurement.
- *Colonel Hassan Ishkal.* He was Commander of the Sirt military region and, because of infighting with Qadhafi during the war in Chad, was liquidated on November 24, 1985.[55]

(2) In-laws of the Qadhafi Family

In this category, the relatives of Qadhafi's second wife, Safia Farkash, stand out. One of her sisters is married to Colonel Abdallah al-Sanusi. Colonel al-Sanusi descends from the Maqarha tribe located in Fezzan (as does Qadhafi's former deputy in the Revolutionary Command Council, Staff-Major Abd as-Salam Jallud). He has been one of Qadhafi's closest colleagues since the 1970s, identified as one of the perpetrators of the UTA attack in September 1989, and has been head of the *Jamahiriya Security Organisation* since 1992.[56]

(3) Members of Qadhdafi's Tribe

Since the 1980s, tribal origin has played an increasingly significant role well beyond the immediate family and relatives of the Libyan leader, a development that was linked to the military and security policies designed to safeguard the regime. Mansour El-Kikhia, supported by numerous reports, confirms that Qaddafi preferred to use members of all six tribes of the Qadadfa tribal community and younger recruits from the tribes to form the security organizations or to control the coordinating points that still guarantee the existence of the regime. In this respect, the most important Qadadfa tribal members—aside from the Qadhaf al-Dam brothers—already mentioned are:

- *Brigadier General Mas`ud Abd al-Hafiz Ahmad*: Commander of the Libyan troops in Chad; Commander of the Security Battalions from 1995–98; Commanding Officer of Military Security from 1995 to 1998; and, since 1998, Secretary of the People's Committee of the Sha`biya Sabha.
- *Colonel Ali al-Kilani*: *worked* in the Liaison Office of the Revolutionary Committees' Movement *in the 1980s*, and is currently in charge of security for Qadhafi's residences.
- *Colonel Misbah Abd al-Hafiz Ahmad.*
- *Colonel Sa`d Mas`ud al-Qadhafi.*
- *Captain Muhammad al-Majdhub al-Qadhafi*; *Ahmad Ibrahim al-Qadhafi*;[57] *Ali Mansur al-Qadhafi*: all are all high-ranking leaders within the Revolutionary Committees' Movement.

(4) Members of Tribes Allied to Qadhafi's Tribe

This fourth circle is comprised of tribes allied to the Qadadfa. The most important of these are the *Warfalla Tribe* (to whom there are blood ties) and the *Maqarha Tribe* that dominates the southern province, Fazzan. In particular, the Maqarha occupy several sensitive posts in the security apparatus, despite Abd al-Salam Jallud's departure from the Revolutionary Leadership in 1995:

- *Colonel Abdallah al-Sanusi.*
- *Colonel Ahmad Aun.*
- *Brigadier in the General Staff Ahmad Fathallah al-Muqassibi*: for many years, he has occupied high-ranking posts in the General Staff. Since October 1, 1998, he has been Secretary of the People's Committee of the politically insecure *sha`biya* Darna.
- *Brigadier al-Mahdi al-Arabi Abd al-Hafiz*: Commander of the Border Guards, former General Coordinator of the People's Social Leadership Committees.
- *Brigadier in General Staff al-Hadi al-Tahir Imbirish*: former Commander of the People's Resistance Forces and, after October 1, 1998, Secretary of the People's Committee of *sha`biya* Sabratha/Surman).
- *Brigadier Ali al-Rifi al-Sharif.*

The procedure for assigning posts suggests the following conclusion: even if the lack of information, the variations in the spelling of people's names. and the rapid rotation of posts and functions do not make it possible to sketch an accurate picture of who controls or commands which organization at each given moment, it has been possible since the beginning of 1980s to make out a trend within Libya. This trend may be called the "re-tribalisation of Libyan society."[58] It is highly unlikely this will change in the medium term.

Conclusion: The Future Roles of the Informal Actors in Libya

Those informal actors within the *jamahiriyya* that are closely bound to the revolutionary sector will continue to play a dominant role whether the revolutionary regime retains its current form or not. As long as revolutionary Leader Qadhafi lives, and thus personally embodies revolutionary legitimacy, the *jamahiriyya* will not require a constitution, and revolutionary control of the Libyan "sovereign" will continue. The use of actors loyal to the revolution was last visible in the government's reaction to the first *National Conference of the Libyan Opposition* (June 25–26, 2005) in London. In Libya, the revolutionary youth organizations and the Basic People's Congresses were mobilized by the Social People's Leadership

Committees and the Revolutionary Committees to organize counter-demonstrations, some of which even demanded "death to the traitors." The rhetoric and attitudes were reminiscent of the gestures used by the Revolutionary Committees at the beginning of the 1980s.

However, even if Revolutionary Leader Qadhafi were to die, the existent informal groups would continue to dominate decision making. This is, in part, due to the lack of a constitution. Who would take over the role of revolutionary leader? Would this position continue to exist? Qadhafi himself has commented on this in a speech given on March 2, 2000, in which he said that, in an emergency, the General Coordinator of the Social People's Leadership Committees could take over as head of state. This would partially explain why a high-ranking officer of Qadhafi's tribe usually occupies the post of General Coordinator, as did, for example, Saiyid Ahmad Qadhaf al-Dam in March 2004. Whoever is to succeed Qadhafi at the head of Libya's leadership will undoubtedly need the support of the influential *Free Unionist Officers Movement*, the *Forum of the Companions of Qadhafi*, and the most important tribal representatives to assume this post, and to shape the subsequent period of transformation. In a post-Qadafi power struggle, it is those who already occupy key decision-making functions, and who use these to represent their own interests and those of their families and tribes, who will be better placed to continue to exert political influence and to occupy leading posts. Taking these factors into account, Saif al-Islam al-Qadhafi, the son of the Leader of the revolution, seems to have few chances of success.

Notes

1. The five point manifesto included: (1) The abolition of all laws that contradicted the spirit of the revolution; (2) The "cleansing" of the country of the "politically ill" (i.e., counter-revolutionaries); (3) The arming of the "(revolutionary) masses"; (4) The implementation of an administrative revolution (setting up of People's Committees); (5) A cultural revolution.
2. The name of a collection of Qadhafi's speeches starting in 1972–73.
3. *Green Book Part 1: The Solution of the Problem of Democracy: The People's Power* (January 1976); *Part 2: The Solution of the Economic Problem: Socialism* (November 1977); *Part 3: The Social Base of the Third Universal Theory* (June 1979).
4. Refers to the founding of the *jamahiriyya*.
5. See the World Center for Studies and Researches of the *Green Book* in Brief, Tripoli, without year (1996).
6. Interviews, Tripoli, May 2002.

7. Qadhafi said, for example, in a speech on February 12, 1979: "The task of the revolutionary leadership is leadership. That is why it is leaving the General Secretariat of the General People's Congress, just as it left the Council of Ministers some time ago; i.e. it is giving up all administrative work. That doesn't mean, however, that it is giving up the revolution, and that also doesn't mean that the revolutionary leadership doesn't have anymore work: People always believe that administrating or running the executive are the tasks of the leadership, but in fact they are not the tasks of the revolutionary leadership. Its principle task is the revolution." This statement is valid today.

8. *Jamahir* (Arabic for "People's Masses") is the key term of the political ideology of Qadhafi.

9. In dedication to the celebrations, Qadhafi held a speech on March 2, 2005, in which he called for economic liberalization in Libya. See *Agence France Press*, Paris, March 3, 2005.

10. Qadhafi's official title has been "Leader of the Revolution" (*qa'id al-thawra*) since March 2, 1979.

11. The *sha`biya* succeeded the regional levels that had existed before, e.g., the forty-two municipalities (*Baladiyat*) that had been set up in 1975.

12. The secretaries of the different Basic People's Congresses within the *sha`biya* constitute the *People's Conference of the Sha`biya*.

13. The secretary of the People's Committee of the *sha`biya*, nominally elected by the People's Conference of the Sha`biya, is, in fact, nominated by the leadership of the Revolution. Many secretaries of the People's Committees of the *sha`biyat* are high-ranking officers. This highlights, in fact, the undiminished capacity of control of the leadership of the Revolution.

14. The last session on local issues held on the national level took place in July 2005.

15. A General Secretariat prepares the sessions of the General People's Congress and the drafts of the bills submitted to the delegates. The acting General Secretary of the General People's Congress since November 1992 is Zannati Muhammad Zannati

16. That was the case when the Libyan army intervened in Chad in the 1980s and when the Libyan border was opened to let in migrants from sub-Saharan states in the 1990s. Both decisions were not discussed by the Basic People's Congresses.

17. This is, however, not true of the sessions of the Sha'biya People's Congress and the General People's Congress, as their members are elected delegates of the respective subordinated levels.

18. It is also true that, although the participation of the tribes in society is rejected by the *Green Book* Part III, the revolutionary leadership has encouraged re-tribalization of society and politics since the 1990s. They use their tribal members more than before to shore up their own power bases.

19. It is worth mentioning that the revolutionary leadership had to respond to the continuing lack of competence within the hierarchical structure of the system by reorganizing the bureaucracy on a number of occasions.

20. Cf. Mu'ammar Al-Qadhafi: *"Je suis un opposant à l'échelon mondial." Entretiens avec Hamid Barrada* (Lausanne and Paris: Favre and ABY, 1984), 72. A more current example was provided by Qadhafi in June 1999, cf. *Arab News*, Jidda, June 23, 1999: "I'm out of power."

21. Qadhafi even ignored his own suggestion of December 2, 1979, just before the passing of the Declaration on the Separation of Rule and Revolution. At that time, he commented on the redistribution of responsibility by saying: "If a revolutionary leader enters the Jamahiriya, he is greeted by the revolutionary leadership, and if someone is elected to office, he is greeted by a committee elected by the masses" (al-Sijil al-qawmi/National Register 1978–79).

22. See his speeches and interviews in the volumes of *Sijil al-qawmi*; cf. also "Kaddafi et la presse", *Jeune Afrique*, Paris, November 16, 1999.

23. Decision makers in the local, decentralized administrative units are forced by the dual system, and the resulting multiplicity of centers of authority, to show consideration to the revolutionary sector and to the different power centers of the ruling sector (General People's Congress, General Secretariat of the General People's Congress, The General People's Committee).

24. Cf. http://www.gaddaficharity.org.

25. On March 18, 2001, the trial of ninety-eight political prisoners who had been accused of breaking this law began in the People's Court in Tripoli.

26. The current members of the Leadership of the Revolution are Qadhafi, the General Chief of staff General Abu Bakr Yunis Jabir, plus Generals Khuwildi al-Humaidi and Mustafa al-Kharrubi.

27. See Maria Graeff-Wassink, *La Femme en armes. Khadafi féministe?* (Paris: Colin, 1990). A Woman's Police Academy has also been in existence for two years.

28. See Ronald Bruce St John, *Historical Dictionary of Libya* (London: Scarecrow Press, 1991), 67.

29. On the thirtieth anniversary of the September Revolution, there were similar discussions. See the publication "Journey of 4000 days" (in Arabic, Tripoli, 2001).

30. Interview, Tripoli, May 2002.

31. Cf. Musa M. Kousa, "The Political Leader and his Social Background: Muammar Qadafi, the Libyan Leader," MA thesis, Michigan State University, 1978. Musa Kousa is the current head of the Libyan *Jihaz al-amn al-khariji* (foreign intelligence).

32. For details, see Hanspeter Mattes, "The Rise and Fall of the Revolutionary Committees," in *Qadhafi's Libya 1969 to 1994, ed.* Dirk Vandewalle (New York: St. Martin's, 1995), 89–112.

33. The description of tasks for the Revolutionary Committees in 1977 is comprised of the following four points: mobilization and incitement of the masses to "practice their authority" (by participating in the Basic People's Congresses and the election of the People's Committees); the consolidation of the people's authority; supervision of the functioning of Basic People's Congresses and

People's Committees; protection of the September Revolution. Since 1979, the latter two tasks have become predominant.

34. The twenty-second annual session of the Revolutionary committee took place on April 14–15, 2001 in Tripoli: the twenty-third annual conference took place on April 6–7, 2002. For the resolutions, see *al-Shams*, Tripoli, August 4, 2002, 4.

35. At the annual conferences at the beginning of the 1980s, the liquidation of enemies of the revolution was of the highest priority. See Mattes 1995.

36. JANA (April 26, 2004), *The Leader of the Revolution*. The Libyan military intervention in Chad in the 1980s clearly showed that this statement merely reflected the theory and not the practice, since the intervention in Chad was *not* based on the "free will of the *Jamahir*."

37. Qadhafi explicitly confirmed, for example, on June 5, 1996, that the Revolutionary Committees had the right to commit extra-judicial killings of enemies of the revolution in order to "guarantee the revolutionary order."

38. The modifications were triggered by the clash between Libya and the United States in 1986, the defeat of Libya in the Chad war, the drastic fall in crude oil prices in the middle of the 1980s, and the unrest in the population caused by the excesses of the Revolutionary Committees. Following the excesses, the "Revolutionary jurisdiction" was restricted by Qadhafi in 1987. In June 1988, with the passing of the *Great Green Human Rights Charter*, the People's Court took over this function. In April 2004, because of imminent political liberalization and reforms, Qadhafi put the function of the special jurisdiction up for discussion, and subsequently, in January 2005, the General People's Conference abolished the People's Court.

39. Since 2000, the local committees have been meeting also at *sha`biya* level.

40. The first General Secretary, Sheik Mahmud Subhi, was replaced in 1978 by the former Minister for Education, Dr. Muhammad Ahmad al-Sharif, who still holds the post.

41. Cf. Hasan Salaheddin Salem, "The Genesis of the Political Leadership of Libya 1952–1969," PhD diss., George Washington University, 1973.

42. Qadhafi—Qaddadfa tribe/ Sirt region; Jallud—Maqarha Tribe/Fazzan; numerous members of the Warfalla tribe (South-Eastern Tripolitania).

43. Examples for the Warfalla tribe were given in conversations in May 2002 in Tripoli.

44. Omar I. El-Fathaly, *et al.*, *Political Development and Bureaucracy in Libya* (Lexington, MA: Lexington Books, 1977), 10.

45. Omar I. El-Fathaly, *et al.*, 11.

46. Hasan Salaheddin Salem, op.cit., 192–93.

47. Lisa Anderson, "Tribe and State: Libyan Anomalies," in *Tribes and State Formation in the Middle East, ed.* Philip S. Khoury and Joseph Kostiner (London: I. B. Taurus 1990), 297–98.

48. In this period, a civil cabinet came into existence, led by Prime Minister Dr. Mahmud Sulaiman al-Maghribi.

49. Since the dissolution of the Revolutionary Command Council on March 2, 1977, Qadhafi has been the General Secretary of the General People's Congress; since March 2, 1979, he has been *Qa`id al-thawra* ("Revolutionary Leader"), i.e., he is the "protector" of the revolutionary legacy and is responsible to no one.

50. The Revolutionary Command Council was the former Central Committee of the approximately sixty-member strong *Free Unionist Officers' Movement*, which had carried out the September Revolution. These officers still occupy important functions, whether within or outside the armed forces.

51. Currently, al-Khuwildi al-Humaidi is also head of the most important security department of the customs, the *Office of Passages and Gates*.

52. Al-Sharif was already a member of the *Free Unionist Officers' Movement*; temporarily, he was commander of the Air Force.

53. Mansour O. El-Kikhia described him as "one of the most influential people on the current Libyan scene." Cf. Mansour O. El-Kikhia, *Libya's Qaddafi* (Gainesville: University of Florida, 1997), 90.

54. The military region Sirt or, more accurately, the administrative unit (*sha`biya*). Sirt is important because it is the area of settlement of the Qadadfa tribe, accommodates large units of troops, and contains all the oil loading ports.

55. See "Mystery Surrounds Death of Senior Libyan Officer," *The Jordan Times*, December 11, 1985.

56. Exclusively Arabophone and never having traveled abroad, Sanusi had a very Libyan-centred view of the world.

57. Author of *Revolutionary Organization. Revolutionary Committees: The Instruments of Popular Revolution* (Tripoli, 1983); for a time in the 1990s, he was Secretary of Information, Culture, and Mass Mobilization.

58. Re-tribalization means, here, the intensified reversion to members of one's own tribe in order to shore-up the regime.

3

Qadhafi and Political Islam in Libya

Alison Pargeter

Since coming to power in 1969, Colonel Qadhafi consistently attempted to eliminate the threat posed by political Islam, and continues to view it as the single most important internal challenge to his regime. In fact, Qadhafi has displayed a singular personal hatred of Islamists: he still refers to them as *zanadiqa* (heretics), and his public discourse over the years has been peppered by condemnations of political Islam. In 1989, for example, he described them as "more dangerous than AIDS."[1] In one of his short stories, he even mocked contemporary Islamic scholars in a stance few Arab leaders would dare to adopt, writing: "If we were to believe in what the parties of the God coalition say, there is no need for our children to go to schools, higher technical institutes or the Bright Star University of Technology . . . rather, let them out in the open air on sidewalks selling cigarettes and cakes to adults . . . the only important thing to do is to learn the prayer."[2] Despite this attitude, however, and his zero-tolerance approach to Islamist opposition of any nature, he has been unable to prevent political Islam from taking root in Libya.

Like many secular Arab nationalist leaders who took over after the excesses of the colonialist-backed monarchies, Qadhafi tried to limit any potential support for an Islamist opposition by investing more religious authority in his own rule. Shortly after coming to power he tried to "Islamicize" his pan-Arab socialist revolution, introducing certain elements of *sharia* law, including banning alcohol and prostitution, as a means of displaying his commitment to Islamic values.[3] To the dismay of the traditional *ulama* (religious scholars), Qadhafi tried to insist his new revolutionary *jamahiriyya* was compatible with Islamic values. Indeed, as George Joffe has rightly noted: "Islam became the vehicle through which Qadhafi attempted in his usual popular fashion to reject the old religious order and to justify his own ideological alternative."[4]

However, this means of containing support for a potential Islamist opposition was always the icing on the cake, and the main tool Qadhafi used to defeat his Islamist opponents has been outright repression. Immediately after the 1969 revolution, Qadhafi set about dismantling the existing religious elites that had been allied to the sufi-oriented Sanusi order.[5] He also sought to prevent the emergence of an underground Libyan Islamist opposition by dealing with suspects in the harshest of terms. Qadhafi's dual approach, however, was not sufficient to prevent an Islamic revivalism that emerged throughout the region starting in the 1980s. As a result, Qadhafi found himself confronted with growing internal support for groups such as the outlawed Muslim Brotherhood (*Ikhwan al-Muslimin*), as well as for those of a jihadist orientation. Some observers have suggested that Qadhafi may have deliberately overemphasized the scale of this Islamist opposition as a means of justifying generalized repression, and for discouraging internal divisions within the regime.[6] It is true that, at its peak, the formalized opposition was limited in nature and never managed to make any real inroads inside Libya. However, while Colonel Qadhafi's amplification of the problem may have had its own political uses, it would be wrong to suggest that he did—and does not continue—to view political Islam as an acute and dangerous threat to his *jamahiriyya* system. Furthermore, despite his more recent forays into Africa, Qadhafi remains a true Arab nationalist at heart, the descendant of a generation of secular nationalist leaders that viewed Islamists as reactionary agents of the West. Indeed, Qadhafi once described the ikhwan as "the servants of imperialism" and as "members of the reactionary right wing," accusing them of being "comprised of hooligans, liars, bastards, hashish smokers, drunks, cowards, delinquents."[7]

One of the reasons for the regime's ongoing vigilance against its Islamist opponents—despite the fact that it had all but eliminated all the formalized Islamist groups—is that Qadhafi is astute enough to realize that he cannot completely prevent enduring sympathy and support for an Islamist ideology within Libya. The regime remains acutely aware that, given the right circumstances, political Islam could easily flourish once more. Indeed, Libya's rehabilitation into the international community following its decision to abandon its weapons of mass destruction (WMD) programs in December 2003 has raised new questions in this respect. Pressure to implement internal reforms has prompted fears within the regime that the simmering discontent still bubbling away might spill over and prove too difficult to contain. Libya's population continues to display persisting signs of religiosity, frustrated by enduring socioeconomic problems and by the corrupt nature of the ruling elite. In fact, Qadhafi's son, Saif al-Islam, reflected these anxieties when he commented in February 2006 that if genuine democratic elections were held in any Arab country, then the Islamists would sweep to power because "people trust them."[8]

This chapter traces the growth of both the moderate and jihadist strands of the Islamist opposition in Libya and assesses why they failed to make any serious and concrete inroads inside the country. It also investigates why the regime continues to be wary about such opposition movements in the post 9/11 environment.

The Roots of Political Islam in Libya: The Ikhwan

It was during the monarchy of King Idris (1951–69) that the stirrings of a modern politicized Islamist movement were first felt in Libya, in the shape of the international Muslim Brotherhood (hereafter, "the Brotherhood")— a *sunni* movement that was established in Egypt in 1928, largely as a response to the fall of the Ottoman Empire, and that soon spread across the Middle East and North Africa. As in other countries in the region, the Brotherhood was implanted in Libya through Egyptian students and teachers working in the country, and by young Libyans who had returned from their studies in Egypt. In addition, in the 1950s, King Idris famously gave refuge to a group of Egyptian ikhwan who were fleeing persecution in Egypt and who settled in the eastern part of the country.[9] This included Dr. Izzadine Ibrahim, who was to become a key focal figure for the Ikhwan in Benghazi. The Libyan king gave the ikhwan a relative degree of freedom, enabling them, as a result, to spread their own fundamentalist interpretation of Islam which, like the Sanusi before them, advocated a return to the original sources and texts within Islam as a means of dealing with the failings of the *umma* (Muslim community).

Despite its efforts, however, the Brotherhood was not able to garner real support at the grassroots level at that time. Being primarily a cultural and religious organization, its appeal was limited almost exclusively to the intelligentsia. While it was able to attract a number of young educated Libyans, the population at large, like the traditional *ulama*, displayed certain misgivings toward the group. This was partly because of the population's suspicions that, despite the Brotherhood's assertion that it was a purely cultural movement, it also contained an underlying political agenda. These suspicions were heightened by the fact that members of the movement had been imprisoned in Egypt by President Nasser, who viewed them as a threat to his Arab nationalist regime. Moreover, in Libya, where the nationalist revolution came much later than in much of the rest of the Arab world, the religious legitimacy of the monarchy itself meant that there existed little attraction for such an ideology among the population at large. In addition, Libyan society, at the time, remained overwhelmingly tribal and traditional in nature, and proved suspicious of any ideology that had been brought in from outside. As Nikki Keddie noted: "Islamism is not strong in states which are *really* largely traditional and have not experienced a major western cultural impact."[10] Libyan society, during the period of the monarchy, clearly was not ready to take on the ikhwan's ideology at that time, and the few currents of opposition that did exist, including Qadhafi's, were primarily Arab nationalist in nature.

Qadhafi and the Ikhwan

After coming to power, Qadhafi tried to remove the threat posed by the old religious establishment by creating his own type of Islam, which he viewed as more progressive and in line with the spirit of the nationalist era. His new and rather unorthodox ideas aimed at undermining the influence of the traditional *ulama*. They included, under Law No. 16 of March 1973, the abolishing of *waqf* (religiously endowed property), which brought him accusations of heterodoxy.[11] He also sought to quash other potential sources of Islamist opposition and, although they had not developed on a large scale, Qadhafi was quick to target the nascent Libyan Muslim Brotherhood. After coming to power, he immediately sent a number of Egyptian ikhwan back to Egypt and targeted Libyan ikhwan, along with other secularist opponents—such as the small Ba'athist and Marxist currents that had begun to develop—as part of his "cultural revolution" of 1973. Libyans who were associated with the Brotherhood were arrested and tortured. Qadhafi also televised a confession by the leadership of the ikhwan, who were forced to give an oath that they would dismantle the organization and not reform its leadership, in effect effectively finishing off the movement inside the country.[12]

However, this proved insufficient in preventing the movement from rising again. During the 1970s, when Libya was at the peak of its oil boom, the government sent thousands of Libyan students abroad—mainly to the United States and the United Kingdom. For many, this was the first time they had come into contact with the new and exciting ideas that were developing inside Muslim communities in the West, as dissidents and students from across the Muslim world gathered in Europe and the United

States and exchanged ideas and experiences. A number of Libyan students who were attracted to the ideology of the Brotherhood formed their own ikhwani groups in the United States and the United Kingdom and, in 1979, began referring to themselves as the *Jama'a Islamiyya Libiya* (Islamic Group–Libya).

These ikhwan were all too well aware that, unlike their counterparts from other Arab countries who were also in Europe, the Libyan ikhwan had never been able to develop or have any real influence inside Libya. Indeed, according to one Brotherhood member at that time, there were no ikhwan left in western Libya, and only a handful of people who were still prepared to identify themselves with the movement in the east of the country.[13] However, reestablishing the movement inside Libya proved to be more difficult than anticipated. The brothers were hampered primarily by the repressive nature of the Libyan regime that continued to clamp down on any form of opposition movement and that did not permit them the smallest space in which to operate. Furthermore, the movement was plagued by internal divisions and by power struggles that were being played out in Britain, the United States, and Cairo—home to the leadership of the international Brotherhood movement. As Ashur Shamis noted: "There was a lot of internal organizational turmoil in the Brotherhood movement in the late 1970s and early 1980s."[14] In the Libyan context, this turmoil was primarily linked to the setting up of the National Front for the Salvation of Libya (NFSL), established in 1981 by Dr. Muhammad al-Mugariyaf, himself a former ikhwani. The NFSL was a front that sought to draw together opponents of the Qadhafi regime, and that would not be considered an Islamist organization by Western and Arab governments. However, the backbone of the NFSL was the Libyan Islamic Movement that had been set up around the same time, and that was headed by Ashur Shamis. Shamis and a group of other ikhwan sought to establish their own independent Libyan ikhwani group that, unlike most branches of the Brotherhood, did not come directly under the control of the leadership in Cairo. They were supported in this by key Sudanese ikhwan, such as Ahmed Maki and Dr Alamin Osman, who, at that time, were running the Brotherhood branches in the United States and the United Kingdom, respectively. Both Maki and Osman were for the Sudanese ikhwani leader, Dr Hassan al-Turabi, who was embroiled in his own personal struggle with the Brotherhood leadership in Cairo, represented by the Supreme Guide of the time, Omar Telmesani, and his deputy, Mustafa Mashour. Turabi wanted to move away from the control of Cairo, favoring the idea of the Brotherhood operating internationally as a decentralized movement, with each national branch being independent of the leadership in Egypt. The Libyan Islamic

Movement shared this vision and strove to attract Libyans abroad to its ranks. According to Hajj Abdullah Bu Sen, a key Libyan ikhwan who acted as a kind of envoy to the Brotherhood leadership in Cairo, Libyan ikhwan abroad who were part of the international Brotherhood movement were ordered by Ahmed Maki to join Shamis's group.[15] Maki justified this move by declaring that there was no Brotherhood movement inside Libya itself. However, other Libyan ikhwan, namely those who were close to the leadership in Cairo, objected to this suggestion and went on to establish their own group.

This did not prevent the Brotherhood, as a whole, from being blamed by Qadhafi for the NFSL attack on Qadhafi's *Bab Al-Aziziya* residence in Tripoli in 1984, leading to the arrest, by the regime, of a number of ikhwan in its aftermath.

Despite this setback, the ikhwan continued with their strategy of bringing people to their cause, and of trying to create a network across the country that linked the members in the east and the west across the vast empty spaces of desert in between. By 1987, the group had developed sufficiently to set up their own *shura* (consultation) council, as well as an executive committee inside the country. It chose lawyer Idris Mahdi, who was part of an important Benghazi tribe, as the group's head. By 1991, the group had further developed to enable the ikhwan to hold a highly significant meeting in Tripoli that was attended by members from across the entire country. This was the first time the group was able to bring themselves together in such a big and formalized way, and they elected a new *shura* council and a general guide, Abdulmajid Burween, a professor of electrical engineering.[16]

This relative expansion in the movement's organization coincided with a difficult period in Libya. During the 1980s, the country was suffering acute socioeconomic problems, and people had become increasingly frustrated and restless when the regime proved unable to extend the same level of services and benefits they had enjoyed during the boom years of the 1970s. In fact, the limited ideas behind Qadhafi's revolution had all but exhausted themselves after a decade in power, and looked increasingly anachronistic. Moreover, Libya, like the rest of the Arab world, was experiencing an Islamic revival that, by the end of the 1980s, had gathered real momentum. The *salafist*-inspired interpretation of Islam that was advancing across the region appealed to certain parts of Libyan society that had never been comfortable with the kind of revolutionary progressive ideas that Qadhafi had foisted upon them.[17] Libyans, like their Arab counterparts, began to display increasing signs of religiosity, spurred on by the Islamic consciousness that developed as a result of the Iranian revolution of 1979 and because of the events in Afghanistan in the 1980s. For most Libyans, however, this religious revivalism did not automatically spill over into the political arena. And, unlike Algeria, where the ikhwan's ideological equivalent, the *Front Islamique du Salut* (FIS), were able to form themselves into a political party, the Libyan Brotherhood was not able to capitalize on this development in any meaningful way.

There were several reasons for this. The Brotherhood, worldwide, has traditionally appealed to the professional classes, and was primarily the domain of the petty bourgeoisie across the Arab world. In Syria, for example, the Brotherhood was strong among the artisan and merchant classes. In Egypt and elsewhere, the ikhwan were, and continue to be, found among middle class students, engineers, civil servants, and university lecturers. This was also the case in Libya: those who joined the movement were primarily members of the professional or middle and lower middle classes who found, in the ikhwan's message, a more solid alternative not only to the eccentricities of the *jamahiriyya* system, but also to the large scale corruption and patronage networks that underpinned the regime. Unlike in countries such as Algeria, Egypt, or Syria, however, the Libyan Brotherhood was never able to truly develop beyond the confines of this intelligentsia, or to create the kinds of social networks found in other countries. As a result, it was never able to develop a broad-based appeal that would enable the movement to persist despite the regime's repression.

Like their counterparts in the rest of the Arab world, the Libyan ikhwan sought to establish an Islamic state under *sharia* law, with a comprehensive Islamic economic system. They believed that the best way to achieve this was to work from the bottom up, preparing society for such an eventuality, and educating them according to Islamic ideas. This dated back to the thoughts of the movement's founder, Hassan al-Banna, who emphasized the idea that "personal piety and the good community [were] the conditions' for a good Islamic state."[18] A crucial element in the success of the ikhwan in other countries was not so much their political role, but, rather, their ability to dominate each country's social infrastructure by running professional syndicates, trades unions, and university associations. In Egypt, for example, the ikhwan were able to gain control of the student bodies and, as Giles Kepel has noted, by the mid-1980s, the majority of Egypt's twenty-two professional guilds had come under the control of their Brotherhood members.[19] Similarly, in Algeria, the FIS succeeded in creating a network of mosques run by their own people. These kinds of activities enabled the Brotherhood to make some headway in controlling each country's public space.

Due to the nature of Qadhafi's *jamahiriyya* system—prohibiting any professional organization or trades union from operating outside the framework of the state, as well as the fact that civil society activity has been even more restricted in Libya than in other countries of the region—the Libyan brothers had no such channels open to them. This was also the case at the Libyan universities where, despite the presence of individual ikhwan, they were unable to develop a real power base, as Qadhafi had staffed this sector and the student bodies with members of the Revolutionary Committees movement. Therefore, the ikhwan was forced to attempt pushing their agenda at the local level.

Even more importantly, the Libyan ikhwan were denied, perhaps, the most powerful tool that the Brotherhood was able to wield in other countries. This was the ability to carry out welfare and charity work through local networks, and to step in where state provision often proved woefully inadequate. In other countries, the ikhwan could draw on the financial support from their rich supporters in the Gulf, and in Saudi Arabia in particular, who were keen to spread the type of ideology promoted by the Brotherhood. As a result, the ikhwan were able to spread their influence among the population at large by handing out food, charity, and medicine, and, at the same time, giving away Islamic clothes, literature, and cassettes promoting their message. They also worked to promote free Islamic education. In some instances, the Brotherhood was able to conduct charity work on a large and impressive scale. In Algeria, the FIS responded immediately to the disastrous earthquake that occurred in Tipasa, near Algiers, in 1989. They did so in a fashion that was both faster and more effective than that of the Algerian authorities. As Jeremy Harding observed: "When the earthquake struck in Tipasa, the FIS had only been in existence for about six months. It arrived on site with its own teams of rescue workers, nurses and doctors, in ambulances carrying the party insignia."[20] As such, the FIS was virtually able to operate as a state within a state.

The Libyan regime's vigilance and intrusion into the smallest aspects of everyday life meant that the Libyan Brotherhood was severely restricted in the type of charitable work it could carry out. They attempted to do so, particularly after succeeding in holding their first major meeting in 1991. They found ways to increase their welfare and educational work and, throughout the 1990s, succeeded in running a number of schools where they followed the national curriculum, but also focused on a more Islamic education. They also managed to run a few student camps, although clearly not identifying themselves openly as members of the Brotherhood. In addition, they also tried to develop a base in Libya's mosques by working alongside *imams* in assisting people with their daily problems. Yet, these remained small-scale efforts, and, despite their aspirations to work from the bottom up, the Libyan ikhwan were never able to really get a strong foothold in the country.

To make matters worse, despite their limited numbers, the Libyan ikhwan who were active inside the country continued to be hampered by internal divisions that, in some cases, proved disastrous. One such setback resulted from a disagreement that broke out in the early 1990s, prompting a group of ikhwan to break away and form their own group, the Islamic Gathering (*Harakat Al-Tajamaa Al-Islami*), in the eastern part of the country. This conflict arose out of a squabble over who should lead the ikhwan. The then General Guide, Idris Mahdi, and his deputy, Mustafa Jihani, who was the de facto leader, were effectively pushed out of the ikhwani leadership by another faction led by Abdelmajid Burween and Dr. Alamin Belhaj.[21] After being pushed out, Mahdi and Jihani created their own group that widened its support base beyond the ikhwan. They allegedly began associating with some of the jihadist groups that were active at that time. However, due to their careless approach that was not sufficiently security-conscious, in 1995, the regime arrested the group who, under torture, revealed the names of a number of leaders of the Brotherhood. These revelations prompted a large number of ikhwan to flee the country. According to one Libyan analyst, this clampdown paralyzed the movement until it was given a boost by other brothers who returned to Libya after they had completed their studies abroad around the same time, and who took over much of the leadership of the organization.[22] The movement appears to have flourished for a couple of years following this clampdown and looks to have focused mainly on reorganizing itself and on carrying out *dawa*.[23] According to one senior member, in the three years following 1995, the Brotherhood was able to increase its membership four- or fivefold.[24] Their numbers, however, remained small. It is, as yet, not clear whether this expansion was permitted or not by the regime as a means to gather information about those involved. Certainly, in 1998, perhaps as a result of such infiltration, the movement was dealt a deadly blow that marked its end as an active organization inside the country. In June 1998, the regime launched a mass arrest campaign specifically against the Brotherhood and, in sweeps across the country, arrested 152 members including its General Guide, Dr. Abdullah Ahmad Izideen, and his deputy, Dr. Salem Mohamed Abu Hanek. Those who escaped arrest immediately fled the country. The prisoners, meanwhile, were held incommunicado and, at a brief session before the People's Court in April 2001, were accused of belonging to an outlawed organization under Law No. 71 of 1972. After a long, drawn-out mass trial, Dr. Abu Hanek and Dr. Abdullah Izideen were finally sentenced to death in February 2002, thirty-seven of the accused were sentenced to life imprisonment, and others were sentenced to lengthy prison terms.[25]

The movement never recovered from this blow and, while it may have had some sympathizers left inside the country, the arrests marked the end of the group's operating as a formal body. Indeed, in July 2005, the movement's General Guide, Suleiman Abdel Kader, who now lives in Switzerland, told the *Al-Jazeera* satellite television channel that there were no members of the organization left operating in the country.[26] The ease with which the regime had succeeded in arresting almost the entire leadership, as well as most of the group's members, served to demonstrate the ultimate flimsiness of the Libyan Brotherhood. While the ikhwan's ideology might well have appealed to a population in the grips of Islamic revivalism, as a movement, it proved unable to secure a strong enough base in the country to really make its presence felt.

The Jihadist Strand

While the ikhwan's more intellectual approach might have appealed to some of Libya's intelligentsia, the idea of patiently preparing for the eventual establishment of the Islamic state was not enough for activist youth who sought a more militant alternative. As in many countries, the jihadist strand in Libya appeared in the 1980s when small cells of Islamists began to group around their own *shaykhs*, who advocated taking up arms against the authorities. One of the first groups in Libya was established by Amir Awad al-Zuwawi in 1982. Al-Zuwawi, a former student at the education college in Tripoli, whose father was a Libyan artist, traveled around the country preaching *dawa* and *jihad*. His group consisted of around fifteen to twenty people, mostly in their late teens and early twenties with limited education levels, who were swayed by the heady ideas of the jihadist cause.[27]

These individuals had been inspired by events in Afghanistan, where scores of young men traveled from across the Arab world to fight against the Soviet superpower in the defense of their "fellow Muslims." For many disaffected Arabs, Islam had, by this time, become the answer to the failures of their own regimes. While some opted for the lofty ideals of *jihad*, others saw the trip to Afghanistan as a real life adventure, an escape from the humdrum routine, and, in some cases, the opportunity to find employment in the many humanitarian outfits that were created to support the mujahidin. Regardless of the motives, the struggle against the infidel communists, and taking up arms for the cause of Allah, came to represent an exciting new possibility that was felt throughout the Arab world. In the

Libyan case, the jihadists were also inspired by the teachings of *Shaykh* Mohamed Abd al-Salam al-Bishti, the popular imam of Tripoli who had been appointed by King Idris. When Qadhafi came to power in 1969, al-Bishti could not accept his unorthodox "Islamic" revolution or his attempts to reduce the power of the formal religious establishment. Although he did not explicitly preach *jihad* against the regime, he was the first public figure to articulate the idea that Qadhafi's rule was not legitimate in an Islamic sense, and, as such, he became a highly inspirational and influential figure for those who later went on the challenge the regime more directly. Al-Bishti asserted: "We are living in a time when they are denying the *sunna* [the saying, ways and traditions of the prophet Muhammad] . . . Allah told us that Allah's group are the winners and we only follow that group."[28] In 1980, Qadhafi decided to rid himself of his own "troublesome priest," and al-Bishti was taken from the Al-Qasr mosque in Tripoli and later died in prison. Yet, his sermons came to act as an important reference for the jihadist cells that were springing up in the country.

These cells operated more or less independently, but remained small-scale affairs, consisting of handfuls of young hopefuls who would gather secretly in each other's houses or shops, and exchange videos, cassettes, or pamphlets that had been smuggled into the country.[29] The euphoria of *jihad*, and the kinds of stories coming back from those who had visited the front lines in Afghanistan—such as Awad al-Zuwawi, who made a short visit there in the early 1980s—appears to have inflated their idea of what they could realistically hope to achieve. In 1986, a group in eastern Libya, led by Sheikh Muhammad al-Ushbi, tried to heighten the stakes by capturing and assassinating a leading Revolutionary Committees figure, Ahmed Musbah al-Warfali. They were caught soon after by the regime, and, in 1987, six of them were publicly hanged in a Benghazi sports stadium, while the other three were reportedly murdered in their military barracks.[30]

Even this proved insufficient to convince the jihadists of their own limitations. In fact, by the end of the 1980s, their relative sense of invincibility had been heightened further, not only by the victory against the Soviets in Afghanistan, but also by the ongoing fervor of the Islamic revivalism among the population. These cells appeared to have been convinced that they could launch a struggle against the might of the Libyan security apparatus and that the population would follow their path. In 1989, an amir and imam of a Benghazi mosque, *Shaykh* Fahkih—who had a reputation for being fiery and impulsive—decided to launch his own jihad inside Libya. He was prompted to act after another unconnected cell in Ajdabiya was discovered while practicing rifle shooting, and its members were killed by the regime. By the end of the 1980s, Fahkih had allegedly been able to amass around one hundred followers, and named his group the *Harakat Al-Jihad* (The *Jihad* Movement). After the Ajdabiya incident, Fahkih sent a number of his people to Tripoli to consult with al-Zuwawi and with the ikhwan to ask them to join him in launching a *jihad*.[31] Both groups declined to take part with al-Zuwawi, reportedly telling Fahkih that such actions would result in disaster. However, despite his group's lack of training and expertise, Fahkih was determined to go ahead, and tried to start his own rebellion from Benghazi. The Libyan security services soon moved into the ensuing chaos and were easily able to put down the uprising, killing Fahkih and another of the group's leaders, Saleh Mafouz, in the process.

This misjudgment by Fahkih was to herald a huge clampdown by the regime. The security services immediately launched a mass arrest campaign, rounding up thousands of suspected Islamists and their sympathizers. A mop-up operation in August of the same year resulted in yet more arrests. Among those arrested was al-Zuwawi, who is believed to have been killed in the Abu Salim prison massacre of 1996. This onslaught by the regime temporarily devastated the militant opposition, prompting those who could to flee to Afghanistan. As a result, Qadhafi believed he had defeated his opponents by either quashing them or by pushing them into exile. It was not long, however, before they would rise again in a much more organized and deadly form.

Afghanistan, the LIFG, and Jihad in Libya

The new wave of militancy that came to threaten the Qadhafi regime in the 1990s was largely a product of the Afghanistan experience. Although there are no official statistics, it is estimated that there were between 800 and 1,000 Libyans who joined the *jihad* in Afghanistan during the 1980s, far outweighing the number of Moroccan and Tunisian volunteers.[32] These Libyan jihadists were a mixed group from both Tripoli and Benghazi, and ranged from those who had barely finished secondary school to a handful of graduates. A number of ikhwan also joined the cause, and some went to Afghanistan to carry out humanitarian work. The Libyans set up their own camp in the tribal area between Pakistan and Afghanistan and fought under the command of Abd al-Rasul Sayaf, one of the Afghani mujahidin leaders. According to one Libyan veteran, the Libyans soon gained a reputation for being well-disciplined, excellent fighters.[33]

After the Soviet withdrawal from Afghanistan in 1989, the attention of the Libyan fighters—mirroring that of many other Afghan Arabs—turned toward their own country. Around 1990, a group of Libyan veterans, many who had been followers of Al-Zuwawi in Libya, formed the Libyan Islamic Fighting Group (LIFG), known as *al-Muqatila*. This group worked hard to bring all the Libyan jihadists under one umbrella, and allegedly scoured the front lines looking for reliable Libyan recruits who could join them.[34] Despite its adoption of the discourse of the *umma* (One Muslim nation) and global *jihad*, the LIFG continued to be primarily focused on the struggle against Qadhafi, who they referred to as "Pharaoh." As LIFG spokesman Omar Rashid asserted, "the battle between the Fighting Islamic Group and the Libyan regime from the tactical and practical level relies on armed activity, that is, *jihad* in the path of Allah."[35] The group's spiritual leader, Abu Munder al-Saidi, noted in the group's program, written around 1990: "We took *jihad* in the path of Allah as our way because it is a religious duty and at this time there is every reason for *jihad*."[36]

For security reasons, and unlike other groups that were created in Afghanistan around the same time, the LIFG did not formally declare its existence. They set up their own camps in Afghanistan near Nangahar, close to the Pakistani border, in order to prepare for the struggle back home. These camps were run with rigorous discipline and, as one former LIFG member recalled, "[By 1992] we had our own separate camps and no one could gain access to these establishments without our authorization."[37] The Libyans adopted a focused and organized approach that even drew praise from one of the most important jihadist leaders of the time, the Syrian, Abu Musab al-Suri.

However, actually getting back into Libya proved much more difficult than they had anticipated. While the Algerian Afghan veterans were able to return home and create their own bases inside the country, Libya's stringent border controls meant that much of the group's leadership was forced to remain outside the country and to direct the *jihad* from afar. Moreover, the regime's arrest campaign of 1989 had seriously weakened their support base inside the country. Nevertheless, a number of fighters did manage to return with false documents and worked to spread the LIFG's message inside Libya, mainly tapping into the remnants of the jihadist structures that had escaped the repression of 1989.[38] However, the LIFG was forced to adopt a cautious approach that focused on gathering weaponry and ammunition, as they had little room for maneuver. Even the training opportunities open to them were limited to what could be described as near ridiculous endeavors for a group intent on defeating such a strong and centralized regime. As one veteran explained: "In terms of training we used to send our people to rough areas in the big cities—places infested with gangsters and violent criminals—and tasked them to get into fights and confrontations. We especially encouraged them to get into knife fights and other situations involving extreme and life-threatening violence. The idea was for our people to develop their courage and diminish their sense of fear. We especially used the Abousaleem quarter of Tripoli, which must be one of the roughest urban quarters in the country."[39]

The group's cautious approach appeared to pay off initially, as it appeared that the Libyan security services were unaware of the resurgence of a jihadist movement inside the country, despite the fact that it is estimated that, by 1994, the group had tripled its numbers to around three hundred.[40] In fact, one former LIFG member asserted: "They [the regime] never imagined that there were hundreds of people inside the country—who had never been outside Libya, let alone to Afghanistan—that had been trained by the *Muqatila* and were dedicated enough to give their lives to the cause."[41] While this may represent an optimistic estimation of the strength of the group, as well as of its members' commitment to becoming martyrs, the regime clearly was unable to detect the growing current of militant opposition that was developing internally.

The LIFG leadership, meanwhile, continued to direct the organization from Afghanistan until they were forced out in 1992. Along with other groups, such as Al-Qa'ida, they relocated to Sudan. For the Libyans, this shift to Khartoum was viewed as something positive, as, in theory, it brought them closer to their own country. Indeed, Libyan jihadists in Afghanistan had been making exploratory visits to Sudan from the late 1980s, with a view to using it as a launch pad from which to start the Libyan *jihad*.[42] This aim was probably more a reflection of the optimism of the time rather than any realistic strategy. Likewise, the group's foray into the Algerian *jihad* when, in the mid-1990s, the LIFG sent a group of its mujahidin to fight alongside the GIA in Algeria. The group claims that this step was taken partly to prevent their men from getting rusty, but also as a means of getting closer to Libya.[43] However, at the time, the Algerian struggle was undoubtedly a more appealing prospect and, as Abu Musab al-Suri noted, Algeria was the *jihad* of all *jihads* at that time.[44] Indeed, the LIFG members in London were mixing closely with the GIA representatives there, as well as with other key figures in the jihadist scene, such as Abu Qatada al-Filistini, who came to be known as the Sheikh of the GIA. These individuals were all consumed by the battle in Algeria, which they believed the Islamist fighters were poised to win. The LIFG soon realized, nevertheless, that they had made a grave error of judgment, as internal wrangling continued within the GIA and the Libyans considered some elements of the GIA, including its leadership, to have deviated from the straight path because of the increasingly brutal tactics it was employing. As a result of differences with the GIA, the contingent of LIFG fighters found themselves in increasing difficulties, and it would appear that a number of them were killed by the GIA, whilst others were forced to flee.

This naivety on the part of the LIFG also had important repercussions inside Libya. A gross miscalculation by one of the LIFG's commanders in eastern Libya, around the same time, was to mark the beginning of the end for the group in Libya. Commander Wahid staged a rescue of one of the group's members from the hospital where he was being held under armed guard after having been knocked unconscious trying to steal a government car. Concerned about what the injured man might reveal under torture once he regained consciousness, Wahid decided to launch a highly theatrical rescue operation that reflected the amateur nature of the movement inside the country. He sent ten LIFG fighters, disguised as members of the security services, into the hospital, who promptly tied the guard to a bed and carried the injured man out with them. Such an overt and unusual display was soon reported to the regime. Following the tip-off, the security services discovered a farm in eastern Libya that was operating as an LIFG base. Upon being discovered, one of the members of this cell, Saleh al-Shaheibi, blew himself up to avoid capture.[45] Through the interrogation of the rest of the group, the Libyan security services finally woke up to the fact that they were facing a network of cells intent on overthrowing the regime. They began hunting down LIFG members. Clashes soon erupted between the security services and the LIFG in the eastern part of the country. Although its leadership tried to distance itself from the operation, and presented Wahid as acting on his own initiative without getting clearance from the leadership, the debacle reflected the operational difficulties of attempting to direct such a struggle from outside the country.

After its discovery, the group decided, in October 1995, to officially declare its existence and, in a communiqué published in their *al-Fajr* magazine that was produced out of London, the group announced itself and called for the overthrowing of the Qadhafi regime, which they declared was "the foremost duty after faith in God."[46] In the summer of 1996, the regime launched major offenses throughout the east of the country, and carried out ground and air attacks on LIFG bases in the mountains. It also arrested scores of suspected Islamists and their sympathizers. In November 1996, the LIFG staged an assassination attempt against the Libyan leader— Muhammadd Abdallah al-Ghrew threw a grenade at Qadhafi while on a visit to the desert town of Brak. This failed attack was seemingly a last-ditch attempt to defeat the regime before the movement's final demise. By 1998, the regime clearly had been victorious. Aware that it was failing, the LIFG's *shura* council elected to call an end to the struggle. However, this decision only came after the council had dismissed a hugely ambitious and unrealistic plan put forward by some members of the council to bring all the group's outside fighters into Libya.[47] Instead, the leadership ordered all members of the organization to leave, prompting those who were able to flee abroad to go to Afghanistan and to Europe, especially to the United Kingdom.

In his public discourse, Qadhafi tried to belittle the jihadist movement and to make them appear little more than stooges of the U.S. intelligence services. In a television interview in 1997, he declared: "The simple-minded Arabs fought for America in Afghanistan. The American CIA oversaw [the training of] those false witnesses, those simple-minded people. After the issue of Afghanistan ended America told them: Now, you go back and launch jihad in your countries. . . . As they fought on behalf of America in Afghanistan they fight in Libya on behalf of America."[48] In reality, Qadhafi was deeply shaken and stunned by what had happened. Yet, in comparison to neighboring Algeria and Egypt, Libya had, in fact, escaped relatively unscathed from its Islamist opposition, and Qadhafi was able to repress both the moderate and more radical elements with relative ease. It seems that, despite the widespread frustrations of much of the Libyan population, the LIFG was never able to develop any serious support base inside the country. As such, the LIFG was never able to muster the same kind of support or reputation as the GIA in Algeria. This was, in part, because the GIA developed out of the well-established FIS networks that were not present to the same extent inside Libya. Moreover, the militant groups in Algeria had a greater degree of legitimacy among the Algerian population because of the experiences of the cancelled elections that the Islamists were set to win in 1992. As such, it appeared to be more acceptable for Algerians to fight against their own regime, than for Libyans to take up arms against Qadhafi.

Despite their alleged accolades for producing top fighters in Afghanistan, the Libyan jihadists operating inside the country remained a somewhat amateur outfit characterized by sudden, panic-driven decisions that ultimately led to the movement's downfall. As one Libyan observer noted: "The *jihadis* were desperados and their insurgency was badly planned and doomed to failure from the start."[49] In addition, like the ikhwan, the LIFG was a movement essentially directed from outside the country, limiting its internal appeal. Furthermore, also like the ikhwan, the jihadists' primary support base remained in the eastern part of Libya—a traditionally conservative region long rebellious to the rule of Qadhafi's tribe. Indeed, despite the call for loyalty to the *umma*, even these Islamist movements were unable to overcome the regional divisions reflected more widely among the Libyan population.

9/11 and the War against Terror

By the end of the 1990s, Qadhafi had succeeded in virtually annihilating all forms of organized opposition in Libya. The events of 9/11, however, combined with Libya's rehabilitation into the international community following Qadhafi's decision to abandon WMDs in December 2003, enabled the Libyan leader to effectively finish off what remained of the Libyan Islamist movements. The regime moved quickly to seize the opportunities that resulted from the attacks on the United States, offering its support in the immediate aftermath, with Qadhafi even organizing a "blood drive" to help the victims. The leader also proved ready to share information with Western intelligence agencies about suspected Libyan jihadists. Although these moves should be regarded in the context of the regime's efforts to bring about a rapprochement with the United States and with other Western powers, they were also directly related to Libya's domestic security concerns.

For Qadhafi, 9/11 meant that the international community now shared the same enemy he had been struggling against for over a decade. For him, the attacks against the United States somehow seemed to vindicate the tough measures he had taken against his own Islamist opponents. He pointedly reminded the international community that he had warned the world about Osama Bin Ladin as early as 1995, but that he had been ignored. As such, the Bush administration's decision to freeze the assets of the LIFG on September 25, 2001, was a major victory for the Qadhafi regime, extended further when the United States designated it a terrorist organization in December 2004. Likewise, the willingness of the United States, and the international community more broadly, to explicitly name the LIFG as an Al-Qa'ida affiliate—despite the very tenuous relations between the two groups—enabled the regime to emphasize that the difficulties Libya had experienced in the 1990s were of an international nature rather than simply a local problem directly related to the regime's own failings.

More importantly, Libya was now viewed as an ally in the war against terror, which enabled Qadhafi to get his hands on some of the remnants of the militant opposition groups that had managed to escape. The bombing of Afghanistan in November 2001 flushed out a number of LIFG members who had been sheltering under the protection of the Taliban. This included the group's Emir Abdullah Sadeq and its spiritual leader, Abu Munder al-Saidi, who were arrested in the Far East. With the help of U.S. security agencies, they were reportedly handed back to Libya in March 2004. In addition, Britain's willingness the following year to designate the LIFG as a terrorist organization and to arrest five suspected LIFG members on terrorism-related charges provided a further boost to Qadhafi.[50] More importantly however, Britain signed a highly controversial agreement with Libya under which Libyan terrorist suspects arrested in the United Kingdom could be returned to Tripoli. This agreement was particularly significant for Qadhafi, as he had repeatedly accused Britain of harboring Libyans who were intent on overthrowing his regime. Indeed, in a treatise on terrorism that he posted on his personal website shortly after the 9/11 attacks, Qadhafi commented: "If we believe that youths that trained in Peshawar, who entered Afghanistan, accompanied Bin Laden, and who spread across the four corners of the earth are members of the so called *Qa'ida* organization, then Britain has the lion's share."[51]

These moves clearly dealt an enormous blow to the more radical strands of the opposition abroad, so much so that by the end of 2006 the regime, under the auspices of Saif al-Islam's charitable organization, had entered into a dialogue with the LIFG leadership in prison as part of his "reform and repent" program. The regime sought to convince the LIFG to agree to renounce violence in return for their release. The LIFG leadership was happy to enter into such a dialogue, although their doing so was not well received by the handful of Libyan militants still active in the Afghanistan-Pakistan border area. At the time of writing, this dialogue was still ongoing. Qadhafi also took steps to neutralize the more moderate elements of the Islamist opposition, including the Brotherhood. In March 2006, after months of wrangling, discussion, and differences within the regime, Qadhafi finally released the brothers who had been arrested in 1998 under an initiative spearheaded by his son, Saif al-Islam. This was partly an attempt to demonstrate to the West that the regime had transformed itself and was now showing genuine respect for human rights and was deserving of its newfound respectability. It was also, however, a shrewd means of neutralizing the organization and of weakening the opposition abroad. Just prior to the release of the brothers, their convictions were upheld in the Supreme Court, meaning that they were still considered guilty and were only released on the clemency of the leader himself. More importantly, they were forced to agree that, once released, they would not engage in any political activities outside of the framework of the *jamahiriyya* system. The regime was clearly confident that under such pressure, these ikhwan would not dare to attempt to engage in any activism again. Moreover, the Brotherhood's willingness to accept such conditions resulted in some criticism against it for having caved in to the regime. At the same time, the Brotherhood's unwillingness to put the regime's promises to release their members in jeopardy led to their absence from a major opposition conference held in London in June 2005, thereby further dividing an already split opposition.

However, these victories do not mean that Qadhafi can rest on his laurels. Indeed, the pressures to reform that have accompanied Libya's opening up to the world have made the regime even more acutely aware of its vulnerabilities. As a result, Qadhafi has sought to repeatedly shore up his own regime, citing the threat of international terrorism in his public discourse as a justification for beefing up his internal security apparatuses. In April 2004, the Libyan leader gave the Libyan police military powers in order to better fight terrorism, citing European governments as examples of how clamping down on civil liberties and using police repression were acceptable means. He also ruled that the *Al-Amn al-Shabi* (People's Security) was to be increased and made more efficient. In March 2005, Qadhafi declared that one hundred thousand to two hundred thousand Libyans currently in office jobs were to be drafted into the security services to combat terrorism.[52] Moreover, the regime continues to divide the country up into security squares, and regularly brings in suspected Islamist supporters who are warned against engaging in any anti-regime activities and told that if any attack occurs in Libya they will be held personally responsible.[53] The decision in 2007 by the Groupe Salafiste pour la Prédication et Combat (GSPC) in Algeria to change its name to Al-Qa'ida in the Islamic Maghreb has also thrown up new challenges for the regime that is concerned about the appeal of such a group among Libyan youth. It is difficult to see how such a trans-regional group could operate inside Libya, given the pervasive security apparatus. However, there are clearly still militant elements that may be inspired by such developments. Indeed, in August 2007, Saif al-Islam acknowledged that three Libyan militants had exploded themselves in a house in Derna when they came under siege from the security services.[54] Although there is nothing to suggest that this group had any international linkages, such events, as well as the steady trickle of Libyan volunteers who have made their way to Iraq to join the jihad there, must weigh heavily on the regime.

While international terrorism is clearly on Qadhafi's mind, it is still the threat of a potential Islamist resurgence inside the country that preoccupies him. He is fully aware that, despite the absence of formalized Islamist opposition, the Libyan population remains receptive to the kind of ideology promoted by the Brotherhood. Indeed, the regime's imposed isolation upon its population for so many years served to create a sense of cultural bleakness and introspection. This cultural void has been easily filled by a simple black-and-white vision of Islam that continues to appeal more to the population than the outdated revolutionary slogans of the regime. Qadhafi understands that if the Brotherhood or a similar type of movement were allowed to operate freely or to take advantage of the uncertainties of the rehabilitation period, they would most likely have the support of large sections of society, especially among the professional and merchant classes.

Despite all the regime's talk of reform, therefore, Qadhafi is unlikely to take any chances and will stick to his tried and tested formula that was given a boost by the war on terror, relying on the security apparatuses as a means of defeating political Islam. He has not abandoned his longstanding tactics for simultaneously repressing the Islamists and investing more religious authority in himself. In fact, he has taken his bid to be the leader of Islam to Africa, and has invested huge sums of money into promoting his Islamic credentials in the continent while continuing to clamp down on Islamist activists at home. This dual strategy has proven successful for Qadhafi during the last three decades, and is unlikely to be abandoned soon.

Notes

1. Hanspeter Mattes, "The Rise and Fall of the Revolutionary Committees," in *Qadhyafi's Libya 1969 to 1994, ed.* Dirk Vandewalle (New York: St. Martin's, 1995), 109.
2. "A Prayer for Last Friday" in Mu'ammar Al-Qadhafi, *The Village . . . The Village . . . The Earth . . . The Earth And the Suicide of the Astronaut* (Sirte: Ad-Dar Jamahiriya, 1996).
3. George Joffe, "Qadhafi's Islam in Local Historical Perspective," in *Qadhafi's Libya 1969 to 1994,* ed. Dirk Vandewalle (New York: St Martin's, 1995), 146.
4. *Ibid.*
5. The Sanusi were a religious order founded by the religious scholar, Sayyid Muhammad bin Ali al-Sanusi in Mecca in the early nineteenth century that aspired to purify and revitalise Sunni Islam. The order was established in Libya in 1843 after the Sanusi were forced to flee. For further details, see Joffe, "Qadhafi's Islam."
6. See Lisa Anderson, "Qadhafi's Legacy: An Evaluation of a Political Experiment in Qadhafi's Libya 1969–1994," in *Qadhafi's Libya,* 234.
7. François Burgat, "Qadhafi's Ideological Framework in Qadhafi's Libya 1969–1994," in *Qadhafi's Libya,* 49.
8. *Die Presse.* Interview with Saif al-Islam. February 2006. Quoted in Libya Focus. Menas Associates. February 2006. See http://www.menas.co.uk.
9. Al-Hajj Faraj al-Najar, *Ikhwan Libyia fi Ayoun al Misreen [Libyan Brothers through Egyptian Eyes].* December 21, 2004. Available in Arabic at http://www.ikhwanonline.com.
10. Nazih Ayub, *Political Islam: Religion and Politics in the Arab World* (London: Routledge, 1991), 70.
11. Joffe, "Qadhafi's Islam," 148.
12. They were later offered two choices—either to be released from prison, but on the agreement that they would not engage in any activity related to the

Brotherhood, or to leave the country and spread Islam in Africa. After eighteen months, many were freed, some became *imams* and others left the country, but the regime's efforts had served to finish the movement off inside the country.

13. Interview by author with Dr. Alamin Belhaj. January 2006.

14. Mahan Abedin, "Libya, Radical Islam and the War on Terror: A Libyan Oppositionist's View," *Jamestown Foundation* 3, no. 3 (March 25, 2005).

15. Interview by author with Hajj Abdullah Bu Sen. London, September 2007.

16. Interview by author with Dr. Alamin Belhaj, January 2006.

17. For example, Qadhafi's insistence on maintaining a corps of female bodyguards, and of encouraging women to join the armed forces, did not sit comfortably with the traditional elements of Libyan society.

18. Sami Zubaida, *Islam, the People and the State* (London: Routledge, 1989).

19. Gilles Kepel, *Jihad: The Trial of Political Islam, rev. ed.* (London: I. B. Taurus, 2004), 279.

20. Jeremy Harding, "The Great Unleashing," *London Review of Books* 24, no. 14 (July 25, 2002).

21. Interview by author with Hajj Abdullah Bu Sen. London, September 2007.

22. Saleh Mansour, "Qadiya al-Ikhwan: Al-inbiath al-sijin wal ifraj" ["The Ikhwan Case: Emergence, Prison, and Release"], *Al-Manara*, June 16, 2006.

23. *Dawa* literally means "call," and is used in the context of bringing people to the faith.

24. Interview by author with Dr. Alamin Belhaj, January 2006.

25. Political prisoners and disappeared victims in Libyan prisons. Libya Watch. Undated. Available at http://www.libya-watch.org/lw_paper_hl_eng.html.

26. Al-Jazeera. Bila Hudoud (Without Restriction). July 31, 2005.

27. Interview by author with Noman Ben Otman, former member of the LIFG, London, January 2006.

28. http://www.libya-almostakbal.com/letters/drFathiF030105P1.htm.

29. Interview by author with Noman Ben Otman, former member of the LIFG, London, January 2006.

30. Information and executions documented at http://www.libyanet.com/feb 1987.htm.

31. Interviews with former member of the LIFG and member of the Libyan Muslim Brotherhood. London 2005.

32. Interview by author with Noman Ben Otman, former member of the LIFG, London, January 2006.

33. *Ibid.*

34. *Ibid.*

35. Interview with the Spokesperson for The Fighting Islamic Group in Libya, Brother Omar Rashed. *Nida'ul Islam Magazine* 26, April–May 1999. Available at http://www.fas.org/irp/world/para/docs/fig-interview.htm.

36. *Khutout aritha fi manhaj al-Jama'a al-Islamiyah al-Muqatila al-Mabhath al-raba limatha al-jihad? [An outline of the Islamic Fighting Group's Manhaj. Part*

IV. Why Jihad?]. Abu Munder al-Saidi. Undated. Available in Arabic on www.almuqatila.com. Site now disabled.

37. Mahan Abedin, "From *Mujahid* to Activist: An Interview with a Libyan Veteran of the Afghan Jihad," *Jamestown Foundation* 3, no. 2 (March 22, 2005).

38. Interview by author with Noman Ben Otman, former member of the LIFG, London, January 2006.

39. Mahan Abedin, "From *Mujahid* to Activist."

40. Interview by author with Noman Ben Otman, former member of the LIFG. London January 2006

41. Mahan Abedin, "From *Mujahid* to Activist."

42. *Al-Afghan al-Libyoun: Mohattaat al-Muqatila wa khilaf Zeitouni ma al-Qa'ida.* [*The Libyan Afghans: Muqatila's base and differences between Zeitouni and Al-Qa'ida*], Camille Tawille. Part 4 of 5. *Al-Hayat.* September 18, 2005.

43. *Al-Afghan al-Libyoun*, Camille Tawille Part 1 of 5. *Al Hayat.* September 15, 2005.

44. Abu Musab Al-Suri. *Muqtasa shahaditi ala jihad fi djazair1998–1996 (A Brief Testimony on jihad in Algeria, 1996–98).* Available at http://www.fsboa.com/vw/index.php?subject=7&rec=25.

45. *Al-Afghan al-Libyoun.* Camille Tawille. Part 2 of 5. *Al-Hayat.* September 16, 2005.

46. Gary Gambill, "The Libyan Islamic Fighting Group," *Jamestown Foundation* 3, no. 6 (March 24, 2005).

47. Mahan Abedin, "From *Mujahid* to Activist: An Interview with a Libyan Veteran of the Afghan Jihad," *Jamestown Foundation* 3, no. 2 (March 22, 2005).

48. Interview with Libyan Leader al-Qadhafi by Hamdi Qandil in the Sirte Conference Center. Broadcast live on the Libyan Television Network in Arabic 29 Aug 97. Available in English on http://southmovement.alphalink.com.au/countries/Libya/Qadhafi-ATV.htm.

49. Mahan Abedin, "Libya, Radical Islam and the War on Terror: A Libyan Oppositionist's View," *Jamestown Foundation* 3, no. 3 (March 25, 2005).

50. Britain arrested another group of Libyan suspects allegedly linked to the LIFG in May 2006.

51. Brother Leader of the Revolution Moammar Ghadhafi presents an analysis about the actual crisis the world is passing through about terrorism. Undated. Available on http://www.algathafi.org/terrorism/terrorism.htm.

52. Libyan leader says if he were dictator Libya would be "paradise." Broadcast on Libyan Television. BBCMEP–BBC Monitoring Middle East, March 4, 2004.

53. Interviews conducted during research visit by author to Libya, June 2005.

54. Interview available online at http://news.bbc.co.uk/1/hi/programmes/hardtalk/6927651.stm.

4

Political Elites
in Libya since 1969

Amal S. M. Obeidi

The study of elites constitutes an essential means of understanding change within societies. However, carrying out such research in Libya has been very rare and difficult.[1] This is due to the nature of the political system and its political ideology, based officially on the structure of the "authority of the people's system" or "direct democracy" since 1977. In theory, the Basic People's Congresses are a central element of authority, constituting the main decision-making institution through which people are involved in the political process at the grassroots level. However, in practice, one of the main characteristics of the political system in Libya is the phenomenon of what can be called a *"temporary elite"*: this category describes those whose elite status has been created by the regime in order to help implement the regime's programs. The composition of this temporary elite is continually shifting with the needs of the regime. This has been true in Libya ever since the regime came to power in 1969.

The key concern of this chapter is to explore this process of elite change in Libya from 1969 to 2007. The development of the political system in the *jamahiriyya* since 1969 is significant for an understanding of the mechanism of elite formation in Libya; within each subperiod, attention is given the composition of elites within the executive and the legislative arms of government. Between 1969 and 1976, legislative authority formally rested with the Revolutionary Command Council, while executive power lay with the Council of Ministers. Between 1977 and the present, formal legislative authority has been with the General People's Congress (led by its Secretariat), and formal executive authority has been wielded by the General People's Committee. Although these elements of the political elite are not the only ones in existence today, they do merit particular attention.

Studying Elites in Libya: A Critical Analysis

Even though carrying out research on the elite in Libya might be useful in understanding the process of change within the political system, and within the elite structure itself, such research in Libya has been very rare and difficult. This is due to a number of problems. First, the regime itself does not recognize the existence of elites, and therefore provides no information on them. The state's ideology and the political system have presented a system without elites, especially since March 1977 when Qadhafi's *Green Book* came to form the basis for the Libyan political structure, based on the idea of direct democracy and the "state of the masses."

The second problem has been the reality mentioned above: the fact that, since 1969, the Libyan elite has shifted considerably. It is significant that the names of post holders in the country's political system are not regularly mentioned in the press, except when they are first appointed. After that they are referred to simply by their titles, i.e., "The Brother Secretary of the General Secretariat of Economics and Trade." This system prevails at all levels, except in regard to the Leader of the Revolution, the remaining members of the Revolutionary Command Council, and the Leader's sons.

Third, the influence of members of the various elite elements does not depend only on the role of that particular elite element. Not all of the members of an elite element, therefore, wield an equivalent influence. It is, therefore, sometimes difficult to identify the borderlines between different elite circles.

Finally, the instability and the structural changes related to the institutions of the political system in Libya make it difficult to describe elite developments, in part because of the abolition, separation, and fusion of some of ministries at the executive level since 1977. The fate of the Ministry of Education and the Ministry of Economics and Finance provide good examples of the instability and rapid administrative changes they were subject to.[2]

The Development of the Political System since 1969

In order to understand the mechanism of elite formation and change in Libya, it is important to focus on the nature of the political system and its development since 1969. In doing so, it is important to distinguish between three main historical stages: first, from 1969 until 1973; second, from 1973 to 1976; and, finally, from 1976 until today.

During the first stage, when the revolution consolidated itself, the military played a crucial role as an instrument of change and as a basic element in the structure of authority. One of the main elements that shaped the political system and the ideological infrastructure at this stage was the establishment of the Arab Socialist Union (ASU) on June 11, 1971, as a primary link between the people and the government. This experiment was based on the Egyptian political structure introduced by Gamal Abdul Nasser. The revolutionary regime hoped that creating the ASU would motivate, encourage, politicize, and mobilize the population toward the development goals of the revolution. However, this experiment failed, especially with regard to mobilization and participation for at least three reasons. The first was the complexity of the organizational structure, which confused the public. The second was the failure to understand the traditional outlook of the people and the role of traditional leaders in development. Finally, there was a failure to coordinate nationally with the newly modernizing local officials.

The second period from 1973 to 1976 began with Qadhafi's declaration of "Popular Revolution" on April 15, 1973. As a result of the failure of the initial ASU experiment, Qadhafi announced a five-point program that initiated the cultural revolution, and was intended to revolutionize the administrative structure of the government by turning the masses against the inefficient and corrupt bureaucracy. As a result of the declaration of the Popular Revolution, the Popular Committees were established as new institutions throughout the country. The Popular Committees were to become the official authorities in the governorates and municipalities, and also in the management of institutions, public corporations, companies, faculties, and universities. However, although the Popular Committees gave people the opportunity to participate in the selection of local leaders, and to take part in the policy-making process, it did not bring about mobilization, participation, or development. The new political leaders "were often poorly prepared to exercise their tasks, were guilty of negligence, incompetence or indiscipline, or took the Popular Revolution as merely an opportunity to leap to positions of power, without showing much concern for popular service."[3]

Accordingly, Qadhafi expressed dissatisfaction not with political participation or the expertise of the bureaucracy, but with popular mobilization. One of the difficulties in developing a capacity for mass mobilization was rooted in the conflict between the Arab Socialist Union and the Popular Committees, which were the central institutions for popular mobilization.[4] As a consequence of this failure of the Popular Committees in the mass mobilization process, Qadhafi embarked upon another method of mobilization and institution-building in an attempt to encourage the masses toward participation, especially after the break-up of the Revolutionary

Command Council in 1975. This new structure was based on the "Basic Popular Congresses." The third period from 1976 onward is a very important one, as the Declaration of the Establishment of the People's Authority was issued on March 2, 1977. The latter is significant in understanding the country's political system because, despite all the practical changes that occurred within the system since 1977, it is based largely on the structure of the Popular Congresses and Popular Committees.

The main event during this stage was the publication of the first part of Qadhafi's *Green Book* in January 1976. The *Green Book* has formed the basis for *the jamahiriyya's* political structures since 1977. Qadhafi proposed a system of direct democracy, or the so-called authority of the people, based on Popular Congresses and Popular Committees. The formation and the numbers of the Basic People's Congresses vary. Since 1998, the Basic People's Congresses have been constituted in units at the local level. In 1998, there were 381 Basic Congresses in which all citizens were registered. Each local unit has a people's committee responsible to the People's Congresses and exercises an administrative role within the community. At the level of the twenty-six *Sha'abiya* (municipality) in 1998, similar congresses and committees existed, consisting of individuals appointed by the basic people's congresses and committees and by the professional associations and unions.

At the national level, the General People's Congress represents the formal authority. It appoints the General Popular Committee, a body that corresponds to the cabinet in other countries.[5] The General Popular committee represents the highest executive authority in the country and is nominated by Qadhafi. It has usually consisted of twenty secretariats (ministries). In March 2000, the General Peoples' Committees were reduced to seven Secretariats: services affairs; production affairs; justice and public security; foreign affairs and international co-operation; finance; information, culture, and tourism; and African unity.[6] The thirteen others were transferred to the authority of the twenty-six *Sha'abiya*. The idea behind this was to increase decentralization within the country, and to hand more responsibility to the local level. By 2003, the number of *Sha'abiyat* municipalities increased to more than thirty, and the number of Basic Popular Congresses grew to 450. Moreover, within the General Peoples' Committee, a total of ten Secretariats were created. In March 2006, the numbers of municipalities was reduced to twenty, and the formation of a new cabinet in March 2006 recreated those ministries that had been abolished in 2002.[7]

While the framework outlined hints at a clear structure of political decision-making, two other institutional developments—the Revolutionary

Committee movement and the Popular Social Leadership movement—make the system of authority and decision-making considerable more complex.

The Revolutionary Committees

The Revolutionary Committees (RC) are formally regarded as a temporary phenomenon and not officially a part of the structure of people's authority. The rise of the RC movement started in the late 1970s when Qadhafi gave up his post as a Secretary-General of the General People's Congress and renounced all other official positions and titles except that of Leader of the Revolution. This introduced the notion of the separation between revolutionary and people's authority. As the leader of the revolution, he devoted his time to revolutionary activities. In this role, in 1977, Qadhafi called upon Libyan revolutionaries to form committees all over the country: in every educational institutions, offices, armed forces, and in the Basic People's Congresses in order to "help the masses take a firm grasp of the reins of power and all sources of power within society."[8]

The membership of the Revolutionary Committees is open to anyone who believes in Qadhafi's ideology, encapsulated in the *Green Book*, and is therefore not based on any kind of election. The members of the Revolutionary Committees operate outside the framework of the Popular Congresses. They are regarded as a temporary movement, performing duties that are temporary, and were envisioned to disappear when the "state of the masses" came into existence. The Revolutionary Committees rapidly became Qadhafi's direct link with the masses and his tool for spreading new ideas and new initiatives among the masses. Secondly, the committees developed a broad power within Libyan society and became tools to destroy the opposition (the enemies of the revolution) inside and outside the country. The Revolutionary Committees also became one of the main sources of elite recruitment in the Popular Committees at the Basic Popular Congresses level, and within the General People's Committees at the local and national levels. Finally, the Revolutionary Committees became an important source of elite recruitment since their establishment in the late 1970s.

The Popular Social Leadership

In 1993, for the first time since the 1969 revolution, the revolutionary regime created a role for the traditional elite in managing and controlling the population. This was done through establishing a new institution within the framework of the political system, the so-called Popular Social Leadership system. This was defined as a national organization, with an emphasis on incorporating tribal leadership into national decision-making. Its members were "respected natural leaders" of local communities who, in turn, would chose a group of "coordinators" for three years.[9] Among them, a general coordinator was chosen to represent the area in the popular social leadership at the Sha'abiya (municipality) level. A general coordinator at the national level was chosen for every six-month period from among the twenty-six coordinators at the municipal level.

Although the texts that announced the introduction of the new institution left the concept of "respected natural leaders" somewhat unclear, the main duties of the popular social leadership involved countering corruption, deviation, conspiracy, the spreading of "revolutionary culture," resolving local conflicts, maintaining contact with the popular congresses and committees, and following up on development plans for the local area.[10]

In general, the General Coordinator of the popular social leadership is considered by Qadhafi as the formal head of state. This was very clear in his speech in March 2000, when he made a suggestion that "Libya actually should have a head of state again, like other countries, in case something happens, like a catastrophe, a war, or whatever." He suggested that the job might go to the coordinator of the General Popular Social Leadership, a post that theoretically rotates every six months. In practice, since the establishment of the Popular Social Leadership, thirteen General Coordinators have been appointed since 1994. Through analyzing the data from 1994 until 2006, one can identify the main characteristics of this particular group as follows:

1. Only two of the General Coordinators were civilians, and eleven had a military background, mainly as colonels and generals.
2. Only two of the General Coordinators were from the eastern part of the country. One was from the south, near Kufra. Two were from the middle of the country, around Sirte. Eight were from the western part of the country.
3. In practice, the time in service of each member varies. Some of the General Coordinators were in their posts for six months, some for almost two years. Moreover, some were appointed for a second time in the same position. The case of Said Qadhaf al-Dam, who is from Qadhafi's tribe, is an example. He was appointed in 1995–96 and, for the second time, in 2004 until the present.

Identifying the Libyan Elites since 1990

State ideology in Libya emphasizes that power is in the hands of the people through the Popular Congress and People's Committees. However, the formal structure does not reflect the realities of influence and distribution of power (for greater detail on this, see Chapter 2). This is clear from the final sentence of Part One of Qadhafi's *Green Book*, where he concludes that, "[T]heoretically, this is genuine democracy. But realistically, the strong always rule, that is the stronger part in society is one which rules."[11] In reality, then, the Libyan experiment created such "stronger" groups after 1969. This becomes particularly relevant after 1990 when the increasing role of Qadhafi's sons raised the question of succession in Libya. The growing role of the tribes also brought back the traditional elite to the country's political system after years of marginalization and hostility. This was done through the Popular Social Leadership system.

In general, there was no change of top leadership between 1969 and 2006. Qadhafi remains the dominant figure within the elite structure in Libya. As Leader of the Revolution, he stands above mass institutions, at the center of three concentric circles of power around him, as explained in Mattes's chapter in this book. Clearly, Qadhafi stands at the core of the first circle. The second circle's influence is arrived from their closeness to the leader, and they are those with whom Qadhafi discusses policy options and positions. This circle is called the *Rijal al-Khaimah* (Men of the Tent). In recent years, this group has been dominated by members of Qadhafi's tribe, especially those occupying senior positions in the army and security services.[12] However, this group was also a part of the elite structure in previous periods, but the members remain very difficult to identify, as they were rotated from time to time. For instance, in the early years of the revolution, these were largely members of the free officers. In the mid-1970s, more were drawn from the ranks of the revolutionary youth. The latter were young activists to whom Qadhafi appealed to bring about social and economic transformation, and from among whom he formed the leadership of the Revolutionary Committees after 1977. Although the role of the revolutionary committees was downgraded at the end of the 1980s, its old leadership remains integral to the inner circle.[13]

Within the second circle, a set of intermediary elite groups has also emerged. The first group consists of the remaining members of the Revolutionary Command Council, referred to as Members of the Historical Leadership. They are part of this second circle, although most of them do not have any real influence in the decision-making process. Only Kharubi, al-Humaidi, and Jabir are still active in the political scene, although their role is a minor one. Jallud was considered second in command in the Libyan regime before he suddenly disappeared from the political scene in the mid-1990s after expressing criticism of Qadhafi's internal and external policies.[14]

The second subgroup consists of those individuals represented on the Popular Social Leadership committees. The majority of these, as stated above, have been from a military background. The third subgroup within the second circle is the central leadership of the country's Revolutionary Committees. The role of the Revolutionary Committees has, however, been restricted in recent years, after a wave of dissatisfaction emerged among many segments of society as a consequence of the heavy tactics used in silencing any opposition.

The Revolutionary Committees, in general, nowadays are not concerned with their formally normal duties, such as inciting the masses to exercise authority and agitating the popular congresses, but they have become local security forces. Despite everything, the central leadership of the Revolutionary Committees has remained strong, in part because they possess a Liaison Committee that has its own structure for reviewing policymaking in all major spheres of government.

The third circle consists of three distinct groups. The first is the General Popular Committee, which functions as the "Administrative Machinery" of the country. It represents the highest executive authority in the country, and is usually nominated by Qadhafi. Although this cluster of individuals has relatively little concrete power, as an institution, the General Popular Committee has survived all the changes within Libya's elite structure over the years. The importance of the group derives from the technical and professional expertise they possess, which is needed to implement policies. Its influence has depended, to a substantial degree, upon the importance of issues that are linked to the country's economic survival. This particular cluster of individuals is the easiest to identify, and possesses clear characteristics, unlike other groups within Libya's elite structure. Moreover, twenty of its members represent the core of the country's technocrats and, thus, exert a large amount of influence: many have been recycled several times over the years, and some have more than twenty years of experience.[15]

The second group within the third circle is the General People's Congress, which meets annually, or at least periodically and is was made up of the Secretariat of Basic Popular Congresses, the people's committees, the unions, the syndicates, and all professional associations. Theoretically, the duty of the individuals within the General People's Congress is to plan and organize the annual meetings of the GPC, to preparing its agendas, to solicit comments, and to review its members' comments. In reality, it represents the highest legislative authority in the country, and is nominated by Qadhafi.

The final group within the third circle is the Secretariat of the Basic Congresses. Libyan citizens are allocated to Basic People's Congresses on the basis of their residence. All citizens register as members of the Basic People's Congress in their areas. Every Basic People's Congress chooses, from its members, a committee to lead the congress (Secretariat of the Congress) at the local levels. The latter group is theoretically considered as the carrier of the people's decisions between the Basic People's Congresses and the national General People's Congress. In general, official ideology in Libya has emphasized that power and influence should be within the Basic Congresses and the People's Committees at the local level. One should expect that these two agencies are powerful and have influence beyond that of other groups within the elite structure. However, in reality, these two institutions do not constitute a major channel for policies within the *jamahiriyya*. Within the elite structure, they have no influence or power, although their role focuses on projecting and enhancing the regime's legitimacy.

The Legislative and Executive Elites

The legislative and executive elites of the *jamahiriyya* are important because they have been a constant element of the political system, even though they have not necessarily always wielded real authority. Although, together, they represent, at least nominally, the highest level of legislative and the executive power in Libya, their real power has varied from one period to another, depending on the individuals who are part of the groups. However, this does not mean that they have no influence on the decision-making process. For instance, within the executive group, their influence stems from their advisory role in technical matters and their long association with the regime.[16]

The legislative elite has consisted of the Revolutionary Command Council (RCC) from 1969 until 1977, and the Secretariat of the General People's Congresses from 1978 onward.

The Revolutionary Command Council originally consisted of the twelve officers of the Free Officers Movement who carried out a military coup on September 1, 1969, in Libya. It consisted of Colonel Mu'ammar al-Qadhafi, Major Abd as-Salam Jalud, Major Bashir Hawadi, Captain Mukhtar al-Gerwy, Captin Abd al-Munim al-Huni, Captin Mustapha al-Kharubi, Captin al-Khuwaylidi al-Hamidi, Captain Muhammed Najm, Captain Awad Hamza, Captain Abu Bakr Yunus Jabir, Captain Omar al-Muhayshi, and Captain Muhammad al-Mugaryef. The group was carefully selected, and Qadhafi had nurtured some of them for several years prior to the revolution.[17] According to details provided at the time of the revolution, this relationship, as in the case of Jalud, found its origins in the late 1950s when Qadhafi established the first political study cell in Sebha, and later in Misrata, in order to discuss Gamal Abdul Nasser's ideas and speeches broadcast by The Voice of the Arabs in Cairo. Moreover, some of this group joined him at the military academy in Benghazi, and all graduated in 1963–64.[18]

According to Article 18 of the Constitutional Proclamation issued on December 11, 1969, the Revolutionary Command Council constituted the supreme authority of the Libyan Arab Republic. It exercised power over national sovereignty, promulgated laws and decrees, decided the general policy of the state, and made all decisions necessary for the protection of the revolution and the regime.[19] From 1969 until 1977, the Revolutionary Command Council, led by Qadhafi, was considered as the core elite. However, only five of the officers remained politically active after 1975: Qadhafi, Abdel Salam Jalud, Mustapha al-Kharubi, Abu Bakr Yunus Jabir, and al-Khwayldi al-Hamidi. The majority of those politically inactive lost out in intra-elite conflicts since 1969.[20] Although Qadhafi emerged as the dominant figure within this elite structure. and his influence was clearly represented in most policies implemented by the regime during this stage, the other members of the RCC were also initiators of policy and enjoyed wide supervisory jurisdiction over most areas of political and economic life in Libya. Moreover, one of the important characteristics of the RCC during the initial years of the revolution was that it very much remained a collegial body where most decisions were made collectively.[21]

Table 4.1 shows some of the characteristics of the RCC as the supreme authority of Libya during the period 1969–75, including its social profile and its regional and educational background. As far as the social profile is concerned, the leaders of the Libyan revolution came from mostly modest social backgrounds. Qadhafi came from a lower-class Bedouin family. As al-Fathaly and Palmer indicated in earlier research in 1980, al-Muhayshi was the only one among the group who could e considered upper-middle class, while four others—Muhammad Najm, Mukhtar al-Gerwy, Abd al-Munim al-Huni, and Muhammad al-Mugaryef—were from the country's middle class, while seven, including Qadhafi, were poor.[22]

The regional background of the Revolutionary Command Council differed substantially. They came from different areas within the country, with 42 percent from western Libya, 33 percent from the eastern part of the country, 17 percent from the south, and 8 percent from the middle part of the country around Sirte. The educational background of the revolutionary elite was mainly military. As Hinnebusch has indicated, none of them went

Table 4.1 The Revolutionary Command Council as a supreme authority in Libya from 1969 to 1975

Name	Position	Region	Social background	Educational background
M. al-Qadhafi	Chairman of RCC	Middle	Lower	Military
A. Jalud	Member of RCC	South	Lower	Military
*M. al-Mugaryef	Member of RCC	East	Middle	Military
*B. Hawadi	Member of RCC	South	Lower	Military
A. Yunus	Member of RCC	East	Lower	Military
A. al-Himidi	Member of RCC	West	Lower	Military
M. al-Kharubi	Member of RCC	West	Lower	Military
*O. al-Muhayshi	Member of RCC	West	Upper-Middle	Military
*M. al-Gerwy	Member of RCC	West	Middle	Military
**A. al-Huni	Member of RCC	West	Middle	Military
*M. Najm	Member of RCC	East	Middle	Military
*A. Hamza	Member of RCC	East	Lower	Military

*Intense policy conflicts occurred in 1975 between Qadhafi and a coalition of RCC members. The numbers of RCC decreased due to the death of some, and due to conflict with Qadhafi, which led numbers to withdraw from the RCC.

**After being a member of one of the opposition groups who lived in exile for a time in Cairo and London, Al-Huni was appointed as a permanent representative to the Arab League in September 2000. This can be seen as one of the policies that the regime initiated in order to bring opposition back to the regime.

beyond high school and a two-year period of military training. At this stage, the revolutionary elite lacked advanced military training, which many of the Egyptian free officers had acquired for instance.[23] Among the group, none seemingly tried to acquire a further education in order to become "officer-technocrat," which had been a prominent feature among the Egyptian military elite. However, some of the remaining members of the Revolutionary Command Council, such as Jalud, acquired administrative training through the positions they held over a number of years.

Age was one of the important common characteristics of Libya's elite during this early stage. At the time of the revolution, most of the Revolutionary Command Officers were in their late twenties and early thirties. In addition to this, all were junior officers. By 1977, only five of the Revolutionary Command Council members were still politically active. However, a resolution issued by the General People's Congresses abolished the Revolutionary Command Council, and their duties were given to the General People's Congresses Committee. From then on, the remaining members of the RCC acted within the system as so-called Historical Leadership Members, and enjoyed a minor role within the elite structure.

Since the Declaration of the Authority of the People on March 2, 1977, the formal political system in Libya has been based on the structure of People's Congresses or Direct Democracy. One of the main institutions since then has been the General People's Congress (GPC), which meets annually or when convened by Qadhafi. The members of the General People's Congress are described as being liaisons between the lower-level congresses and associations and the GPC. The General People's Congress also selects a General Secretariat, whose duty is to plan and organize the annual meetings of the GPCs, to prepare agendas for those meetings, to solicit comments, and to review members' comments. Moreover, some of the functions normally exercised by a head of state, such as the acceptance of ambassadorial credentials, rest with the secretariat of the congress.

After the Declaration of the Authority of the People on March 2, 1977, the General People's Congresses appointed Mu'ammar al-Qadhafi as General Secretary of the GPC and leader of the remaining Revolutionary Command Council. Jalud, El-Hamidi, Jabir, and al-Kharubi became members of the General Committee of the GPC, and the original cabinet changed its name to the General Popular Committee. In March 1979, when Qadhafi announced the separation of the revolution and the authority principle, he insisted that the revolutionary leadership give up all its official posts. Qadhafi and the remaining members of the RCC resigned, as a consequence, from the General Secretariat of the GPC. The GPC then appointed Abd al-Ati al-Obeidi as the General Secretary of the GPC. As a result, also, since 1979, the role of the military as a source of elite recruitment at the legislative level disappeared. Table 4.2 shows some of the General People's Congress Secretariats since 1977, numbers of the GPC members, their periods in the office, and dates of their creation.

Representation of legislative elites, according to gender since 1969, shows that the vast majority (89 percent) were males. Among the fifty-four members who served in the General Committee of the People's Congress since 1977, only six were females (see Table 4.3). This weak representation contradicts the official political discourse in Libya, which has lauded the growing role of women in all aspects of society. At the same time, women have played a minor role in the political affairs of Libya at the higher levels of government. Those who were appointed as secretaries (ministers) were restricted to Women's Affairs and Social Affairs. At the local level, within the Basic Popular Congresses, women tend to be more involved and active, although their role, again, did not go beyond the Secretariat of Social Affairs and the Secretariat of the Media and Culture.

As far as the regional background of Libya's legislative elite is concerned, 46 percent of the group was from the western part of the country, 28 percent

Table 4.2 Secretaries of General People's Congress, numbers of the General Committee members, and the periods in office per day from 1977 to 2006

Date of formation	General People's Congress Secretaries	Numbers of General Committee members	Periods in the office by day
Mar. 2, 1977	M. Al-Qadhafi	4	730
Mar. 2, 1979	A. Al-Obeidi	4	310
Jan. 6, 1980	M. Z. Rajab	4	1,502
Feb. 16, 1984	M. Al-Usta Omar	4	1,496
Mar. 22, 1988	M. Al-Usta Omar	4	352
Mar. 9, 1989	M. Al-Usta Omar	5	577
Oct. 7, 1990	A. Al-Sawsa'a	4	773
Nov. 18, 1992	A. M. Al-Zanati	6	437
Jan. 29, 1994	A. M. Al-Zanati	6	1,135
Mar. 9, 1997	A. M. Al-Zanati	6	295
Dec. 29, 1997	A. M. Al-Zanati	6	793
Mar. 1, 2000	A.M. Al-Zanati	11	760
Mar. 22, 2001	A.M. Al-Zanati	8	387
June 13, 2003	A.M. Al-Zanati	6	814
Mar. 2, 2006	A. M. Al-Zanati	7	1054

Source: Survey by the author based on numbers of Libyan Official Gazette since 1977.

from the east, 13 percent from the south, and only 13 percent from the area around Sirte. It is also worth noting that, since 1992, the main posts of the legislative group were held by members of Qadhadfa tribe—by men like Al-Zanati Muhammad al-Zanati (the General Secretary of the GPC) and Ahmad Ibrahim, Assistant Secretary of Popular Committee Affairs. This provided a clear indication of the increasing importance of a tribal dimension in Libyan politics. The level of education of the legislative elite from 1977 until 2006 remains one of its most significant characteristics: 57 percent of the

Table 4.3 The gender representation in the legislative elite from 1969 to 2006

Sex	Representation in legislative	Percent
Male	48	89
Female	6	11
All	54	100

Source: Survey by the author based on numbers of Libyan official Gazette since 1969

group holds a university degree, 19 percent of the members are PhD holders, 9 percent hold military academy degrees, 9 percent of the group have only a high school diploma, while 6 percent have a master's degree.

Another characteristic of the legislative elite since 1977 has been its basis for recruitment. In general, the most dominant source of recruitment has been the Revolutionary Committees. This indicates the continuing importance of ideological commitment as a source of recruitment. Table 4.4 illustrates the phenomenon: 69 percent of the group belonged to the Revolutionary Committees, 22 percent of members were technocrats, and only 9 percent had a military background.

As far as their educational background is concerned, 59 percent of the group had social science and humanities backgrounds, while, once more, only 9 percent came from the military. Nine percent of the members had a legal background, while 9 percent only had a high school education. Only 7 percent of the group had a business and economics background, and only 7 percent had a medical or engineering background. The influence of each group, however, was unequal. Those with a military background, for example, dominated the elite structure until 1979. Those with a revolutionary background dominated the elite structure from the end of 1970s, through the 1980s, until the mid-1990s, and again in 2006. The numbers of technocrats increased during the 1990s and beyond. This was, in part, due to the economic and political problems the country faced during this period of U.S. and multilateral sanctions (see Chapters 1 and 9 in this book).

The Composition of the Executive Elite

The executive elite in Libya, during the period from 1969 to 2006, comprised the Council of Ministers until March 1977, and the secretaries (ministers) of the General People's Committee from 1977 until today. The first

Table 4.4 Source of recruitment in the legislative elite from 1977 to 2006

Source of recruitment	Frequency	Percent
Military	5	9
Revolutionary Committees	37	69
Technocrats	12	22
All	54	100

Source: Survey by the author based on network approach.

government after the 1969 revolution was announced on September 7, 1969, and consisted of two army officers who were not members of the RCC and who held the portfolios of Defense and Interior, as well as seven civilians.[24] It was headed by Dr. Mahmud Suleiman al-Maghrabi, who had a leading role in the strike of dock workers during the Arab-Israeli war of 1967. As Ruth First mentions, apart from al-Maghrabi and a couple of his colleagues, the other appointments were of relatively obscure personalities.[25]

One of the main problems of the new regime in 1969 was the lack of a systematic program, which influenced relations between the Cabinet Ministers and the Revolutionary Command Council. A reshuffle took place at the beginning of 1970 when five RCC members, including Qadhafi, joined eight civilians on the council.[26] Table 4.5 demonstrates, first of all, the rapid changes that took place within the Council of Ministers. For example, there were four distinct Councils of Ministers between 1969 and 1971. It also shows the domination of the cabinet by the military through the presence of RCC members. This reflected the power of the RCC within the legislative and executive authorities in Libya, which lasted until 1977 when the Declaration of People's Authority was announced. The table also indicates the dependence of the regime on technocrats, despite the ideological, revolutionary orientation of the regime. Finally, it also indicates the growing numbers of ideologically committed individuals (primarily Revolutionary Committee members) throughout the 1984–94 period.[27]

Table 4.6 shows the regional backgrounds of the executive elite from 1969 to 2006. The regional distribution of the cabinet members, and of the members of the General People's Committees, was roughly equal to the size of the population in each of the country's regions.[28] The appearance of a Tunisian minister (al-Shitwi) as Minister of Labor and Social Affairs during 1969–70, and of an Egyptian minister (Amin Hilmi Kamil) as Minister of Light Industries in 1989, among the cabinet members reflected the ideology of the state and the political discourse at the time, focused around Arab unity and Arab nationalism.

As can be seen from Table 4.6, at the beginning of the 1970s and at the end of the 1980s, 44 percent of the cabinet members were from the western part of the country, 30 percent from the eastern part, 17 percent were from the middle of the country around Sirte, 7 percent from the south, mainly from Sebha, as well as a Tunisian and an Egyptian secretary. One interesting fact is that the vast majority of the members (98 percent) were males and only 2 percent were females (see Table 4.7). Among the 132 members of the executive elite, only three women held office during the 1969–2006 period. Fatima Abdulhafiz was the Secretary of Education from March

1989 until October 1990, Fawziya Shalabi was a Secretary of Culture and Media in 1995, as well as Secretary of Media and Mass Mobilization from 1997 to 2000, and Bakhita El-Shalwi was appointed as the Secretary of Social Affairs in March 2006.

Such a small representation once more clashed with the official ideology of the regime, which encouraged women to play a significant role in the social, political, and economic development of Libyan society.[29] Table 4.7 accentuates the reality of women's roles within Libyan decision-making structures.

Table 4.5 Ministries-committees, number of Cabinet-GPC members and the periods in office from 1996 to 2002

Date of formation	Prime Minister-Secretary	Number of Ministries-Committee	Cabinet Members-GPC	Periods in the office by day
Sept. 7, 1969	M. Al-Maghrabi	11	9	131
Jan. 16, 1970	M. Al-Qadhafi	13	13	243
Sept. 16, 1970	M. Al-Qadhafi	13	13	331
Aug. 13, 1971	M. Al-Qadhafi	16	13	338
July 16, 1972	A. Jalud	19	17	851
Nov. 14, 1974	A. Jalloud	21	21	839
Mar. 2, 1977	A. Al-Obeidi	25	25	730
Mar. 2, 1979	J. Al-Talhi	20	20	677
Jan. 7, 1981	J. Al-Talhi	21	21	420
Mar. 3, 1982	J. Al-Talhi	18	18	719
Feb. 16, 1984	M. Z. Rajab	19	19	446
May 2, 1985	M. Z. Rajab	18	18	300
Mar. 3, 1986	J. Al-Talhi	10	10	364
Mar. 2, 1987	O. Al-Muntasir	10	10	366
Mar. 2, 1988	O. Al-Muntasir	13	13	372
Mar. 9, 1989	O. Al-Muntasir	18	18	577
Oct. 7, 1990	A. Dawrda	21	21	773
Nov. 18, 1992	A. Dawrda	12	12	437
Jan. 29, 1994	A. Al-Q'awd	14	14	1,135
Mar. 9, 1997	A. Al-Q'awd	19	19	295
Dec. 29, 1997	M. Al-Manqoush	20	20	793
Mar. 1, 2000	M. Al-Shamikh	7	7	760
Mar. 22, 2001	M. Al-Shamikh	7	7	550
Sept. 1, 9.2002	M. Al-Shamikh	8	8	286
June 13, 2003	Shukri Ghanem	9	9	263
Mar. 2, 2004	Shukri Ghanim	17	17	730
Mar. 2, 2006	El-Baghdadi.A. El-Mahmoudi	18	18	59

Source: Survey by the author based on numbers of Libyan Official Gazette since 1969.

Table 4.6 The regional backgrounds of the executive elite from 1969 to 2006

Region	Frequency	Percent
West	58	44
East	40	30
Middle	22	17
South	10	7
Tunisian	1	1
Egyptian	1	1
All	132	100

Source: Survey by the author based on network approach.

Table 4.7 The gender representation in the executive elite from 1969 to 2006

Sex	Representation in cabinet	Percent
Male	129	98
Female	3	2
All	132	100

Source: Survey by the author based on network approach.

The level of education of cabinet and committee members during the 1969–2006 period shows that more than half possessed university degrees; 22 percent held doctorates, and 9 percent had a military degree. As far as their educational background was concerned, the most prominent field of study was social sciences and humanities, followed by engineering and then by business and economics degrees. The growing number of business and economics degrees throughout the period can be explained by the fact that members of these backgrounds were needed to execute and carry out some of the economic policies the regime initiated by the end of 1970s. In general, the majority of the executive group elites got their degrees from Libyan universities and institutes, mainly from the University of Benghazi (later renamed the University of Garyounis) and al-Fatih University in Tripoli. One-fourth of the group received their higher education in the United States, Britain, France, Germany, Egypt, Tunisia, and the former Eastern Europe.

Those cabinet members who held higher degrees in engineering and economics were the most dominant within the group. At least two of those who held higher degrees were represented in each cabinet since 1969, and the number increased to four in each cabinet at the end of 1980s. One of the main characteristics of the executive elite since 1969 is the basis of their recruitment. In general, the technocrats represented 61 percent of the cabinets, distributed equally over the years. This can, of course, be explained by the nature of their field of study, needed to implement many of the regime's economic policies. However, the increasing accent on ideology as a factor for recruitment since 1977 is a significant finding. Thirty percent were revolutionary committee members. Furthermore, many of those with so-called revolutionary backgrounds were appointed more than once. For instance, Mohammed Sharaf al-Din was responsible for the Culture and Media secretariat in 1985 and 1986. He was responsible for the burning of western music instruments in 1986. Ahmad Ibrahim was responsible for bringing the educational system and its curricula in line with the regime's revolutionary rhetoric. He was responsible for banning the teaching of foreign languages, affecting the fate of students during the 1980s and 1990s.

Using the longevity of time served in office as a criterion of influence, roughly 20 percent of core technocrats were able to hold onto the most important portfolios over time.[30] This is proven by the fact that these individuals are holding the most important portfolios, and they are being shifted from one position to the other. Perhaps the best example is Abd al-Ati Al-Obeidi, who held posts both within executive and legislative elite circles during the 1970s and 1980s, and who was repeatedly "recycled" into other positions within the system.

Studying the main characteristics of the legislative and executive elites between 1976 and 2006 yields some significant comparative findings. In both cases, technical and professional expertise, needed to implement policies and to assure ideological loyalty, were crucial. But, since 1969, this technocratic elite has been very narrow within both legislative and executive circles. Military personnel, rather, have dominated both the legislative and executive elite during the 1970s through the Revolutionary Command Council.

In general, the composition of the executive group, represented by the Council of Ministers until 1977, and the Secretariat of the General People's Congresses since 1977, has changed substantially. By comparison, the legislative group elites are much more stable: the composition of the cabinet members, for example, has changed twenty-seven times from 1969 to 2006, but the composition of the legislative group has changed only fifteen times since 1977, and most of the General Committee members remained in their positions. One of the most important developments within the legislative and executive elite since 1977 is the heightened role that ideological commitment has played. The dominant mechanism for recruitment to the legislative group has been membership of the Revolutionary Committees. Fully 69 percent of the legislative elite group belonged to the committees, in comparison to only 30 percent of the executive group. Another difference has been the previously mentioned increasingly important role that tribes have played, but particularly within the legislative elite group.[31] Both Muhammad Al-Zanati and Ahmad Ibrahim are from Qadhafi's tribe, and their role reflects the growing influence of the al-Qadhadhfa in the army, in security organizations, as well as among the legislative and executive elites.

Conclusion

In theory, the current Libyan government has based its legitimacy on a populist ideology that dates back to its origin in 1969. The Basic People's Congress system is one of the main elements of People's Authority, and the main decision-making institution through which the Libyan people are involved in the political process at the grass roots level. In reality, the rapid changes within the elite structure of the country since 1969 have created a temporary elite situation that more accurately describes the actual situation. The position and authority of these temporary elites indicates, first of all, that the regime has become increasingly narrow in structure and more hierarchical. Second, the role of the military and of the security apparatuses, connected mainly with the al-Qadhadhfa tribe, has increased dramatically. Furthermore, the regime based its legitimacy primarily on a specific ideology that remained unchanged until the late 1980s. Since then, it has increasingly relied on a social dimension that centers around tribes and tribalism. The latter have become an important source of legitimacy, and of elite recruitment, reflecting the growing role of tribes in Libyan politics in recent years.

Although ideology remains important for regime legitimacy, and for elite recruitment at the domestic level, it has lost its role within Libya's international policies. Among other reasons, this can be traced back to the collapse of the Soviet Union and of its ideology. Also, the United Nations sanctions starting in 1992 had a major impact on Libya economically, socially, and politically. Finally, there was also the impact of globalization and the fact that Qadhafi accepted that the period of national revolutions had disappeared with the arrival of the age of globalization.[32]

Identifying the politically relevant elite in Libya remains difficult. We can only clearly point at the two groups who successfully survived all the changes within the country's elite structure: the legislative and the executive elites. By exploring the fate of these two groups from 1969 to 2006, we can observe that their significance was based on their technical expertise in economic and social affairs. As such, they represented a valuable asset for Qadhafi in advising, justifying, and implementing different economic and social policies and decisions of the regime.[33] It seems that the continuing influence of the two groups stems from this advisory role, from their long association with the regime, and from the ideological attachment and loyalty to the regime that has been especially visible within the legislative group after 1979. Change in power within Libya is, for the time being, not contemplated. The growing role of the leader's sons has essentially doubled the size of the core elite. In the long term, it is likely that the Popular Social Leadership system may play a crucial role in transferring power within the family in order to solve the question of succession.[34]

At the domestic level, the country has suffered since the end of the 1970s because of impractical and failing domestic policies that led to a state of chaos in many sectors of the country's economy. The emerging top elite surrounding the leader has no clear agenda to solve many of these domestic challenges. But one could suggest that Qadhafi's sons might carry forward some of their father's agenda to bring about some economic liberalization.[35] One can see the sons' growing influence—particularly that of Saif al-Islam—in the structure of the cabinet members, for example, in 2002, when Shukri Ghanem, a technocrat with long experience in OPEC, was appointed as a minister for economics and trade in June 2003. Ghanem, however, was removed in March 2006 after a long struggle with members of the Committee of the General People's Congress, some of whom contested his liberal and reformist policies, which remain unpopular popular among a large number of Libyans. Moreover, it is important to mention that the formation of the 2006 cabinet shows that the influence of the so-called old guard remains strong.

It is also worth noting that the characteristics of the current socio-professional profile of the emerging elites show significant differences with those of the old generation's elite. The fields of their studies, the places where they studied, other features such as mastering foreign languages, and the time this new elite now routinely spends in the West will have an effect on their agendas, on their worldviews, and on their own ideas and ideology. Moreover, one can expect that this new elite may be more pragmatic and less ideological than the old generation. The change in language and, in particular, elements of the ideology of the regime, expressed in Qadhafi's own political discourse, may well be a harbinger of the changes taking place within Libyan politics. This change in state ideology, however, will not be easy to achieve and implement in light of the fact that, for more than three decades, it has constituted the very legitimacy of Libya's political system.

Notes

1. See Omar El-Fathaly and Monte Palmer, *Political Development and Social Change in Libya* (Lexington, MA: Lexington Books, 1980); see also Raymond

A. Hinnebusch, "Libya: Personalistic Leadership of a Populist Revolution," in *Political Elites in Arab North Africa: Morocco, Algeria, Tunisia, Libya, and Egypt,* ed. William I. Zartman, *et al.* (New York: Longman, 1982), 177–222. See also Omar I. El-Fathaly and Monte Palmer, "The Transformation of the Elite Structure in Revolutionary Libya," in ed. E. G. H. Joffe and K. S. Mclachlan, *Social & Economic Development of Libya* (Kent: Menas, 1982), 255–79.

2. Generally speaking, the lack of stability and structural changes started since 1977 through separation and fusion of a numbers of ministries.

3. Hinnebusch, "Libya: Personalistic Leadership," 199.

4. Omar I. El-Fathaly *et al.*, *Political Development and Bureaucracy in Libya* (Lexington, MA: Lexington Books, 1977), 95.

5. Although the committee plays the role of a cabinet or council of ministers, its members carry the title of "secretary" rather than "minister," and ministries are referred to as "secretariats."

6. Resolution of General People's Congress No: 3-2000, for reorganizing the Secretariat of General People's Committee, March 2000. *Al-Jarida al-Rasmyia* [*The Libyan Official Gazette*] 6 (April 29, 2000), 187.

7. See the new formation of the cabinet at the *al-lajna al-Sha'biya al-a'am* Web site: http://www.gpc.gov.ly.

8. Mu'ammar Al-Qadhafi, "Legislation and the Crisis of Power," *Commentary on the Green Book* (Tripoli: Global Centre for Study and Research on the *Green Book*, 1984), 126–27.

9. Subhi Qanwus *et al.*, *Libya al-Thawra fi Thalathwon Amman: al-Tahwulat al-Siyasiyya wa al-Iqtisadiya wa al-Ijtima'iya 1969–1999* [*Revolutionary Libya in Thirty Years: Political-Economic-Social Transformational 1969–1999*] (Misrata: A-Dar al-Jamahiriyya lil-Nashir wa al-Tawuz' wa al-I'alan, 1999), 150.

10. Ibid., 150.

11. Mu'ammar Al-Qadhafi, op.cit., 30.

12. Tim Niblock, *Pariah States and Sanctions in the Middle East: Iraq, Libya, Sudan* (Colorado: Lynne Rienner Publishers, 2001), 62.

13. See Tim Niblock, "The Foreign Policy of Libya," in *The Foreign Policies of Middle East States, ed.* Raymond Hinnebusch and Anooushiravan Ehteshami (Colorado: Lynne Rienner Publishers, 2002), 220.

14. Ibid., 89–91.

15. See Mohamad Zahi al-Mogharbi, op.cit., 173–79.

16. Mohamed Zahi El-Mogherbi, "The Structure of the Libyan Executive Political Elite 1969–2000," op.cit., 174–78.

17. El-Fathaly and Palmer, "The Transformation of the Elite Structure," 262.

18. El-Fathaly and Palmer, *Political Development*, 38–40.

19. According to Article 18 in the Constitutional Proclamation, issued December 11, 1969. Libyan Arab Republic, Ministry of Justice, "Constitutional Proclamation," *al-Jarida al-Rasmiyya* [*Libyan Official Gazette*] N.3, (December 15, 1969), 3.

20. See Raymond Hinnebush, op.cit, 180–81. See also El-Fathaly and Palmer, "The Transformation of the Elite Structure."

21. El-Fathaly and Palmer, *Political Development*, 262.

22. Ibid., 46.
23. Raymond Hinnebush, op.cit., 184.
24. John Davis, *Libyan Politics: Tribe and Revolution* (London: I. B.Tauris Publishers, 1987), 132.
25. Ruth First, *Libya: The Elusive Revolution* (Middlesex: Penguin Books, 1974), 120.
26. Ibid., 121.
27. Moncef Ouannes,"Elite et pouvoir en Libye: participation et execlusion 1969–1999," in *Les Elites au Maghreb Congres*, op.cit., 210.
28. Total of Libyan population in 1998 (5.3 million), according to the World Bank Reports. See *World Development Indicators, 2000* (Washington: The World Bank, 2000), 39.
29. For more details see chapter 7, "The Role of Women in Society: A Radical Transformation," in Amal Obeidi, *Political Culture in Libya*, op.cit., 168–97.
30. Mohamed Zahi El-Mogherbi, "The Structure of the Libyan Executive Political Elite 1969–2000," op.cit., 176–77.
31. For more details about tribe and tribalism, see chapter 5, "Tribe and Tribalism: An Alternative to Civil Society," in Amal Obeidi, *Political Culture in Libya*, op.cit., 108–35.
32. Ray Takeyh, "The Rogue Who Came in From the Cold," *Foreign Affairs* 80, no. 3,(May–June 2001), 64. For instance, Al-Qadhafi has proved this move in 1999 when he announced that "we can not stand in the way of progress . . . no more obstacles between human beings are accepted. The fashion now is the free market and investments . . . now is the era of economy, consumption, markets and investments. This is what unites people irrespective of language, religion, and nationalities." There are some other dimensions that can be seen as evidence on the changes of the political discourse. This dimension related to the Libyan policy toward the United States and Israel. Al-Qadhafi announced in a speech in August 31, 2002, that "There is no Libyan policy. This is an African policy . . . in the old days, they called us a rogue state. They were right in accusing us of that. In the old days, we had a revolutionary behavior . . . we acted like an independent state and we put up with the consequences."
33. Ibid.
34. The question of succession has never been raised officially, the justification being that the Libyan political system is based on the idea of Direct Democracy's, which is based on the People's Authority.
35. For more details see, Dirk Vandewalle, "The Failure of Liberalization in the Jamahiriyya," in *Qadhafi's Libya 1969 to 1994*, ed. in Dirk Vandewalle (New York: St. Martin's, 1995), 203–22.

5

The Libyan Economy in Transition

Opportunities and Challenges

Ronald Bruce St John

Following three decades of socialist experimentation and two earlier (and failed) attempts at economic liberalization in 1987 and 1991, Libya, after 2000, turned toward the implementation of a series of sweeping changes to attempt, once more, to turn around its stagnant and highly inefficient command-style economy. The government's most recent promises of economic liberalization have generated understandable and considerable interest in, and enthusiasm for, changes in the oil and gas sectors. Exploration and production sharing agreements remained at the forefront of Libyan efforts to encourage hydrocarbon investment, but the terms of the new round of agreements have been modified to provide enhanced incentives to bidders in a more open, competitive environment. In the country's other economic sectors, the speed and scope of reform to diversify the country's economy, and to make it more efficient so far, have proven less successful, the halting progress perhaps suggesting that meaningful reform in these areas will be much more difficult. In all sectors, the regime's actions taken during the earlier years of its self-styled revolution continue to pose significant barriers to the implementation of the new economic strategy.

Policy Revolution

Oil exploration in independent Libya began in 1955, and deposits in commercially viable quantities were first discovered in 1959 when American prospectors confirmed their location at two separate locations in Cyrenaica. The following decade witnessed dramatic increases in both production and revenues, but not in the posted price of oil, the basis of taxable income for producing countries. Like most oil-producing states, Libya considered the posted price to be undervalued and unjust. Nevertheless, it accepted a volume-oriented, as opposed to a price-oriented, policy because it feared that a confrontation with the oil companies over posted price levels might slow industry development.

At the outset, revenues from petroleum exports increased rapidly, growing more than fifteen-fold from $40 million in 1962 to $625 million in 1967. Within eight years of its first shipment, Libya had become the world's fourth largest exporter of crude oil, a rate of growth previously unknown anywhere in the industry's history. In the process, Libya moved from a stagnant to an exploding economy, from a capital-deficit state to a capital-surplus state, from an aid recipient to an aid extender. By the time King Idris I was overthrown in 1969, Libyan oil exports exceeded 3 million barrels per day (bpd); however, the revenue received per barrel of oil remained one of the lowest in the world.[1]

After the Free Unionist Officers seized power on September 1, 1969, the Revolutionary Command Council (RCC), headed by Mu'ammar al-Qadhafi, began to implement a socioeconomic and political revolution in Libya. In early 1970, the RCC opened negotiations with the oil companies working in Libya, eventually gaining a majority control in all of them through modified participation agreements or outright nationalization. Thereafter, it pursued a two-pronged policy of controlled production to conserve reserves and price escalations to maximize revenues. The RCC was notably aggressive in its oil-pricing policy, even when higher prices were not necessarily in its best interests, because it viewed petroleum as its most effective political weapon.[2]

In dealing with the oil companies, the RCC pursued a strategy of confrontation to call the bluff of the international oil cartels and the Western consuming nations. In so doing, it successfully wrestled from them additional taxes and revenues. Unfortunately, the RCC misinterpreted the lessons to be drawn from its negotiations with the oil industry to the detriment of domestic policy in other areas. Pleased with the results of its direct approach, the RCC applied the same management style elsewhere, only to find that none of the nation's other resources were amenable to such aggressive policies. For example, the revolutionary government managed rangeland pasture and water, two highly precious resources in a largely desert state, throughout the 1970s without regard to their sustained use.[3] The increased revenues stemming from the new oil policy also encouraged the RCC to set expanded foreign policy objectives, from the promotion of Arab unity to support for the Palestinian cause to opposition to the regional policies of the United States, most of which proved well beyond its diplomatic and other resources to achieve.

Libyan Socialism

Socialism was a part of most twentieth century revolutions, especially those in the Middle East, and Libya proved no exception. From the outset, Qaddafi and his colleagues on the RCC trumpeted the revolutionary trinity of freedom, socialism, and unity, depicting socialism as the solution to the economic problems of humankind. Libyan socialism was doctrinal, as opposed to pragmatic, and highly nationalistic in a region where socialism and nationalism have often been found together. Early on, Qaddafi made the nationalization of the oil industry and other sectors of the economy a prominent policy because it helped solidify his regime, in addition to being a first step on the road to socialism. His early policy statements also emphasized the indigenous nature of Libyan socialism, describing it as both an integral part of Libyan political culture and a necessary corrective action. Qaddafi's approach here reflected contemporary practice in the Middle East where the origins and character of socialism have frequently been discussed in the context of local history and customs.[4]

As early as 1973, the RCC took tentative steps to turn its socialist rhetoric into practice; however, concerned with domestic opposition, it delayed implementation of the more radical elements of its socialist program until the second half of the decade. Initially, economic policy emphasized social welfare programs, like increased housing and improved health care that enjoyed widespread popular support. Regime support for education was comparatively less and somewhat selective. Following an initial wave of investment in education, health care, and housing, government spending declined due to the limited absorptive capacity of the economy, a shift in resources from development to reserves, and the cash flow problems compounded by mounting arms expenditures.[5]

The Libyan approach to socialism clarified in the second half of the decade with the publication in 1978 of *The Solution of the Economic Problem: "Socialism,"* the second part of Qaddafi's *Green Book*. The socialist theories outlined therein were gradually translated into law, tightening controls over private enterprise. After the *Green Book* defined man's basic needs as a house, an income, and a vehicle, renting housing and hiring vehicles were denounced as forms of domination over the needs of others. When Qaddafi urged greater self-management of public and private enterprise in the fall of 1978, workers rushed to take over some two hundred companies. A widespread redistribution of land on the Jefara plain, west of Tripoli, began in 1979, and continued into 1980–81. In May 1980, Libya declared all currency in denominations larger than one dinar to be void, giving citizens one week to exchange their cash. With the maximum exchange set at 1,000 dinars, all deposits in excess of that amount were frozen. The demonetization campaign was a straight-out socialist measure, redistributive in intent and effect. Libyan author Hisham Matar later provided a vivid description of the impact of the currency exchange in his critically acclaimed novel, *In the Country of Men*, setting the event in his fictional work one year earlier than it occurred in real life.

> In 1979, a few days after I was sent to Cairo, the entire Libyan population was given three days to deposit liquid assets into the National Bank. The national currency had been redesigned, they were told, to celebrate the revolution's tenth anniversary. People deposited pockets of coins and others suitcases of notes and some a truckful of money only to be told afterward that individual bank withdrawals would be limited to one thousand dinars annually. My parents were badly affected by this, their monthly output alone was in excess of that amount. The following year, private savings accounts, which were effectively what most accounts had become, were eliminated, and my parents watched their money vanish "like salt in water."[6]

Finally, the General People's Congress (GPC), the Libyan equivalent of a parliament, announced in early 1981 that the state would take over all import, export, and distribution functions by year's end.[7]

If socialism is defined as a redistribution of wealth and resources, a socialist revolution clearly occurred in Libya after 1969 and, most especially, in the second half of the 1970s. The management of the economy was increasingly socialist in intent and effect, with wealth in housing, capital, and land significantly redistributed or in the process of redistribution. Private enterprise was virtually eliminated and largely replaced by a centrally controlled economy.[8] In the process, the Libyan approach to socialism became more fundamental than that found in neighboring states. Whether or not Qaddafi intended, in 1969, for it to become as radical as it had become by the early 1980s is open to question. What is clear is that precept and theory generally preceded practice in the case of Libya. It is also clear that the domestic turmoil produced by the regime's increasingly radical policies had an adverse impact on its development goals. The widespread redistribution of power and wealth in the second half of the 1970s also affected the economic well-being of many people, resulting in mounting opposition to the regime.[9]

Revolution within the Revolution

The socialist process in Libya continued into the second half of the 1980s, when Qaddafi adopted a more moderate tone and signaled an interest in returning to a more open, free enterprise system. In February 1987, after GPC delegates criticized regime economic policies, Libyan involvement in Chad, and the zeal of the Revolutionary Committees, in March, Qaddafi announced a package of economic and political reforms, calling them a "Revolution within the Revolution." In May 1987, he called for reform in both the agricultural and the industrial sectors, including a reversal of import substitution policies and the adoption of modern management practices. He later called for a new role for the private sector, as well as increased liberalization. Qaddafi also promoted a form of self-management, encouraging the creation of cooperatives in which partners could contribute either capital or labor. In response, some 140 companies had been turned over to self-management committees by August 1988.[10]

In March 1988, a Ministry of Mass Mobilization and Revolutionary Leadership was created to limit the role of the Revolutionary Committees. The power of revolutionary courts was curtailed two months later. In June, the GPC adopted the "Great Green Charter of Human Rights in the Jamahiriya Era." Largely based on prior statements by Qaddafi, the charter guaranteed Libyans some rights and freedoms but did not protect civil and political rights as they are understood under international law. Libya later implemented a few of the provisions in the charter; nevertheless, the real position of religious and political dissidents in Libya was unchanged in the post-charter era. In September 1988, Qaddafi called for an end to government control over trade, abolishing the state import and export monopoly. He also lifted injunctions against retail trade, and markets and *souks* in urban areas began to reopen. The hydrocarbon sector and heavy industry were exempt from the new privatization measures, but Qaddafi did call for greater efficiency in state enterprises.[11]

A complex web of economic and political factors was behind this sudden moderation in the socialist policies of the regime. The state-run supermarket system, plagued with endemic shortages, was faltering under the weight of corruption and a disorganized distribution system; and, the unofficially tolerated black market, where everything was available at a price, provided little relief to the average Libyan. The expulsion, in 1985, of large numbers of expatriate workers, a political decision with severe economic consequences, brought the agricultural and service sectors to a virtual standstill. Finally, as oil prices fell in the first half of the 1980s, oil revenues plummeted, constraining the regime's ability to support extravagant socialist policies.[12]

The impact of these economic issues was intensified by Libya's growing political isolation in the mid-1980s. After closing its embassy in Tripoli in 1980, Washington, in 1982, suspended travel to Libya, prohibited Libyan oil imports, and expanded controls on goods destined for export to Libya. Already stung by a military defeat in Chad and diplomatic setbacks throughout the Arab world, Libya's confrontation with the United States culminated in the American bombing of Benghazi and Tripoli in April 1986. Following the attack, Washington imposed economic sanctions, froze all Libyan assets, and ordered American oil companies operating in Libya to cease operations. At the time, American firms were central players in the Libyan oil industry, and this latter decision threatened the overall health of the entire Libyan economy.[13]

Experienced in reading public opinion, and ever sensitive to political imperatives, Qaddafi realized internal discontent was approaching an explosive level, and responded with corrective measures, moderating many of the socialist policies he had advocated since the outset of the 1969 revolution. His ability to execute a policy *volte-face* at a vulnerable time was facilitated by the April 1986 bombing raid. Designed by the United States to destabilize the regime, the attack had the opposite effect, strengthening Qaddafi's hold on power. The raid did little to rally the masses around Qaddafi, but it invigorated a radical minority, most especially members of the Revolutionary Committees. At the same time, it discredited and demoralized regime opponents inside and outside the country, many of who worried openly that they could be perceived as little more than tools of U.S. policy. Qaddafi seized on the moment to consolidate his domestic political position, even as he continued to oppose the international status quo.[14]

In the so-called Revolution within the Revolution, Qaddafi had envisioned an expanded role for the private sector, accompanied by limited political reforms. This early attempt to promote economic liberalization proved a harbinger of things to come one decade later, but, at the time, it failed to generate widespread public support. On the contrary, delegates to the March 1990 General People's Congress rejected regime efforts to reduce public expenditures, calling instead for lower taxes, free health care, cheaper housing loans, and increased spending on state-owned industries.[15]

In the interim, on December 21, 1988, Pan Am flight 103 exploded over Lockerbie, Scotland, killing 259 passengers, together with eleven people on the ground. Nine months later, UTA flight 772 exploded over Niger, killing 179 passengers. When the Qaddafi regime failed to cooperate in investigating these terrorist attacks, in 1992, the United Nations imposed sanctions on Libya, blocking arms sales and air travel. In 1993, the Security Council toughened the sanctions in place, freezing Libya's overseas assets, banning some sales of oil equipment, and tightening earlier restrictions on air travel.[16]

The UN embargo generated mounting discontent and increasing privation in Libya, reflected in unpaid salaries, decreased subsidies, cuts in army perks, and a shortage of basic goods. Military unrest led to an unsuccessful attempt, in 1993, to assassinate Qaddafi. The regime also faced opposition from various tribal factions, principally in Cyrenaica, as well as ideological movements, mostly operating outside the country. However, the most serious threat to the regime came from militant Islamist forces, especially active in the mid-1990s. Inspired by counterparts in neighboring countries, these groups attempted to destabilize the Qaddafi regime.[17]

Once Libya remanded the two Lockerbie suspects in April 1999, the United Nations immediately suspended its sanctions regime. The United States took the opposite course, announcing its bilateral sanctions would remain in place. The complex rationale behind the Libyan decision to hand over the Lockerbie suspects, having resisted that action for seven years, remains a subject of debate; however, the dire need for economic reform was likely center stage. By 1999, the Qaddafi regime had largely corralled its domestic opposition, but it still faced an ailing economy. Oil production had flagged throughout the decade for a variety of reasons, including the imposition of multilateral sanctions, falling demand, and aging oil fields. With domestic support tied closely to economic issues, Qaddafi clearly recognized the need to revitalize the economy, but he was understandably reluctant to initiate broad economic reforms as long as the country was subject to sanctions. Therefore, the domestic political repercussions of remanding the two suspects was likely of minimal concern when compared to the desperate need to open the economy and attract foreign capital.[18]

Piecemeal Reforms

As the decade of the 1990s closed, the Libyan economy responded positively to the relaxation of UN sanctions, stronger demand for petroleum products, and improved oil prices. Hydrocarbon-based revenues increased sharply, contributing around 50 percent of GDP, 97 percent of exports, and 75 percent of government revenues during the period 1999–2003. Heavily dependent on the oil and gas sector, the economy remained mostly state-controlled, with the IMF estimating in March 2005 that 75 percent of employment continued in the public sector, while private investment remained low at around 2 percent of GDP. The Libyan economy also faced a mounting unemployment problem, compounded by a high rate of population growth and a low rate of job creation.[19]

Once the United Nations had suspended its sanctions regime, Qaddafi launched a wave of new initiatives in Africa and Europe, aimed at ending Libya's economic and political isolation. By the beginning of the new millennium, Libya had succeeded in reestablishing commercial and diplomatic ties with a large number of states. At home, domestic opposition remained a concern, but less so than in the previous decade, as the regime took advantage of its enhanced international status to co-opt opposition groups in and out of Libya. A stronger economy, benefiting from relaxed economic sanctions and higher oil prices, helped dampen popular dissent.[20]

Libya seized the international spotlight to market new investment opportunities. In so doing, its spokespersons soon became expert in using terms, like "transparency," "partnership," and "diversification," largely foreign to them in the past. Emphasis was placed on foreign direct investment in sectors like agriculture, tourism, and trade. A Free Trade Act established free trade zones to promote exports and technology transfer agreements, and Libya attracted some overseas interest in hotel and tourism projects. At a government-sponsored investment conference in November 2000, Libyan officials called on investors to play a larger role in its $35 billion, five-year development plan to liberalize the economy. Qaddafi chimed in one week later, describing his country as the best place in the world for investment.[21]

At the same time, a mid-September 2000 report in *Al-Zahf al-Akhdar*, a publication widely viewed as the mouthpiece of the Basic People's Congresses, strongly criticized foreign companies operating in Libya, labeling them a threat to Libyan society. Attacks on the West were hardly new in Libya, but the timing of this release suggested it might prove a precursor to a move to reduce foreign activities. While some observers dismissed the report as simply another example of the unpredictability of the Qaddafi regime, it proved an early indication that significant segments of official Libya were uncomfortable with the sudden turn toward economic liberalization.[22]

In September 2001, Qaddafi launched a strong attack against corruption, calling for a halt in government expenditures until the problem was addressed. Given the opaque nature of the Libyan policymaking milieu, the rationale behind his remarks were unclear; however, they proved significant for several reasons. First, they added uncertainty to the privatization process, as some observers viewed them as another sign of a pending crackdown on private sector activity. After Qaddafi criticized corruption in the public sector, the People's Court found the finance minister and other authorities guilty of bribery, forgery, and damaging public property. His remarks also paved the way for his subsequent call for a reduction in the number of civil servants. Finally, Qaddafi again demonstrated his ability to read public opinion, successfully disassociating himself from public discontent over corruption and the inefficient use of oil resources before it hardened into outright opposition.[23]

Over the next two years, Libya continued to promote economic liberalization, focused on diversification, privatization, and structural modernization; however, real performance never approached official rhetoric. Hydrocarbons still accounted for approximately 95 percent of exports and some 75 percent of government revenues. Potential investors faced many obstacles, including inadequate legal protection, ambivalent attitudes toward foreign workers, regular bouts of policy uncertainty, and a dearth of Libyan private sector business partners, all consequences of the prolonged socialist experiment. At the same time, risk-adverse Libyan officials remained hesitant to repeat earlier efforts at diversification, efforts that had failed miserably when oil and gas production was expected to increase and oil prices were at relatively high levels.[24]

Stating the nation's public sector had failed and should be abolished, in 2003, Qaddafi called for the privatization of the oil industry, together with other sectors of the Libyan economy. Pledging to bring Libya into the World Trade Organization (WTO), he replaced Prime Minister Mubarak Abdullah al-Shamikh with Shokri Ghanem, a vocal proponent of liberalization and privatization. In October 2003, Prime Minister Ghanem published a list, drawn from a variety of economic sectors, of some 360 state-owned enterprises targeted for privatization or liquidation. His government also unified the multi-tiered exchange rate, a much needed currency devaluation that both increased the competitiveness of Libyan companies and attracted foreign investment. Efforts at privatization accelerated in 2004 after Libya, in late December 2003, renounced unconventional weapons and the means to deliver them, and the United States began to ease the bilateral sanctions still in place.[25]

Addressing an Arab strategy conference in Dubai, in December 2004, Prime Minister Ghanem outlined a development strategy for Libya, centered on economic diversification. Acknowledging that hydrocarbon revenues would be the growth engine, he stressed the need to look for alternative sources of income and to develop new industries so that oil and gas revenues could become a reserve for the economy. Elsewhere, in May 2005, Libya dropped a decades-long requirement for visitor travel documents to be translated into Arabic; and, in July 2005, it lifted customs tariffs on 3,500 imported commodities. In June 2006, after the IMF reported only 66 of the 360 state enterprises slated for privatization or liquidation had been sold, Libya announced the creation of a stock market to support privatization of public companies. In January 2007, Libya accepted the use of foreign languages on roadside billboards, commercial notice boards, and tourist forms; and, in March 2007, it inaugurated a stock market.[26]

Even as Libya reiterated its commitment to a course of economic liberalization, real progress in the non-petroleum sectors of the economy remained tentative, subject to much uncertainty and occasional reverses. Public criticism of liberalization policies increased after May 2005 when the government imposed a 30 percent hike in fuel prices and doubled the price of electricity for consumers of more than 500 kilowatts a month. A related decision to lift customs duties on more than 3,500 imported commodities raised concerns about job security in local factories ill-equipped to meet foreign competition. Adding to public concern, elements of the reform process were implemented in an *ad hoc*, unclear manner, and were often compromised by human capacity constraints.

In response, Qaddafi reshuffled the cabinet in early March 2006, replacing the reform-minded Ghanem with his more malleable deputy, Ali Baghdadi al-Mahmudi. As part of the change, the energy ministry was eliminated, and Ghanem was named chairman of the National Oil Corporation (NOC). The cabinet shake-up was widely viewed as a victory for conservative hardliners, and the much-trumpeted privatization program, which, in the non-hydrocarbon sectors had gained little traction under Ghanem, slowed to a crawl. In the wake of the reshuffle, Prime Minister Mahmudi refrained from attacking Ghanem's polices or attempting to reverse them, but he also said or did little in support of the economic reforms touted by his predecessor.[27]

Following the cabinet reorganization, a series of statements by Qaddafi compounded confusion as to the speed and direction of reform policy. In June 2006, after Libya's planning minister encouraged international companies to look beyond the oil sector and think of investing in construction, health, or tourism, in a July speech, the Libyan leader said he wanted to curb the role of foreigners in the economy to ensure Libya's wealth remained at home. One month later, he scolded the nation for its overreliance on oil and gas revenues, foreigners, and imports, telling the Libyan people to start manufacturing the things they needed. In a speech marking the thirty-seventh anniversary of the One September Revolution, Qaddafi subsequently encouraged unemployed Libyans to emigrate to Africa, warning them they must move quickly before the best paid jobs were taken by Chinese and Indians. Adding to the confusion, the regime later arrested several Libyan businessmen on grounds they were monopolizing the commercial environment and violating the principles of "people's socialism," a new term employed by official Libya to emphasize economic liberalization must be consistent with the *Green Book*. Difficult to interpret, Qaddafi's colorful, but contradictory, remarks did nothing to reassure potential investors in Libya.[28]

A report by the National Democratic Institute for International Affairs (NDI), based on a visit to Libya in April 2006, captured the uncertainty gripping the economy. Outside of the oil sector, large-scale private enterprise is practically nonexistent, and citizens remain dependent on the government for any income they receive. The delegation noted an absence of the high levels of poverty that afflict some states in North Africa, while, at the same time, there were few signs of prosperity or economic dynamism. Despite the fact that relations with the West have improved in recent years, and despite the clear potential for investment in industries such as tourism and construction, there has been little foreign investment outside of the oil sector. Observers of the economic situation told NDI that this is an area where the regime would like to make changes, but as the political system is based on a state-run economy, the way forward is not clear.[29]

An IMF report published at the same time as the NDI report reached a similar conclusion: "Progress in developing a market economy has been slow and discontinuous nonetheless, and the government has yet to clearly break from past shortcomings in policy formulation and implementation."[30]

Oil and Gas the Exception

In stark contrast to the uncoordinated, piecemeal approach to reform which characterized other sectors of the Libyan economy, the reform process in the hydrocarbon sector was more efficient from the start. Libya has long been an attractive investment target for Europe, given its proximity to major European markets, high quality crude oil, and relatively low extraction costs. This was especially true once the UN sanctions were suspended, and the U.S. embargo continued to block American companies from returning to Libya. When the National Oil Company offered forty new oil blocks in May 2000, in addition to almost one hundred blocks offered in November 1999, a number of European operators, including Royal Dutch/Shell, TotalFinaElf of France, Lasmo of the United Kingdom, and Lundin Oil of Sweden, sought expanded acreage in Libya.[31]

In conjunction with its renewed emphasis on the oil sector, Libya also began to promote the natural gas industry. At this point, the Western Libya Gas Project (WLGP) was its most important natural gas opportunity. The project was designed to move natural gas and condensate from the onshore

Wafa field, near the Algerian border, and the offshore Bahr Essalam field (Block NC-41), off the Mediterranean coast, to a new processing plant on the coast at Melitah. Following completion of a 322-mile pipeline from Libya to Sicily, a project known as Green Stream, Libya was expected to provide some 30 percent of Italy's energy needs. The pipeline came on line in October 2004, with the commencement of production from the Wafa field, and trial production from the Bahr Essalam field began in August 2005. According to the World Bank, Libya's proven natural gas reserves total 51.3 billion cubic feet, third highest in Africa behind Algeria and Nigeria, with unproven reserves estimated to be as much as twice that amount.[32] The WLGP aptly demonstrated there were both market demand and the requisite production and distribution facilities available for Libyan natural gas.

In the oil industry, a modest increase in output followed suspension of UN sanctions in April 1999; however, it soon became clear the American oil companies would have to participate to generate the desired level of investment. Libya needed leading-edge exploration and development technology, as well as the enhanced oil recovery (EOR) techniques necessary to soften the natural decline in maturing fields, a decline estimated to be as much as 7–8 percent annually. By 2003, Libyan officials were targeting $30 billion in foreign investment by the end of the decade in order to expand oil production from 1.5 million b/d to 3.0 million b/d by 2015. Since then, the target year for reaching 3.0 million b/d has bounced around, depending on the Libyan official being interviewed, from 2010 to 2012 to 2015, with 2015 remaining the most realistic date.[33]

Libya's renunciation of unconventional weapons and related delivery systems in December 2003 opened the door for American oil companies to return to Libya. The U.S. government lifted some trade sanctions the following April, and restored diplomatic ties in June 2004. Virtually all remaining trade sanctions were lifted in September 2004. At that point, the only sanctions still in place were certain export restrictions related to Libya's retention on the Department of State's list of state sponsors of terrorism. These export controls, which made it difficult to ship essential oil-field equipment to Libya because of dual-use restrictions, were eventually lifted when Libya was removed from the terrorism list in May 2006. Responding to the relaxation in trade restrictions, foreign direct investment in Libya totaled $4 billion in 2004, up six-fold from the previous year.[34]

Improved commercial and diplomatic relations enabled U.S. oil companies to resume activities in Libya. Actually, members of the Oasis Group (ConocoPhillips, Amerada Hess, and Marathon Oil), together with Occidental Petroleum, received permission from the U.S. government to start negotiations with Libya in late 2003. Initial hopes for a speedy return to their acreage, held in trust by Libya after 1986 in so-called standstill agreements, were soon dashed. The NOC insisted the Americans return on the same terms they left in 1986, while the oil companies pushed for new, improved terms, including an increase in profit share and an extension of the ten-year leases agreed to under the standstill agreements. The companies argued the productive acreage held in trust by Libya since 1986 had become, by 2003, enhanced oil recovery projects, and the terms for their return should reflect this decline in productivity. Production at the Oasis Group's Waha concession in Sirte was estimated to be around 350,000 to 375,000 b/d in 2003, compared to a peak of one million b/d in the 1970s. Occidental Petroleum eventually negotiated its return to Libya in July 2005, and the Oasis Group followed at the end of the year, agreeing to pay the NOC $1.83 billion to resume oil production.[35]

The principal vehicle used by Libya to stimulate foreign investment was a new round of Exploration and Production Sharing Agreements (EPSA), intended to provide open, competitive bidding and enhanced incentives for both gas and oil exploration. In August 2004, Libya announced EPSA-4, the fourth since 1973, and the first since 2000. In response to an offer of fifteen onshore and offshore exploration areas covering fifty-eight blocks, NOC officials indicated in mid-October they had received applications from more than 120 oil companies. Libyan authorities later narrowed the field of potential bidders to sixty-three, including several large U.S. oil groups. When tender results were announced on January 29, 2005, American oil companies Amerada Hess, ChevronTexaco, and Occidental Petroleum, alone or in partnership with other companies, were awarded eleven of the fifteen exploration areas. The other winners, Petrobras of Brazil, Indian Oil and Oil India of India, Medco Energy International of Indonesia, Oil Search of Australia, Verenex Energy of Canada, and Sonatrach of Algeria, reflected global interest in the Libyan market.[36]

EPSA-4, round one, marked a significant shift in the way Libya conducted business, validating the claims of then Prime Minister Shokri Ghanem that Libya was committed to opening its business environment and streamlining its approval procedures. The introduction of a new process, incorporating the public opening of bids with automatic awards based on preset criteria, was a welcome change from the previous system in which the NOC negotiated in parallel with competing bidders, a process which lacked transparency and often slowed agreement. European bidders were disappointed with the results of the first licensing round, and some observers felt the winners had paid a relatively high price; however, most participants agreed Libya had conducted a generally transparent auction, awarding exploration areas on the basis of the financial terms offered by the bidders.

In late January 2005, after releasing the results of the first round of licensing, the NOC announced plans in March to offer an additional forty blocks in EPSA-4, round two. One month later, Libya postponed this second bidding round in order to revise the terms of the licensing process. The new framework was designed to boost incentives for companies that employed locals and linked upstream (exploration and development) and downstream (production and distribution) activities. NOC officials stressed they were particularly interested in additional investment in refining operations.[37]

Eventually, in May 2005, the NOC offered forty-four blocks in twenty-six areas in a second open and transparent round of bidding. Relatively high energy prices, and limited exploration and production opportunities elsewhere, again combined to generate considerable interest in Libya. Some 120 international companies once more expressed interest in bidding, with forty-nine eventually submitting bids. With nineteen successful bidders, the second round marked a greater diversity of winners. Italy's ENI took the largest number of permits. Other successful bidders included Exxon Mobil, the BG Group of the United Kingdom, China National Petroleum, and five Japanese companies.[38]

Following the reshuffle at the National Oil Corporation, in March 2006, Libya announced that EPSA-4, round three, would proceed later in the year. The NOC eventually announced the third bidding round in mid-August 2006, covering fourteen areas and forty-one blocks. In promoting the third round, Libyan officials stressed that only 30 percent of Libya had been explored for hydrocarbons. In the end, twenty-three companies from fifteen countries bid for contracts in round three, with Russia's Tatneft taking three of the fourteen contracts offered, and Russia's Gazprom taking one. Taiwan's state-owned China Petroleum Company, Canada's PetroCanada, and Germany's Wintershall also took one contract each. Bids for three areas, each of which attracted a single bid, were not opened, but the bidders were informed four days later that their bids had been accepted. Four areas received no bids.[39]

With growing international interest in Libya's underdeveloped gas sector, including the potential for liquefied natural gas, in March 2007, NOC chairman Ghanem indicated that EPSA-4, round four, would focus on areas thought to contain significant deposits of natural gas. Three months later, the National Oil Company announced the fourth round of bidding, which included onshore contracts in Sirte, Ghadames, Cyrenaica, and Murzuq, as well as several offshore contracts. Libya later prequalified thirty-five foreign companies as operators and another twenty-one as investors in EPSA-4, round four.[40]

In early September 2006, the General People's Committee—the Libyan equivalent of a cabinet—announced the creation of a Council for Oil and Gas Affairs to oversee related policy, including production levels, pricing, and contracts with foreign companies. Two months later, the General People's Committee renamed the body the Higher Council for Oil and Gas, and clarified and delineated its role in regard to the NOC, in effect giving the latter more operational independence. Headed by the prime minister, the council included a number of cabinet ministers, as well as the NOC chairman and the central bank governor. While Ghanem, in his role as NOC chairman, had moved quickly to reassure investors that the new body would not change hydrocarbon policy, its creation clearly represented a dilution of powers long enjoyed by the NOC, suggesting Libyan authorities were dissatisfied with the management of oil and gas policy. On the other hand, it should be noted that creation of the council was not a unique step, as the move echoed similar arrangements in Saudi Arabia and the Gulf, where senior political figures have long overseen the hydrocarbon sector.[41]

In addition to Exploration and Production Sharing Agreements, Libya also developed a bilateral model to stimulate foreign investment and to accelerate the development process. Its negotiations with Occidental Petroleum in 2003–5 and Royal Dutch/Shell in 2004–5 are two successful examples of this bilateral approach. More recently, British Prime Minister Tony Blair, during a May 2007 visit to Libya in which he said commercial relations between Great Britain and Libya were going from "strength to strength," announced a $900 million contract, returning British energy giant BP to Libya well over three decades after its assets were nationalized in 1971. The seven-year exploration and production agreement covered seventeen exploration wells, together with the acquisition of 30,000 square kilometers for survey. BP's development plan also involved investment in gas processing, transport, and liquefaction for the export market. Options included multiple liquefied natural gas terminals at Marsa el-Brega, Ras Lanuf, and Melitah. One month earlier, the NOC and the Dow Chemical Company also announced a joint venture to upgrade and expand the existing petrochemical complex at Ras Lanuf.[42]

The National Oil Company has also shown interest in production sharing agreements, known as Development Production Sharing Agreements, or DPSAs, in which foreign companies revive and expand output at fields that are losing production after decades of use. It has also considered offering service contracts to companies to develop untapped fields previously thought too small to be economically viable. The development of known reserves is attractive to oil companies because it eliminates the risks associated with drilling in new areas.[43]

As relations with the United States worsened in the early 1980s, Libya invested in Tamoil, a leading European petroleum retailing business, to solidify its European connections. Based in Switzerland and 100 percent Libyan owned, in 2007, Tamoil holdings comprised oil refineries in Germany, Italy, and Switzerland, more than 3,000 gas stations in Europe, mostly in Italy, and related businesses in Africa. In April 2005, Libya announced Tamoil was for sale, and in June 2006, Colony Capital, a Los Angeles-based private equity firm, purchased a 65 percent interest in the company. The deal, worth $5.4 billion, was the largest sale of a Libyan-owned asset to that time. Equally important, the sale of Tamoil, together with the bilateral deals struck with Occidental Petroleum, Royal Dutch/Shell, and BP, suggested a revised Libyan business model coming into play in which the state focused more on upstream hydrocarbon operations.[44]

Next Steps

Within Libya, there is little agreement as to the future pace and direction of economic reform, particularly outside the hydrocarbon sector. In contrast, widespread consensus exists outside the country as to the steps Libya must take to broaden and deepen the reforms implemented to date. Recommendations found in the most recent International Monetary Fund and World Bank reports, released in 2007, and in the "National Economic Strategy" completed by the Monitor Group and Cambridge Economic Research Associates in 2006, highlight similar challenges and opportunities. A detailed discussion of these recommendations is outside the scope of this chapter—however, their central arguments can be summarized under four subheadings: sector diversification, business environment, people development, and political regeneration.[45]

According to the International Monetary Fund, the oil and gas sector today represents over 70 percent of GDP, over 90 percent of government revenues, and better than 95 percent of export earnings. Libya thus remains one of the least diversified economies in the world. With only 3 percent of formal employment in the hydrocarbon sector, three-quarters of employment continues in the public sector, and private investment is basically dormant at around 2 percent of GDP. Therefore, the main challenge for Libya is to promote growth in the non-hydrocarbon sectors, spurring economic diversification. To achieve this result, most outside observers agree Libya must increase the productivity and competitiveness of its energy sector, which will remain the engine of growth in the foreseeable future, while prioritizing and sequencing diversification in other sectors. There is also substantial consensus that the requisite diversification can be achieved only if far-reaching reforms are put in place to facilitate private sector development throughout the economy.

The "National Economic Strategy" includes a detailed assessment of so-called clusters, "geographically proximate groups of interconnected companies, suppliers, service providers, and associated institutions, which are linked by commonalities and complementarities." In so doing, it provides the most thought-provoking analysis to date of prioritized diversification in Libya. Based on current size and future potential, it suggests a concentration on five clusters—agriculture, construction, energy, tourism, and transit trade—will lead to economic and social growth. In addition, the report examines several energy-dependent industries, both upstream and downstream, which could be developed to provide future potential growth.[46]

In support of efforts to maintain macroeconomic stability, rationalize use of the country's oil wealth, and accelerate transition to a market economy, general business environment issues include a lack of transparency, corruption, the absence of an agreed-upon plan, and a lack of coordination between government institutions. A core problem in this regard is the lack of a clear vision for foreign investment due to persistent infighting within the government over the speed and scope of reform. In the area of private sector development, key priorities include simplification of the approval process for entry into competitive sectors; lifting remaining restrictions on foreign participation in services like finance; clarifying laws related to renting and owning property; reforming the labor code to add operational flexibility while ensuring sound working conditions; replacing the progressive corporate tax rate with a low flat rate competitive with other countries; and pursuing reforms in customs administration to reduce excessive delays. While Libyan officials are publicly committed to privatizing the state-owned sector, the current strategy of ownership dilution is moving slowly and appears unlikely to lead to the efficiency improvements desired.

On the positive side, the decision in late 2006 to reduce the minimum capital requirement for foreign investments from $50 million to $1.5 million was a smart move as the higher level constituted an effective ban on most of the foreign investment Libya could hope to attract to its non-oil sectors. In contrast, the decree issued by the General People's Committee in November 2006, requiring all direct foreign investment in the non-hydrocarbon sector to be undertaken through joint stock companies with local partners, dampened investor enthusiasm. Foreign companies already invested in Libya wondered how the new requirement affected them, while potential investors rightly viewed it as simply another commercial obstacle to overcome. On the other hand, the merger of twenty-one regional banks, and the planned restructure of public commercial banks, were wise moves. Early steps to reform the banking system were followed at the beginning of 2007 by a decision to allow a foreign bank to own up to a 51 percent stake in the Sahara Bank, the country's largest, majority state-owned, commercial bank. In July 2007, BNP Paribas was selected as Sahara Bank's strategic partner, acquiring 19 percent of the bank's capital with an option to acquire up to 51 percent in three to five years. Plans announced in February 2007 to privatize the mobile phone sector also constituted a commercially sound decision.[47]

Libyans are intelligent, hardworking, entrepreneurial, and capable of the highest ethical standards; unfortunately, the socialist environment of the past did not generally promote and reward these virtues. Instead, advancement in the command economy more often depended on family, clan, and tribal ties or other forms of nepotism and cronyism. Public expenditure on education is relatively high, but there are valid concerns regarding both the quality of education and the efficient use of resources. A rapid improvement in the development of human resources will be necessary to improve productivity, increase diversification, and guarantee competitiveness in the global economy. The government will also need to enhance the quality of life for all Libyans through the targeted provision of health care and housing.

The paucity of technically-skilled laborers, after nearly four decades of revolutionary experimentation, remains a major issue that impacts negatively on all economic sectors, including oil and gas. Employment regulations are designed to provide work opportunities for Libyan nationals, reducing dependence on foreign workers. New jobs that require no special skill or training, like drivers, guards, and maintenance workers, are supposed to be filled by Libyans. Foreign companies are also expected to comply with laws calling for the training of Libyan nationals for more skilled jobs, and to provide all local employees with the same treatment as foreign workers in the areas of wages, medical insurance, and other benefits. With unemployment a serious problem, Libya remains committed to a strict enforcement of these regulations, and the pressure only increased with Prime Minister Mahmudi's announcement in late January 2007 that Libya intends to lay off 400,000 public sector employees, approximately 40 percent of the total. Even though the government plans to give each employee a full salary for three years, and up to $40,800 in loans to start a new business, policies that mandate the hiring of local employees by foreign firms are unlikely to be totally effective until the work force is educated and empowered with the necessary qualifications and skills.[48]

While a high level of consensus exists outside Libya on the need for reform in sector diversification, the business environment, and people development, there is far less agreement when the issue of political regeneration is raised. Commissioned and paid for by the Libyan government, the report jointly prepared by the Monitor Group and the Cambridge Economic Research Associates suggests the Libyan system of direct democracy requires only minor tweaking to support desired economic reforms in other areas. Specifically, the report suggests leveraging information and communication technology, referred to as "e-democracy," and redesigning processes to reduce inefficiencies and to "perfect Libyan democracy." The authors also recommend the establishment of a governance structure, composed of special purpose entities, like the Economic Development Board launched in February 2007, to drive the reform process.

In contrast, both the International Monetary Fund and the World Bank, together with nongovernmental organizations, like the National Democratic Institute for International Affairs and Freedom House, and scholars, like Vandewalle, suggest broader governance issues must be addressed before economic reforms will prosper. According to these observers, issues requiring attention include, but are not limited to, a weak rule of law, an immature legal and court system, and recurrent conflict between municipalities and the central government. The World Bank in July 2006 noted that "various measures of the quality of governance rank Libya very poorly compared to other countries."[49] In turn, the National Democratic Institute for International Affairs highlighted several governance issues, including a lack of transparency in the political system.

Qaddafi has created a system with a highly opaque decision-making process, in which it is difficult, if not impossible, to identify how, and by whom, a decision is taken. In this way, Qaddafi is able to control the country from behind the scenes, while blurring the lines on issues of authority and accountability.[50] In an August 2006 speech, Saif al-Islam al-Qaddafi, often mentioned as a potential successor to his father, also highlighted shortcomings in the Libyan system of direct democracy: "All of you know that the democratic system that we dreamed of does not exist in the realm of reality. Rather, the existing system has its equivocation and misuse of the term 'democracy.' It has a sense of hidden corridors."[51]

Finally, Vandewalle recently concluded little progress toward economic modernization could be achieved without the creation of modern political institutions to administer economic reforms. Arguing the current political system hinders reform because it lacks transparency and commitment to the rule of law, he suggested meaningful economic reform would first require legal reform, which would then stimulate political reform, followed by economic reform.[52]

Prospects for Transition

Libya is a youthful society in which approximately one-third of the population is age fourteen or younger, with the bulk of the remaining two-thirds fifteen to sixty-four years of age. With the One September Revolution in its thirty-ninth year, most adult Libyans have known nothing but a socialist command economy for the bulk of their productive lives. Nurtured since birth on a system of entitlements, from education to housing to healthcare, the sudden embrace of a market economy is unnerving for many, as it threatens to dismantle welfare benefits and lead to a widening income gap between rich and poor. Compounding the situation, civil society in Libya is weak, with family and tribal affiliations dominating attitudes and behaviors. Moreover, the effectiveness of the few existing civil society organizations is undermined by the popular perception that any organization permitted by the regime is an auxiliary of the governmental apparatus and not to be trusted.

The implementation of wide-ranging economic reforms creates anxiety and confusion in any society, and can lead to social instability and a demand for order from above. Earlier attempts at economic reform were sabotaged, in part, by a combination of vested interests and the fear of the unknown. The failure to implement the legal and political reforms necessary to sustain economic reforms also contributed to early failures. Given what has transpired to date, with the oil and gas sector as the exception, there is every reason to believe the latest round of economic reforms could suffer a similar fate.

Experience suggests a free market economy works relatively well within a Western democratic system, characterized by a separation of powers with checks and balances, democratic institutions, political parties, and free elections. Central elements of this process include power sharing, dissent, and loyal opposition. Some elements of a Western-style democracy are found in the Libyan system of direct democracy, but others, like political parties, a loyal opposition, and freedom to dissent, are not. This raises the question of the compatibility of direct democracy with a market economy. Does the structure and function of direct democracy impose any particular limits to the creation of a market economy? Or does it lend itself to a different type of economic system? Can a state be an effective moderator of a market economy in which it participates? When the IMF recently recommended the establishment of a Stabilization and Savings Fund (SSF) to maintain macroeconomic stability and strengthen financial management, for example, Libyan officials did not reject the idea, but noted it would take up to two years to implement, probably an optimistic estimate because it would require a draft law to be discussed by the Basic People's Congresses, and then sent to the General People's Congress. The Libyans also disagreed with the related IMF recommendation that the SSF, in effect the Libyan government, be prohibited from investing in the economy.[53]

Past experience would suggest that Libya will find real limitations to a development model based on the current legal and political system. Therefore, progress toward a market economy will likely come in fits and starts, with dead ends, deviations, and reversals along the way. In support of the move toward a market economy, a slow evolution in the organization and functioning of the direct democracy system remains possible; however, a more likely scenario is the creation of some hybrid economic system, as Qaddafi has suggested in his vague references to "popular capitalism" or "people's socialism," compatible with direct democracy. In the interim, economic liberalization will remain a two-speed process in Libya, with reform in the oil and gas sector moving forward even as it stalls in other areas, increasing the already considerable distance between the two reform paths.

Notes

1. Mustafa Bakar Mahmud and Alex Russell, "An Analysis of Libya's Revenue per Barrel from Crude Oil Upstream Activities, 1961–93," *OPEC Review* 23, no. 3 (September 1999), 215, 221–27.

2. Nathan Alexander [Ronald Bruce St John], "Libya: The Continuous Revolution," *Middle Eastern Studies* 17, no. 2 (April 1981), 210–27.

3. J. A. Allan, *Libya: The Experience of Oil* (London: Croom Helm, 1981), 186–87; Ronald Bruce St John, "The Determinants of Libyan Foreign Policy, 1969–1983," *The Maghreb Review* 8, no. 3–4 (May–August 1983), 98.

4. Mu'Ammar el Qathafi, *Discourses* (Valetta, Malta: Adam Publishers, 1975), 115–16; Libyan Arab Republic, *The Third International Theory: The Divine Concept of Islam and the Popular Revolution in Libya* (Tripoli: Ministry of Information and Culture, 1973), 9–10, 17–18; Ronald Bruce St John, "The Ideology of Muammar al Qadhdhafi: Theory and Practice," *International Journal of Middle East Studies* 15, no. 4 (November 1983), 481–83.

5. Libyan Arab Republic, *The Revolution of 1st September: The Fourth Anniversary* (Benghazi: Ministry of Information and Culture, 1973), 127–33, 158–61; Valerie Plave Bennett, "Libyan Socialism," in *Socialism in the Third*

World, ed. Helen Desfosses and Jacques Levesque (New York: Praeger Publishers, 1975), 99–120.

6. Hisham Matar, *In the Country of Men* (New York: Dial, 2007), 235.

7. *Foreign Broadcast Information Services: Daily Report: Middle East and North Africa* (hereafter, *FBIS-MEA*), Washington, DC, "JANA Reports Al-Qadhdhafi's Review of People's Congresses Agenda," (October 18, 1978), I5; "Al-Qadhdhafi Addresses Agrarian Reform Meeting," *FBIS-MEA* (March 9, 1981), Q1.

8. Allan, *Libya*, op.cit., 244.

9. St John, "Ideology of Muammar al Qadhdhafi," op.cit., 484–85.

10. Dirk Vandewalle, "Qadhafi's 'Perestroika,': Economic and Political Liberalization in Libya," *The Middle East Journal* 45, no. 2 (Spring 1991), 216–28; François Soudan, "Le Kaddafi nouveau arrive," *Jeune Afrique*, no. 1355–56 (December 24–31, 1986), 34–36; "Al-Qadhdhafi Discusses 'Mistakes' of Revolution, *FBIS-MEA* (March 10, 1987), Q1–Q2.

11. Mary-Jane Deeb, "New Thinking in Libya," *Current History* 89, no. 546 (April 1990), 149–52; Ann Elizabeth Mayer, "In Search of Sacred Law: The Meandering Course of Qadhafi's Legal Policy," in *Qadhafi's Libya 1969 to 1994*, ed. Dirk Vandewalle (New York: St. Martin's, 1995), 123–27.

12. François Burgat, "The Libyan Economy in Crisis," in *The Economic Development of Libya*, ed. Bichara Khader and Bashir El-Wifati (London: Croom Helm, 1987), 213–27; Vandewalle, "Qadhafi's 'Perestroika," op.cit., 228–30.

13. Ronald Bruce St John, *Libya and the United States: Two Centuries of Strife* (Philadelphia: University of Pennsylvania Press, 2002), 121–51.

14. Edward Schumacher, "The United States and Libya," *Foreign Affairs* 65, no. 2 (Winter 1986–87), 336–39; Ronald Bruce St John, *Libya and the United States*, op.cit., 144.

15. Dirk Vandewalle, "The Failure of Liberalization in the Jamahiriyya," in *Qadhafi's Libya 1969 to 1994* (New York: St. Martin's, 1995), 203–22.

16. Khalil I. Matar and Robert W. Thabit, *Lockerbie and Libya: A Study in International Relations* (Jefferson, NC: McFarland, 2004), 7–36.

17. Mary-Jane Deeb, "Qadhafi's Changed Policy: Causes and Consequences," *Middle East Policy* 7, no. 2 (February 2000), 146–49; Ray Takeyh, "Qadhafi and the Challenge of Militant Islam," *Washington Quarterly* 21, no. 3 (Summer 1998), 159–73.

18. Nicolas Sarkis, "Les Perspectives Pétrolières Libyennes," *Maghreb-Machrek*, no. 181 (Autumn 2004), 61; Ronald Bruce St John, "Libya in Africa: Looking Back, Moving Forward," *The Journal of Libyan Studies* 1, no. 1 (Summer 2000), 27; Tim Niblock, *Pariah States and Sanctions in the Middle East: Iraq, Libya, Sudan*, (Colorado: Lynne Rienner Publishers, Inc., 2001), 60–92.

19. International Monetary Fund, "Socialist People's Libyan Arab Jamahiriya 2004 Article IV Consultation–Staff Report," IMF Country Report No. 05/83 (March 2005), 5–6 (http://www.imf.org). Data on the Libyan economy is improving

but remains distorted and incomplete; therefore, all statistics in this article should be considered indicative.

20. Luis Martinez, "L'apres-embargo en Libya," *Maghreb-Machrek*, no. 170 (October–December 2000), 3–11; Ronald Bruce St John, "Libyan Foreign Policy: Newfound Flexibility," *Orbis* 47, no. 3 (Summer 2003), 463–77.

21. Mu'ammar al-Qadhafi, "Excerpts from Speech by Al-Qadfhafi at an International Conference on Development and Investment," *BBC News*, November 19, 2000 (http://www.bbc.co.uk); Ronald Bruce St John, "Libya: Coming in from the Cold, Ties Re-established in Europe and Africa," in *Africa Contemporary Record, vol. 27 (1998–2000)*, ed. Colin Legum (New York: Africana Publishing, 2004), B633.

22. Economist Intelligence Unit (hereafter, EIU), *Country Report: Libya* (November 2000), 16; "Libya: Untapped Potential," *Oxford Analytica Brief*, 21 (November 2000) (http://www.oxan.com).

23. "Al-Qadhafi Addresses Congress, Calls for Accountability of Officials," *BBC News*, March 23, 2001 (http://www.bbc.co.cuk); EIU, *Country Report: Libya* (October 2001), 13–14.

24. Ronald Bruce St John, "Libya: Lockerbie Trial Ends, Sparking New Libyan Initiatives," in *Africa Contemporary Record, vol. 28 (2001–2002)*, ed. Colin Legum (New York: Africana Publishing, 2006), B644–B645.

25. Ahmed Mustafa, "Libya economic reforms gather momentum," *Gulf News*, September 4, 2004 (http://www.gulf-news.com); Ronald Bruce St John, "Libya Is Not Iraq: Preemptive Strikes, WMD, and Diplomacy, *The Middle East Journal* 58, no. 3 (Summer 2004), 396–400.

26. Shokri Ghanem, "Libya: Vision for the Future," *Arab Strategy Forum: The Arab World in 2020*, Dubai, December 14, 2004; International Monetary Fund, "The Socialist People's Libyan Arab Jamahiriya: Staff Report for the 2005 Article IV Consultation," IMF Country Report No. 06/136 (April 2006), 9 (http://www.imf.org); "Libya nods at foreign language in tourism sector," *Business Africa*, January 12, 2007 (http://icms.iac.iafrica.com); "Libya opens stock market," *Business Africa*, March 13, 2007 (http://icms.iac.iafrica.com).

27. William Wallis, "Libya's reformist PM is ousted," *Financial Times*, March 6, 2006.

28. Mu'ammar al-Qaddafi, "Untitled Speech to Engineering Activists," *JANA*, July 23, 2006 (http://www.jamahiriyanews.com); William Maclean, "Gaddafi Scolds Libyans for Reliance on Oil," *Reuters*, August 28, 2006 (http://www.reuters.com).

29. National Democratic Institute for International Affairs, "The Libyan Political System and Prospects for Reform: A Report from NDI's 2006 Delegation (April 17–25, 2006)," 7 (http://www.ndi.org).

30. IMF, "Libya: Staff Report for 2005 Consultation," op.cit., 22.

31. EIU, *Country Report: Libya* (November 2000), op.cit., 21–22. For an in-depth look at economic reform in the hydrocarbon sector, see Ronald Bruce St John, "Libya's Oil & Gas Industry: Blending Old and New," *The Journal of North African Studies* 12, no. 2 (June 2007), 239–54.

32. The World Bank, "Socialist People's Libyan Arab Jamahiriya Country Economic Report," Report No. 30295-LY (July 2006), 13 (http://www.world bank.org).

33. Vahe Petrossian, "Libya hits glitch in output plans," *Upstream*, September 1, 2006 (http://www.upstreamonline.com); "Libya Opens Up New Potential for New Players," *Petroleum Intelligence Weekly*, October 25, 2004.

34. Ronald Bruce St John, *Libya and the United States: The Next Steps*, Atlantic Council Issue Brief, March 2006, 4–5.

35. Steve Quinn, "3 U.S. Oil Cos. to End Absence in Libya," *Houston Chronicle*, December 29, 2005 (http://www.chron.com); Sally Jones, "Libya Oil Min: Oasis Group's Return Delayed by Disagreements," *Rigzone*, December 13, 2005 (http://www.rigzone.com).

36. Dave Ebner, "Talisman Questions Cost of Libya Rights Bids," *The Globe and Mail*, March 3, 2005 (http://www.theglobeandmail.com); Kevin Morrison and Doug Cameron, "U.S. oil groups win Libyan permits," *Financial Times*, January 31, 2005.

37. Shokri Ghanem, "These Are Our Priorities for the Upcoming Phase," First interview on the NOC Web site, September 18, 2006 (http://www.en.noclibya .com.ly).

38. Michael Penn, "A Japanese Oil Victory in Libya," *Asia Times*, November 2, 2005 (http://www.atimes.com); Andrew Jack, "Libya awards oil and gas licences," *Financial Times*, October 3, 2005.

39. Ghanem, "These Are Our Priorities for the Upcoming Phase," NOC Web site, September 18, 2006 (http://www.en.noclibya.com.ly); National Oil Company, "Bid Round III Results, December 20, 2006 (http://www.en.noclibya.com.ly).

40. "Libya to unveil gas round details," *Reuters*, May 24, 2007 (http://www.iol .co.za); National Oil Company, "Bid Round 4 qualification results," September 4, 2007 (http://www.en.noclibya.com.ly).

41. "Libya sets up oil and gas council to oversee energy policy," *Platts Commodity News*, September 5, 2005 (http://www.platts.com).

42. Roula Khalaf and Thomas Catan, "BP and Libya in Talks over Gas Project," *Financial Times*, January 6, 2006; "Libya: Dow Chemical in Petrochemical Venture," *The New York Times*, April 19, 2007; "Britain and Libya Unveil Energy and Arms Deals," *International Herald Tribune*, May 30, 2007.

43. Maher Chmaytelli, "Libya May Let Foreigners Own Oil," *Houston Chronicle*, October 5, 2005 (http://www.chron.com); Maher Chmaytelli, "Libya Seeks Partners to Run 300 Small Ooilfields," *Business Report*, February 8, 2006 (http://www.busrep.co.za); Jad Mouawad, "Oil Innovations Pump New Life Into Old Wells," *The New York Times*, March 5, 2007.

44. Elizabeth Douglass, "Colony Capital to pay $5.4 billion for Libya's Tamoil," *Los Angeles Times*, June 6, 2007 (http://www.latimes.com); Nesa Subrahmaniyan and Maher Chmaytelli, "Colony Capital to Buy Libya's Tamoil for EU4 Billion," *Bloomberg*, June 6, 2007 (http://www.colonyinc.com).

45. International Monetary Fund, "The Socialist People's Libyan Arab Jamahiriya: 2006 Article IV Consultation—Staff Report; Staff Statement; Public

Information Notice on the Executive Board Discussion; and Statement by the Executive Director for The Socialist People's Libyan Arab Jamahiriya," IMF Country Report No. 07/149 (May 2007) (http://www.imf.org); The World Bank, "Socialist People's Libyan Arab Jamahiriya: Country Economic Report"; Monitor Group and Cambridge Economic Research Associates, "National Economic Strategy: An Assessment of the Competitiveness of the Libyan Arab Jamahiriya," 2006.

46. Monitor Group, "National Economic Strategy," op.cit., 75–107, quote 75.

47. "Libya to privatize mobile phone sector," *Middle East Online*, February 23, 2007 (http://www.middle-east-online.com); "Update 1–Libya names 6 banks for Sahara Privatization," *Reuters*, March 29, 2007 (http://www.investing .reuters.co.uk); "BNP Paribas selected Sahara Bank partner by Libya," *Khaleej Times*, July 20, 2007 (http://www.khaleejtimes.com).

48. "Libya Says It Will Lay Off 400,000," *The New York Times*, January 22, 2007.

49. World Bank, "Socialist People's Libyan Arab Jamahiriya: Country Economic Report," iv.

50. National Democratic Institute for International Affairs, "Libyan Political System," op.cit., 5.

51. Saif al-Islam al-Qaddafi, "The Speech of Saif al-Islam Al Gaddafi, President of Gaddafi Development Foundation, in the First Forum of the National Organization of Libyan Youth," Sirte, August 20, 2006 (http://www.gdf.org.ly). On human resource development in Libya, see Abdoulhakem Almhdie and Stephen M. Nyambegera, "HRM in Libya," in *Managing Human Resources in Africa*, ed. Ken Kamoche (London: Routledge, 2004), 169–82.

52. Dirk Vandewalle, "Libya: Prospects for Change," *Middle East Institute Policy Brief*, September 18, 2006 (http://www.mideasti.org).

53. IMF, "Libya: Staff Report 2006,", op.cit., 16.

6

The Future of the U.S.-Libyan Commercial Relationship

Ethan D. Chorin

Despite the turmoil that has marked Libyan-American relations over the past thirty-odd years, there exists a pervasive view that the two countries enjoy a "special" commercial relationship, one that extends beyond the simple exchange of money for oil. With the lack of a continuous record of trade with which to prove the point, the whole idea of exceptionality must incorporate something intangible, transcending simple novelty or curiosity about the "other." One thing is clear: if exceptionality exists, it is a complex animal, one that has lived largely underground since the 1970s and exists today within specific segments of Libyan society. The essay begins with a summary assessment of the potential for the United States and Libya to develop a broad-based commercial relationship, then mines the commercial record for evidence and antecedents of the alleged exceptionality. Assuming exceptionality matters, and that there is basis for such feeling, the essay concludes by asking how the U.S. business community might most effectively influence the course of the evolving relationship.

The Mixed Draw of Libya

From the perspective of need and ability to pay, the basic scenario is promising indeed: the majority of Libya's physical plant dates from the 1960s and 1970s. At the same time, the country sits on the largest oil reserves in Africa, at a time when the price of oil is at record highs. In a January 2006 speech, Qadhafi announced that the development budget for the next three years would focus on basic infrastructure. Expectations were high that

Libya would see a near-term building boom in everything from roads to residential housing, to power generation and wastewater treatment plants, all paid for by a cash surplus in excess of $50 billion. While the market for final goods and services is modest (Libya's population is currently estimated at 5.6 million), Libya exhibits strong potential in a variety of capital-intensive industries, from fertilizers, chemicals, and aluminum smelting to transshipment services, all of which derive advantages from Libya's proximity to Europe. With the distinct—and real—possibilities posed by Libya, there exist several enduring impediments to trade: these factors include uncertain political will, pervasive corruption, an almost impenetrable bureaucracy, administrative gridlock, lack of transparency, mistrust of institutions and multinationals, insularity, a lack of information, and a modest retail market.

Economic Uncertainty

There is no doubt that for Libya to make a successful transition from quasi-rentier state to a modern, capitalist economy, the leadership must make decisions that, in the near term, will affect both peoples' lives and the traditional patronage structure negatively. In the transformation from a bloated private sector, there will need to be large layoffs on top of an already hugely impressive unemployment rate. While subsidies on essential goods have been lifted, Libya has yet seriously to implement aspects of the IMF's Article IV Consultation recommendation regarding private sector stimulation and the creation of a social security net. Efforts to pare down the massive, redundant bureaucracy and stimulate employment have been weak. This is particularly critical in the eastern province, which saw politically and economically-motivated riots in early 2006.

Foreign analysts have described the political dynamic as being a struggle between the reformist camp and the old guard. To a large degree, these are heuristics, an attempt to impose a Western logic on an alien system. Foreign companies are at a loss to understand exactly what is going on, what are really the limits of reform, and how secure their investments are.

The Information Deficit

Timely and accurate commercial information is extremely difficult to obtain in Libya. It is common to find government tenders published in one of the four major government-run papers a matter of days before (or after) bids are due, while bidding agents tip off preferred candidates months before. While a few enterprising souls have managed to circumvent related proscriptions, employment agencies remain illegal. Recruiting and retaining quality employees with proper language skills and basic technical skills is extremely difficult, while new legislation has instigated a massive outflow of foreign service-workers. Most establishments in Libya do not have fixed street addresses, making deliveries problematic. Libyan businessmen—again, with the exception of those in the oil sector—rarely use or respond to email. U.S. companies attempting to develop commercial relationships in Libya often find themselves confused about with whom they should be dealing. A member of the political or commercial establishment may be "in" one week and "out" the next. Organizations such as the Libyan Business Council are geared primarily to serve the interests of individual members, not the private sector as a whole. The information problem affects not only foreign companies, but Libyans as well: a representative of the World Bank noted that Libya had literally "forgotten" it was a member of the IBRD, and as such, is eligible for certain services and facilities.[1] With the increase of economic activity, information has become more valuable to more people, even as competition has made individual deals less profitable. With all the problems, there have been some advances, notably the websites maintained by the General Peoples' Congress and the Ministry of Economy.

Corruption and Administrative Gridlock

The Libyan commercial environment remains infused with corruption. Major contracts are made and unmade according to the dictates of those charged with responsibility to negotiate. As one publication noted, *"After three or four decades of hybrid revolution, of which the obsolescence is patently obvious, where the endless struggle against the state only exacerbated tribalism and destroyed the little sense of civic pride which unified Libyans, the hour is for individual enrichment, parasitism remunerated."*[2] The infamous Law No. 15 of 1980, which placed ceilings of between 150 and 500 Libyan dinar per month on salaries, depending on job grade, is often cited as a major inducement to corrupt practices.[3] Corruption remains a major skewing factor in the award and execution of international business contracts.

Insularity/Conservatism

Despite the outward secular character of the regime, even by regional standards, Libya is an extremely conservative society. Libyans are welcoming to foreigners, but are very concerned about the introduction of forces that might impact the local value structure; hence, the ban on alcohol, and slow movement on developing infrastructure that caters to the needs of foreigners, is not simply a sign of disorganization, but emblematic of a very real ambivalence about the consequences of opening the country to free flow of goods and people. One area in which the (at least rhetorical) provincialism is apparent is Libya's long long-standing distrust of multinational enterprises. In the late 1960s and 1970s, observers attributed this view to the psychological impact of multiple colonizations. Yet, half a century later, a noted Libyan academic writes, in the context of a discussion of water policy that "*top level decision makers tend to associate desalination with international companies.*" In a similar vein, in 2006, Qadhafi had this to say regarding the need to protect Africa from genetically engineered organisms: "*These modified seeds form a treacherous and evil plan. It is not directed at Libya alone but against the whole world. There are a number of evil, capitalist companies with billions of dollars and they're supported by political capitalist circles. The goal if this international evil is to control the supply of food of people on this planet. They will control our food supply, they will control our lives.*"[4] The ban on alcohol has a direct effect on the tourism industry, effectively precluding any attempt to market Libya to a mass market. In sum, all elements of Libyan society are handicapped by an archaic worldview, a direct result of the country's relative isolation. Lack of experience with the wider world, as one might expect, manifests itself as Libya-centricism, i.e., the expectation is often that the world must adjust to Libya's eccentricities, rather than vice versa. As we will see later, this situation also has its advantages, particularly where the United States is concerned.

Small Domestic Consumer Market

At only 5.6 million, Libya's domestic market is small. As a measure, one Tripoli based trader noted "*all the diapers in Libya would fit into one Kroeger's.*"[5] The perceived risk of the Libyan market, combined with its size and limited access to startup capital, serve to explain, in part, why we see locals (and foreign companies) engaged in hit and run (low capital intensity), generating interest among American conglomerates. With a few individuals chasing—often with the help of serious connections at the top—a limited pie, and extremely limited access to startup capital, there is an effective ceiling to expansion and competition, whether foreign or domestically funded. The difficulties posed by capital accumulation further impede the growth of the private sector as a whole. As in the previous section, this negative offers some parallel advantages: word of mouth spreads fast, and consumers share information. A solid reputation goes a long way.

In an environment where U.S. companies are caught between opportunity and the unknown, the commodity we refer to here as exceptionality becomes important. Many U.S. companies have cited excessive risk (tied directly to a lack of understanding of the business environment) as a decisive factor in pushing them to invest in more known quantities, such as the Emirates or the former Soviet Union. Most perceptions of Libyan receptivity to U.S. companies are built on very simple, even over-reactions to processes and actions that have little to do with the core issues. If there is a single question on the minds of prospective foreign investors, American or other, as well as many Libyans, it is: Is Libya for real? Are there opportunities here? The answer is, most certainly, "yes." Whether the opportunities are sufficiently attractive for most is a function of tolerance for risk and experience in similar (or similarly difficult) markets. In the next section, we examine a half century of Libyan-American interactions for hints as to the changing flavor of the relationship and factors we might consider the basis of exceptionality.

In Search of American Exceptionality

At independence in 1951, Libyan per-capita GNP was approximately thirty-five U.S. dollars, with 13 percent of value of net exports composed of proceeds from the sale of scrap metal. The most significant exports included peanuts, animal hides, and fodder. Rent paid by the United States and the United Kingdom for airbases formed a non-negligible percentage of Libyan GNP, as well as a major rationale for aid. The majority of Libyans were illiterate, and the country's health system was in complete disarray. Libyans lived primarily on small-scale farming. American foreign assistance, which from 1953–56 amounted to $64 million, played a large role in improving economic conditions in the early days of independence. Gifts of American wheat sustained many Libyan communities in the postwar years.[6] From 1956–60, the amount of American aid was in the neighborhood of $112 million.

The Eisenhower Doctrine, part of a broader effort to stave off communism through direct aid, resulted in an approximate doubling of U.S. assistance to Libya in the late 1950s, the period in which foreign oil companies began serious prospecting in Libya. With oil came investment, new services, and then, inevitably, a range of consumer goods. American companies were broadly present at this time in Libya, and included the major car companies (General Motors, Chevrolet, Chrysler), and consumer goods and electronics (Kraft, Carrier, Westinghouse, General Electric, Motorola). As the old "standby" sources of income lost their significance relative to advances in technology, poor skills, and deteriorating environmental conditions, Libya found itself on the threshold of a transforming event: the discovery and production of oil, the principal factor behind what Wright called Libya's "remarkable" economic progress between 1951 and 1969.[7] The period was the start of what we might call Libya's first economic awakening, in which America, as the undisputed leader in petroleum technology, played a key role.

Esso Sirte (later, Exxon), a decidedly American company, with partners W. R. Grace and Libyan-American Oil Co. discovered or developed most of Libya's large fields, including the Mabruk and Amal fields. Esso built the export terminal at Marsa el-Brega, from which the first Libyan oil cargo departed on August 8, 1961. Among twelve companies awarded sixty concessions in 1957, figured American independents Continental (Conoco), Marathon, Amerada Hess, and Bunker Hunt. By 1969, American companies produced a full 90 percent of Libyan oil. Esso played a crucial role in training Libya's first generation of scientists, managers, and technocrats. Its Accelerated Training Program focused on training Libyans from the towns of Brega, Ajdabia, Jalo, and Misurata to take over maintenance and operations jobs initially staffed by Americans; an Operations Training Center focused on higher-level technical knowledge acquisition, training more than 260 Libyans in the 1970s.[8] While this activity may or may not have had much impact on Libyan public policy, it must be considered a major factor in whatever we call "exceptionality."

Libyan Attitudes toward the United States, 1951–69

Libyan attitudes toward America in the postindependence years evolved in the context of a wave of Arab nationalism, growing U.S. support for Israel, and a fresh Libyan antipathy toward the former colonial powers—Italy, Britain, and France, in particular. At the same time, America represented the culmination of every developing country's dream: global relevance and freedom of opportunity. Diplomatic correspondence from the time indicate Libya's eagerness to engage the United States, even as forces conspired to push the two countries apart. Further, there seems to be evidence that Libyans initially saw the United States as a something of a fair-weather friend, coming to Libya's aid only when clearly in its interest to do so. Former Prime Minister Mustafa Ben Halim claims Libyan requests for specific economic and technical assistance in 1954 were met with bureaucratic indifference. The author goes on to draw a direct link between this and

Libya's flirtation with the Soviet Union.[9] With the establishment of a U.S.-Libya Reconstruction Commission, further and significant American aid was forthcoming. Aid notwithstanding, the discovery of oil created large-scale disruptions within a very traditional society: migrations from the countryside to the cities, as well as dislocations and unemployment caused a considerable amount of pain.

The 1960s and 1970s literary record is full of references to the "American." As Ibrahim Al-Fagih notes, *"The sudden boom was not without its negative aspects. For those without means, this was a time of upheaval. The literature of the period is full of accounts of the 'ugly American,' ignorant of local custom, a broadening chasm between the 'haves' and the 'have nots' and the erosion of traditional ways of life, despite the fact that in 1958, 70 percent of oil revenues were to be spent on economic and social developments."* A story by Libyan author Ramadan Bukheit brings to life the emotional crash that followed early expectations of what oil and the foreigners would do for Libya. "The Company" is understood to be an American oil company: *"Khalifa recalled the early days of that year in the desert. He felt then like he had been given a new lease on life. When he came back to spend his first vacation, his children were happy to see him. He brought them canned food, courtesy of The Company. They got used to expecting him at the end of each month, but he never forgot how excited they were that first time. When The Company stopped distributing the food, he went to buy cans from the shops so as not to disappoint the kids, but they could tell the difference."*[10]

The popular response to these disruptions was often anger, not only at the foreigners, but those who let them in: King Idris was seen as *"an accomplice of the West and therefore of Israel, and as a protector of a newly enriched minority which monopolized revenues drawn from the oil companies."* Libyan ambivalence, again, could be seen springing from a clash at the level of the state between the desire to minimize the impact of Western social structures and mores on the Libyan people, a realization of inherent weakness, and a desire for protection. The monarchy chose to maintain a close relationship with the United States and its allies because it believed they were in the best position to guarantee Libyan security. A growing number of Libyan citizens increasingly distrusted the United States and resented its extensive presence in significant aspects of Libyan internal and external affairs. Libyan writer Sadiq Nayhoum wrote fiery columns in the popular Benghazi paper *Al-Haqiqa* in June 1969, lambasting American materialism: *"Twenty-first century culture, a poison which is responsible for the development of both economic and mechanical culture in the United States, and the export to other countries of nuclear weapons and companies of obscene wealth."*[11] This quote is interesting, for it encapsulates a number of the ideas expressed in previous sections, i.e., the mix of admiration for American technology and progress, as well as a violent, almost knee-jerk repulsion for an entity that many felt was out to remake the world in its own image, an image very alien to traditional Libyan culture.

Libyan Attitudes toward the United States, 1969–82

Qadhafi's Free Officer Revolution brought two opposing trends to the fore: a popular resentment of "Western" exploitation, in all its perceived forms, and an increasing reliance on U.S. technology and market for oil. One Libyan researcher distilled the day to day interactions between Libyans and Americans at this time: "*Most American servicemen are apathetic to service in Libya and almost never leave the airbase. Others, when they do leave, make asses of themselves. The native population is referred to as 'mohab,' and rumors are spread that Christians are killed in the old city of Tripoli. All Libyan customs are interpreted and compared, always unfavorably in terms of the air conditioned, sky-scrapered culture of the United States.*"[12] This view is not completely consistent with other American or other Libyan accounts of the relationship at the time, which tend to focus on relationships in newly-built, and wealthy, suburbs of Giorgimpopoli, where Libyans, Italians, and Americans lived side by side.

By the mid 1970s, Libya and the United States were at each other's throats publicly. At the same time, a clean break was difficult: the United States and Libya were tied to each other by common economic interests that neither, despite frequent threats and warnings from Tripoli, was willing to forego. U.S. technology at this time was, to some degree, irreplaceable. For its part, the United States needed high quality low-sulphur Libyan crude. By 1977, the United States was Libya's largest customer, running a $3,500 million trade deficit with the Great *jamahiriyya*. Libyan exports to the United States rose from $216 million in 1973 to $2.2 billion in 1976. American exports to Libya rose from $104 million to $277 million by 1977, at which time the United States was the largest purchaser of Libyan oil. In short, "*Bilateral economic ties were shaped in large part by mutual economic interest, but political dialogue was determined by forces external to that relationship. Due to his esteem for American power and prestige, Qaddafi often betrayed a need for U.S. recognition of his position and importance.*"[13]

As the Libyan leadership gained confidence, it sought to challenge the status quo, and to change the relationship between the owners of the resource and the producers, which, for the first time, were forced to adopt the policy of owners in determining prices. Qadhafi set an early tone for relations with the West by forcing the United States to abandon its Wheelus airbase on June 31, 1970, prior to the expiration of the lease. It was with the decision to take that critical step farther, i.e., the partial nationalization of U.S. oil companies, that U.S.-Libya relations began a precipitous fall. In the following years, the United States responded by blocking the sale of $400 million in military equipment, including eight Lockheed C130 transports and two Boeing 727-400s. In 1977, the Pentagon put Libya on list of "potential U.S. enemies." It was in 1982, with the Reagan-imposed U.S. embargo of Libyan oil that the commercial and political spheres of U.S. policy were united against Libya.[14]

U.S.-Libya Relations during the U.S. & UN Embargo (1986–2003)

During the embargo years, U.S.-Libya relations were predictably dismal. The Libyan image of the United States was focused on the 1986 bombing of Tripoli and Benghazi, an event that most people over thirty years of age remember vividly. The U.S. impression of Libya was shaped most strongly by the country's implication in various terrorist incidents in Europe, the Pam Am Lockerbie affair, and resulting wrangling over the extradition of suspects. It was during this period that Libya became known to the United States in decidedly extremist terms, and vice versa. Qadhafi and President Ronald Reagan, both charismatic figures inclined to the dramatic, were, in many ways, the perfect foil for one another. The intensity of the exchanges between the two seemed, to some commentators, to indicate a certain utility, if not affection. Here is where the David and Goliath analogy peaks, for as much as Libya took these conflicts seriously, from the U.S. perspective, there was a limit to how much Libya could matter: "*Relations with Libya seldom had any significant influence on U.S. foreign or domestic policy and seldom gained the attention of the American public. Consequently, what was good for Libya not only was not necessarily good for the United States, but often was of no interest to the United States.*"[15] With 9/11, the U.S. invasion of Iraq, and fears of $100 per barrel oil, one could forgive the Libyans for thinking they warranted more of the United States' attention than they had in the past.

Libyan Attitudes toward the United States, 2005

Just as is the case with the United States with respect to Libya, there is not a solid, unified Libyan perception of the United States. What Libyans think of Americans is colored by their position in society, access to wealth, power and patronage, and the strength of their religious beliefs (all of which are related). That said, in 2005, the balance of Libyan sentiment toward the United States vis-à-vis Americans and American products was, in sum, positive, and certainly better than that of the region as a whole.

"*Libyans want to eat McDonald's hamburgers, not uranium.*" This statement, made by Qadhafi's second-eldest son and Libya's most prominent and visible proponent of reform c. 2005, serves to answer part of the question of whether or not American exceptionality exists in twenty-first century Libya.[16] At a time when the United States and Libya had not yet normalized relations, it underscores not only the attractiveness of specific American brands to Libyans, but also the extent to which the Libyan regime felt it was willing to go to rebuild the relationship, not just with the West, but the United States in particular.

Qadhafi's speeches over the last few years are remarkably consistent with those of the early 1970s. They exhibit admiration and defiance, and a forthright acknowledgement of U.S. economic and technological superiority, qualified by a refusal to cede any moral high ground: "*If America were a Jamayirriya, transformed itself into a jamahiriyya with Peoples Congresses and Peoples councils, and leadership from the Shaabiyyat, then it would have something to offer the world, for it has strength of message, strength of capital and economy. With all of these possibilities [the United States] could become a savior to the world,*" Qadhafi said in a 2005 speech.[17] In his public statements since 2004, Qadhafi has toned down the anti-American rhetoric, while insisting that Libya has, thus far, gotten a bad deal from the agreement that normalized relations. The agreement has led to an export value of crude in 2005 that tops $1.1 billion.[18] This rhetoric has hardened in early 2007, as Qadhafi warns other countries like Iran and North Korea not to follow the "Libyan model" of superpower reconciliation. In a March speech commemorating the thirtieth anniversary of the Libyan *jamahiriyya*, or "State of the Masses," Qadhafi returned to old themes, insisting that Libya need not follow the American model, and that his country was willing to cooperate with other governments for mutual benefit.[19]

Even as the Libyans have brought American consulting firms in to help them turn a new leaf, and Libyan power brokers fight over American megabrands like Coke and Caterpillar, Libyans are actively exploring options for increased engagement with other parts of the world. Case in point, Malaysia and Singapore's authoritarian, Islamic, and free-trade orientations have been touted by the Libyan leadership as potentially more appropriate than the relative transparency of the American and European economies. During a January 2006 trip to Malaysia, Saif Al Islam called upon Malaysian companies to invest $7 billion in infrastructure projects in Libya. India and Sri Lanka have made significant gains in Libya in recent years. Chinese oil companies dominated the second round of EPSA. Certainly, it is no coincidence that Qadhafi has turned his back on the Middle East, its problems, and patrons in recent years, preferring to develop his political capital within Africa, as the force behind the African Union (or, as Qadhafi calls it, the Future United States of Africa). In sum, what all of this seems to indicate is that the people who run Libya cannot ignore the United States, and want part of what it has to offer. It also suggests that there are clear limits to the intimacy of this relationship.

The Commercial and Intellectual Elite

In most countries, the most eager constituency for U.S. policy and business is the middle class. Libya would be no exception—if it in fact had a middle class worthy of the name. In early 2004, the Libyan private sector was still but a collection of individuals. As such, it is made up primarily of ex- and current government officials, and other friends of the powerful. What they have in common is capital—usually foreign, but sometimes local—and a solid education (usually gained in the United Kingdom or Italy) or solid connections. A thorough analysis of the few "darlings of the Libyan private sector" will reveal a deep patronage network—some are inclined to pursue deals with America, for reasons more of profit and political exigency than affection; others have thrown their lot in with, notably, Korean, Chinese, and Malaysian companies. In 2005, members of the trading class felt American companies were, in comparison with their European and Asian competitors, unadventurous, overly bureaucratized, and excessively rule-driven. In an environment where, often, the only way to get things done is to bend the rules, the clash of cultures on this score is significant. Unsurprisingly, this group shares a view expressed frequently by higher-level administrators that U.S. companies can be arrogant and culturally insensitive. In the early 2000s, they decried American corporate executives' use of words like "charity" and "aid" in conversations about deal sweeteners, and comparison of Libya with war torn regions like Afghanistan. Libya, they would tell you, is a lot of things—poor is not one of them.

While what we call the "entrepreneurial class" is well connected and highly political, it also contains within it a couple hundred principled, highly successful, and fundamentally pro-American businessmen, lawyers, and civil servants (the line between these categories is also frequently blurred) who serve collectively as the "class conscience." Many are agents for Western companies, they have been outspoken regarding both what they believe to be the worst elements of both the Libyan system, as well as actions of Western companies and governments which they believe are unproductive. This group shares some of the activist ideology of political dissidents, with the notable exception that they do not accept disengagement or abstention as a viable alternative. For them, what is going on now is a war of attrition: a step forward here leads to two steps back, then three steps forward. This latter constituency is absolutely key to the evolving relationship with American firms, and the future of U.S.-Libyan relations. They are the bridge between the Libyan past and present, they understand the stakes, and they are risking their personal, financial, and other welfare on the positive evolution of the reform process.

View from the Masses

A December 2004 Internet poll indicated that 20 percent of respondents in Europe and Canada said they consciously avoided buying U.S. products as a result of policies. "Problem brands," according to the survey, included Exxon-Mobil, AOL, American, CT, UA, Budweiser, Chrysler, Barbie doll, Starbucks, and General Motors. Marlboro was the most problematic. Interestingly, these brands—Budweiser excluded—are some of the most sought after brands in Libya. There is an outlet for Barbie doll-knockoffs on one of the busiest streets in Tripoli; Exxon-Mobil (formerly Esso) has returned; and most Libyans chain smoke Marlboros. Why, when so many other peoples in the Middle East are demonizing America and American products, do Libyans seem perfectly content, for the moment, to think well of entities with image problems outside the *jamahiriyya*? This attitude is clearly important in the search for "exceptionality."

Libyans may be less critical of the United States than other Arabs, and this, despite their conservative bias, precisely because they have been sheltered from much of the incessant negative imagery to which the rest of the region has been exposed over the last decades, focused as it has been on the Israeli-Palestinian conflict. In a similar vein, those Libyans old enough to draw upon memory in forming a view of the other, clearly expected the early twenty-first century American businessman to resemble that of the 1960s. With changes in corporate structure and the advent of the multinational corporation, a Libyan's first contact with a major U.S. brand might now be through a regional representative based in Cairo or Switzerland, rather than a senior U.S.-based executive. This has not gone over well. In a country where personal relationships are key to action, principals expect to speak with the heads of companies, not the foreign-born heads of regional subsidiaries.

At the time the United States eased its economic sanctions against Libya in May 2004, there was a widespread—if unspoken—feeling among

Libyans that the reentry of the United States was a harbinger of better times. Indeed, economic loosening of regulations that had their origins in the late 1980s seemed to be gathering steam. Across Tripoli, there was new activity—relentless cottage industries and outlets sprang up. Where there was nothing five years before, the five-mile Gargaresh Street was now literally covered with shop fronts. Where there were virtually no foreign advertisements in 2004, two years later, the Tripoli Airport had been transformed into a mini-mall of Movenpick ice cream stands, espresso counters, and gift shops full of Qadhafi T-shirts and plates. High-resolution TV screens with LG sponsorship logos replaced hand-painted posters of Qadhafi. The Afriquiyya Airlines logo appears astride photos of "The Leader." The availability of conveniences seemed to improve peoples' moods, even if much of it remained far beyond the means of the average Libyan.

While many Libyans clearly take comfort in the increasing availability of creature comforts, many wonder aloud if a "consumer infitah" is the limit of reform, and even whether or not the influx of foreign attitudes and goods poses a threat to traditional ways of life. In many segments of Libyan society, as in Egypt, outward signs of piety and religiosity appear to be growing. U.S. business ignores these ambivalences and countercurrents at their peril. Whether it is explicit or not, Libyans are wary of exploitation, and look to the new arrivals for assurance—and proof—they are not here to take and run.

American Attitudes toward Libya: 2005

Just as Libyan attitudes toward Americans are not monolithic, neither are those of Americans. Of course, for all the curiosity and "exoticism," Americans' fundamental association with Libya is still the 1989 Pan Am Lockerbie bombing. As for positive currents, however, they exist. In 2004, there were at least five major articles vaunting Libya's tourist potential, including a feature in the *New York Times* Sunday travel section and *Conde Nast* magazine. Despite never having set foot in Libya, Oprah vaunted Leptis Magna as one of the "five places to see before you die."

Just as there is a group in positions of power in Libya who maintain fond memories of the United States, there is a sizeable community in the United States with deep personal attachments to Libya. Every other year since the late 1970s, more than a thousand people gather in Texas for a reunion of American-Libyan expatriates. Members, mostly former teachers and oil workers, gather to sing the club anthem "I will be back again,

Libya." Many of these individuals have indeed made it back to Libya in some capacity, and are staunch advocates for rebuilding relations.

In a speech before the Middle East Institute in 2004, a former Conoco-Philips CEO went as far as to say that the industry could take very little credit for advances of the past few years: "*There are no American names on that list [list of first re- entrants into the Oil and Gas sector] and, therefore, no American credit for restoring Libya's most important export.*" "*The Americans are late,*" a high-ranking Libyan official told *The Export Practitioner* in 2004. The implication, of course, is that the Europeans, whose governments permitted them to do business in Libya many years before U.S. companies were granted access, had the market sown up. While these statements may have had a whiff of truth to them in 2003, they are not accurate descriptions of the current environment. The signing of the former Oasis Group's reentry agreement in January 2006 was a major event, as it reestablished the United States as the dominant foreign presence in the Libyan oil sector. Any fear that the United States has somehow lost out to Europe should be dispelled by one statistic: by January 2007, the United States had regained its position as Libya's largest consumer of Libyan crude. While this is an "import" category, it also speaks directly to the role of U.S. companies in Libya's petroleum sector.

A closer look at European countries' relationships with Libya reveals some significant dissonance: Libya's trade with Italy and Germany has been experiencing a rather dramatic decline in recent years, particularly in non-refined products. Libya is expected to increase its domestic refining capacity substantially in the coming five to ten years, further entrenching this trend. In the Fall of 2004, the British ambassador, before a well-publicized international conference in Tripoli, characterized prospects as "bleak," and blasted the lack of transparency, inaccessibility, and unreliability. Historically, Italy has been Libya's number one import and export destination. Italian exports to Libya held steady throughout the 1990s, at just over 1 billion USD/year—the figure jumped some 20 percent in the years immediately surrounding the lifting of UN sanctions, and has declined somewhat since 2004. Libya has increased pressure on Italy for forms of compensation for war-related damages, including an import tax of 4 percent, the proceeds of which are supposed to fund a social rehabilitation fund. There are areas in which the United States has lost out to aggressive European marketing, but there is no indication that these losses are indicative of something structural in the relationship. The United States sold 350,000 tons of wheat to Libya in 2004 (out of a total 800,000 imports), but was "knocked out of the market" in 2005 by competition from Australia and Europe. From virtually nothing in 2003, the United

States imported $1.3 billion in goods from Libya through October 2005, 98 percent of which was oil, with the residual made up mainly of petroleum derivatives such as ammonia and fertilizers. The United States exported to Libya a mere $66 million over the same period. The seventh largest exporter to the United States in the Middle East, Libya imports the lowest amount of U.S. goods of all countries in the region. Over the years 2004 to 2006, Libyan exports have increased geometrically, while imports have roughly doubled each year to 331.6 million USD in 2004.

In sum, the United States has been making steady gains in the Libyan market, in the face of a rapidly increasing trade deficit. The Asian countries and Russia, as previously noted, have made significant gains over the last two years, primarily through their willingness to undersell the (primarily European) competition. After a tentative showing in the first EPSA round, Japanese and Chinese companies startled their Western competitors by dramatically underbidding on Libyan exploration licenses, prompting one Western Oil company with no little irony to speculate that the EPSA of the future would consist of the Chinese paying money solely for the privilege to bid.[20]

While Corporate Social Responsibility (CSR), the idea that corporations "do well by doing good" is an ill-defined movement, there are few places in the world where the argument for business intangibles goes farther than in Libya. Libya will open, in the long run, only through the concerted action of several constituencies, working together to develop infrastructure that they—and the public—need to operate, and for which the government has no consistent policy or vision for producing public goods, i.e., projects where the benefits accrue to the Libyan community and the community of foreign companies as a whole, not to individual companies.

In the last few years, American companies such as IBM, Cisco, and others have made contributions to essential infrastructure, including core banking technologies, a sine qua non for an efficient and transparent banking sector. American accounting and consulting firms have established relationships with Libyan partners, and have been working, albeit slowly, with those entities to bring their practices up to international standards. These are all examples of businesses doing good by doing their work well; other companies have taken additional steps to educate and train Libyans: U.S. consumer products giant Procter & Gamble, for example, offers seminars in health maintenance for women, as well as small business management. Many of these activities are in the company's direct interest—they create points of sale that the company uses to market goods.[21] Exxon Mobil, presumably working off the huge success of its training programs in the 1970s and 1980s, has been looking again at how to use education to build goodwill and a pool of local technical expertise.

The fact that there are no Libyan NGOs in the traditional sense of the term allows for, and one might say mandates, an even broader scope of corporate social engagement. This is a tricky situation, as we have already seen, as such initiatives must be presented as "part of business as usual" (e.g., as "deal sweeteners," explicitly part of a contract proposal), as opposed to anything that might be construed as "charity." At the same time, one has the interesting situation where the host country is requesting "cooperation" and "technical assistance"—which, in large companies, is the purview of corporate governance departments—in an environment where ethical standards will very likely constitute a short-term impediment to U.S. advances in the Libyan market. Here is an area where the Europeans and Asians do have a competitive advantage, for they are often willing to engage in practices that are explicitly prohibited by the Foreign Corrupt Practices Act.

U.S. companies must recognize that efforts to build infrastructure will rarely be amenable to a photo opportunity. Nor will it always be welcomed with open arms by the government. Some clever strategy and industriousness is required. Yet, as European chocolate manufacturers are dumping products in a country with one of the highest incidences of Type 2 diabetes; in an environment where Europeans and North African reexporters, during sanctions, were known to have sold Libya substandard agriculture equipment and heavy machinery; where the market is full of counterfeit goods, some of which pose serious health risks, U.S. companies, even those with the "worst" international reputations, have an opportunity to distinguish themselves.

Depending on the particular line of business and the related commercial imperatives, community development initiatives may not be standard operating procedure. At the same time, they should also internalize the fact that, in the circumstances under which the West has chosen to engage with Libya, policies of refusal and ultimatums will rarely work. Companies looking to make profits in Libya will do best to consider it a long-term investment, and be willing to accept lower than optimal short-term returns in exchange for future gains. What U.S. business has, at the moment, is a chance to convince the Libyans that they are, as they were in the past, on Libya's side. U.S. companies must recognize, as well, that how Libyans remember us is often not what we have become.

Conclusion

Before the United States lifted remaining sanctions and took Libya off the "terror list" in 2006, the most obvious source of "exceptionality" was the fact that the United States, within the community of Western states, was the lone holdout for full diplomatic relations. Libya wanted what full reentry symbolized: a welcoming back of Libya into the fold of the international community. The problem with this form of "exceptionality"—and the attention it engenders—is that it is not convertible, i.e., once the blessing is given, it cannot easily be taken back. This we might call the most superficial layer of exceptionality. The next layer of exceptionality is that born of commercial-economic necessity: as was the case in the late 1950s and 1960s, both parties have things the other needs—the United States is still technologically superior in a number of critical fields, the petroleum sector foremost among them; Libya has a political and social culture that is sufficiently "different" from many of its neighbors, as to make it potentially more "friendly" to U.S. interests in the region, particularly in the context of the War on Terror.

With the internationalization of commerce and technology, however, and the aggressive approach of countries like China, this second layer is increasingly assailable. The third form of exceptionality, and perhaps the most critical, comes from a form of shared worldview—or at least, a perceived form of shared values—dating back to an age which increasingly few Libyans remember. These convictions are not evenly spread throughout the population, but, for the moment, exist in the hands of those with the most to lose from the failure of liberalization—part of the commercial elite, and on some level, a good fraction of ordinary Libyan citizens.

Insularity has both disadvantages and advantages: Libya's hibernation shielded it from "progress," but also the kind of political anti-Americanism that much of the rest of the region is prone to. The more Libya opens to the region and to the world, the more it will lose its individuality in outlook. The pro- U.S. demographic, the ones who benefited from direct contact with U.S. firms and studied in the United States in corporate training programs, is nearing the age of retirement. A new generation, more who are more familiar with the United Kingdom or who have very little experience with the West, will take their place. They admire certain things about the West, but have no basis for nostalgia. The United States cannot count on the long life of whatever exceptionality currently exists being long-lived in the absence of strong efforts to update perceptions and create new bases for exceptionality.

In this chapter, we have identified a basis for exceptionality, an influential locus of native support, and a pattern of behavior that seems a viable path to change, albeit long-term change. Together, this presents a challenge to the U.S. business community. To protect its own interests, and increase the probability of return, the U.S. business community would do well to band together to create pressure points or lobbying groups for specific types of economic reform, and then to hit those notes over and over.

The lone efforts of one company may not make a difference in the near term, but the efforts of several companies over long periods of time have been shown to produce results; sustained, incremental progress is what one can expect from Libya under current conditions. Above all, empty public relations exercises, of which one can identify a couple of prominent cases, are to be avoided. Fundamentally, Libyans have expectations of the United States. The worst thing the United States could do now in Libya is to fail to meet past and present "exceptionality" with an exceptionality of its own.

Notes

1. World Bank Draft Report, "Socialist People's Libyan Arab Jamahiriya Country Economic Report," Report no. 30295-LY (Washington: The World Bank, July 2006).
2. *Jeune Afrique L'Intelligent* No. 2280.
3. The Libyan dinar (LD) is pegged to a basket of currencies. For the past few years, it has floated around 1.4 LD/$.
4. Qadhafi, Mu'ammar, Al-Mu'tamar, January 12.
5. An American supermarket chain.
6. Gwyn Williams, *Green Mountain*, Dar Al-Fergiani reprint (orig. London: Faber & Faber, 1963), 89.
7. John Wright, *Libya: A Modern History* (Washington, DC: Johns Hopkins University Press, 1981), 83.
8. Gidney, Dennis, "Esso Standard Libya Inc (ESL) Training and Development Program pre-1982," unpublished
9. Mustafa Ben-Halim, *Forgotten Pages From Libya's Political History: The Memoirs of Mustafa Ahmad Ben-Halim* (Arabic Version) (London: Alhani International Books, 1992), 188–93.
10. Ramadan Bukheit, *Hikayat Al Madi Al Qarib: Qisas Qasira*, (Benghazi: Dar Al-Kutub Al-Wataniyya, 1996), 114.
11. Sadiq Nayhoum, *Al-Awdat Al Mahzan Ila Al-Bahr*, 57.
12. Ali Mohammed Shembesh, "The Analysis of Libya's Foreign Policy, 1969–1973" (PhD diss., Emory University, 1975), 56–60
13. St John, *Libya and The United States*, 10.
14. Ibid, 126.
15. St John, 10.
16. Saif Al-Islam Al-Qadhafi, "Libyan-American Relations," *Middle East Policy* 10, No. 1, Spring 2003.
17. Qadhafi speech,11/6/05, Al-jamahiriyya
18. U.S. Foreign Trade Statistics, U.S. Census Bureau.
19. Komfie Manalo, "Gadhafi Blasts U.S. for Allegedly Imposing U.S. Policy On Others," March 1, 2007, http://allheadlinenews.com.

20. Given the size of the first-round bonuses in the last 2006 EPSA IV round, this may effectively have already happened.
21. Further, wide penetration of satellite TV has allowed companies to cut back on advertising expenditures.

7

Libya and Its
North African Policy

John P. Entelis

The initial orientation of postrevolutionary Libyan foreign policy ranked North Africa, with Egypt at its core, as the primary area of interest, followed by the rest of the Arab Middle East and sub-Saharan Africa.[1] The Islamic world held moderate interest, while the West was shunned altogether, save for the narrow instrumentalist benefits related to oil. The Communist bloc served more as an anti-Western agent than as a preferable region of association. Today, North Africa including Egypt, ranks last in the hierarchy of Libyan foreign policy concerns, with sub-Saharan Africa and, most recently, Europe and the United States emerging as the priority actors and preferable partners in foreign affairs. Why and how did this dramatic reversal take place? Given the physical proximity, common colonial legacies, cultural attachment, religious and linguistic affinity, and uniform identification with the Palestinian cause that the states of North Africa represent, one would have thought that deepening, rather than distancing, Libya from its Maghrebi neighbors would have characterized Libyan foreign policy in the last forty years. As with all things Libyan it is difficult to explain this contradictory, if not illogical and counter-productive, approach toward foreign affairs.

While many factors may be identified, personality and petroleum may well best explain Libya's view of, and attitude toward, Algeria, Morocco, and Tunisia. These two configurations are immune to revision, or change as they are rooted in circumstances peculiar to Libya that defy "normal" political discourse and diplomatic bargaining. This chapter begins by identifying the systemic context within which Libya sees itself, and then elaborates on how this context impacts the country's relationship with its Maghrebi neighbors. It concludes with some tentative projections of future Libyan-Maghrebi ties.

Personalistic Rule in Libya

The Libyan leader, Colonel Mu'ammar Qadhafi, is the longest-lasting political head of state in the Arab world, having come to power in a coup d'état in September 1969. Only in his mid-60s, he is projected to continue ruling for another decade or two, unimpeded by institutional constraints or demands for democratic change. Having long ago lost his charismatic appeal and the "heroic" image he first inspired, he rules today through a combination of tribal patronage, coercive force, and economic incentives made possible by an excess supply of hydrocarbon revenues. He has neither built a viable Libyan national state, nor established the legal institutions necessary to insure the country's survival in the post-Qadhafi era. Indeed, his decades-long political purpose has been to deinstitutionalize the state in the name of "people power," as espoused in his convoluted "third universal theory" that serves as the ideological centerpiece of his *Green Book*.

Composed of an indigestible mixture of socialist principles and Islamic belief, the regime's ideological text is, more than ever, ignored by both its founder and practitioners. A form of nomadic socialism has been replaced by a "popular capitalism" intended to jump-start a stagnant economy and animate a lethargic society. Regardless of the mercurial character of the man and his policies, one thing has remained constant: Libya is thoroughly dictatorial with virtually no semblance of democratic life, either within civil society or the state. And despite the numerous positive gestures undertaken in foreign affairs, especially the country's elimination of its weapons of mass destruction (WMD) program in 2003, none of these efforts has impacted domestic politics in any progressive way.

What Political System?

Libya represents, in its most basic sense, a "tribe with a flag": a society composed of diverse tribal groupings incorporated into three regionally-defined provinces of Tripolitania, Cyrenaica, and Fezzan, but never fully integrated into a Libyan nation-state in which citizens are governed by their duly elected representatives. Neither the nation-building nor state-building process was ever realized either under the monarchy (1951–69) or under the leadership of Qadhafi (1969 to present). For the last four decades, charismatic authority has never been permitted to evolve into a rational-legal system of rule, nor has it fully eradicated the traditional bases of legitimacy in which tribal identity, family ties, and Islam have remained powerful constants in the lives of ordinary Libyans.

The discovery of oil in 1959, and the enormous revenues it has generated over the decades, has worked to further ensconce the status quo, rather than serving as the economic engine for social and political change.[2] Indeed, Libya remains the quintessential rentier state, one in which rulers have had the luxury of ruling without the consent—or the tax revenues—of those being ruled. Capping this retrograde system of state-building has been Qadhafi's unique vision of what constitutes the legal order—the *jamahiriyya*, a blend of romantic tribalism that gives primacy to the tribal values of solidarity and equality. For Qadhafi, the *jamahiriyya* represents the ultimate expression of "true" democracy, in which the people govern themselves freely from the constraints of the impersonal bureaucratic state. The result has been neither democracy nor bureaucracy, but rather a chaotic and unpredictable pattern of elite-directed initiatives that have little to no connection with popular aspirations or rationally determined developmental policies. Even the so-called liberalization of the economy undertaken in the beginning of the twenty-first century has been more rhetoric than reality and, in any case, has had no direct impact on the domestic political order that remains thoroughly dictatorial. Even the abandonment of the WMD program in December 2003 has not completely eliminated the country's revolutionary orientation, and global activism, including the goal of assassinating unfriendly foreign leaders, as was the case in the failed attempt to murder then Crown Prince, now King Abdullah of Saudi Arabia, in 2003.

The Depoliticized State

Consistent with the "Brother Leader's" vision of the idealized polity, there is no Libyan "government" or cabinet "ministers," but only the people expressing their democratic wishes through popular assemblies, known locally as the Basic People's Congress (BPC). Each BPC selects its own representative to the national-level body, the General People's Congress (GPC), serving as the functional equivalent of a "legislative" body. At the executive level, there are parallel structures, known as the Basic People's Committee and the General People's Committee, the closest equivalent to a governmental cabinet. Yet even these so-called governmental institutions have low levels of legitimacy among the general public, whose participation, in any case, is extremely low. Technically, the GPC is empowered to choose the secretaries who are appointed to the General People's Committee, but, in reality, those chosen for these positions are first approved by Qadhafi himself, with the Congress simply rubber-stamping the results. Not trusting anyone except those closest to the leader himself has resulted in the same few individuals holding the same positions of power for consecutive decades, with Qadhafi simply alternating their posts. Even these individuals, however, serve more as technocrats than politicians, since ultimate decision-making authority remains with Qadhafi himself and his small circle of close advisors drawn from tribal affiliations, military associations, and high-level business contacts. This is all by way of saying that the Libyan Jamhiriyya is, more than ever, a depoliticized entity run by the few for the benefit of the few, all rationalized under the ideological mantra of "people power."

Political parties or any kind of independent political or civic associations are strictly forbidden, with life-threatening consequences for those contemplating such activity. Public accountability is virtually nonexistent, and civil liberties forever in jeopardy. If activists within civil society initiate any kind of independent political action, as the case of the twelve journalists currently on trial for charges of attempting to overthrow the political system clearly demonstrates, the penalties can be harsh, including the use of torture and long-term prison sentences.

Despite the surface appearance of total political control at home, however, there are clear signs that challenges have emerged to contest the authority of Qadhafi and his belief system. Indeed, it is believed that virtually all the positive gestures undertaken in the international arena—compensation for the victims of the Pan Am 103 bombing; cooperation with international authorities regarding the adjudication of the airline explosion; the abandonment of the WMD program; the turning away from terrorist practices and policies; the willingness to cooperate more openly with the West in encouraging business ventures and other opportunities for normal global exchanges; and the release of the Bulgarian and Palestinian health workers condemned to death for having infected Libyan children with the HIV virus—are responses to serious challenges developing at home. Among the major domestic challenges facing the regime are: a moribund economy despite the oil wealth, the lack of employment opportunities for a rapidly expanding youth population, the decrepit conditions of the country's basic infrastructure, and the rise of Islamist appeals among an increasingly alienated mass public. All have forced Qadhafi to rethink, but not fundamentally alter, his strategy of governance. His willingness to collaborate with the United States in the latter's "War on Terror," including participation in intelligence gathering and other sharing of information involving alleged Al-Qaʻida activities in the Sahara and the Saharan-Sahelian corridor, all speak to the pressure for change forcing itself on the "Great Leader."

It is uncertain, at this point, whether Islamic radicalism has taken a firm foothold in the country sufficient enough to undermine Qadhafi's fast waning charismatic appeal and the coercive apparatus associated with it. In any case, the absence of legitimate institutional structures intended to secure the system's longevity leaves the regime vulnerable to sudden, if not violent, overthrow. Also uncertain is the status of Qadhafi's son, Saif al-Islam, as the designated successor to his father, despite his high profile within the country, including his leadership of the Qadhafi Development Foundation, a charitable organization intended to serve as Saif's power base within civil society. Whatever economic reforms the regime does or does not undertake, they will have little impact on the manner in which Libya is ruled with political power still concentrated in the hands of the security and intelligence apparatus and the revolutionary committees, both still under the control of Qadhafi. The more things change, the more they remain the same.

The Foreign Policy Connection

Given the unchanging and authoritarian character of domestic politics, it is no surprise to see the Libyan leader roam the world for political advantage, justified in the name of some larger ideological principle, whether it be anti-imperialism, anticolonialism, anti-Zionism, Pan-Arabism, Pan-Africanism, or Pan-Maghrebism. It is to the latter that we now turn our attention.

Arab unity and support for the Palestinian cause have long inspired the Arab masses across both the Machrek and Maghreb. This, in particular, has been the case for Libya, in part due to the weak sense of national identity held by its tribal people. Thus, Qadhafi's pan-Arabist orientation reflects not only the man's personal belief, but responds to a broader, deeply held sentiment within Libyan society itself, regularly confirmed in both attitudinal surveys and political behavior.[3] Given this "reality" of cross-border Arab sentiment for unity, Qadhafi thought it only "natural" that unification would be desired both as a matter of principle, but also as politically advantageous by other Arab leaders, beginning with Libya's neighbors in northern Africa.

From the moment he achieved power, and even long before, Qadhafi aspired to achieve what his political idol, Gamal Abdel Nasser, never succeeded in achieving: unifying the Arab world into a militarily strong, economically powerful, politically important, and culturally influential global actor capable of meeting the challenges presented by imperialism, colonialism, and Zionism. Believing that his charismatic appeal and oil wealth were sufficient to achieve these goals, the Libyan leader pursued a single-minded policy of "take it or leave it," in which Arab states were being asked to subsume their national interests in the name of some larger, but undefined, pan-Arab entity organized under Qadhafi's leadership. When neither personal charm nor financial incentives succeeded, a policy of confrontation, coercion, and conflict was adopted, none more disruptive than that applied to Libya's immediate neighbors—the Sudan, Chad, Egypt, Morocco, Tunisia, and Algeria.

The Nasserite Imperative

From the moment he assumed power, Qadhafi sought union with Egypt at almost any cost. Nasser, the man, and pan-Arabism, the ideology, served as passionate inspirations for the young Qadhafi, who literally hand-delivered Libya to the Egyptian leader, if only the latter was willing to take it. This contrasts dramatically with Egypt under Sadat, whom Qadhafi viewed as seeking to completely overturn the Nasserite idea of Arabism. As one commentator has observed: "Qaddafi gave Libya to Nasser, then tried to 'steal' Egypt from Sadat."[4]

Within four months of the 1969 revolution, Libya joined Egypt and the Sudan in signing the Tripartite Agreement, or Tripoli Charter. While not officially constituting a unity scheme per se, the charter did serve as a preview of Qadhafi's ambitions for political acceptance, power, and notoriety, best achieved through close and immediate association with the Arab world's most inspirational leader, notwithstanding the dramatic defeat Nasser experienced in the 1967 war with Israel.

Between September 1970 (Nasser's death) and October 1973 (Arab-Israeli War), Qadhafi entered into a rash of unity schemes and merger efforts. Most noteworthy was the Federation of Arab Republics that brought Syria, Egypt, the Sudan, and Libya together in November 1970, later reduced to three members in April 1971, when the Sudan withdrew. Despite his misgivings about Sadat in the years immediately following Nasser's death, Qadhafi "pursued a relentless policy of greater rapprochement with Egypt and called for a merger between the two states."[5] This impulse was crowned on September 1, 1973, when the United Arab Republic (1958–61) was revived with Libya and Egypt, proclaiming political unity one month before the outbreak of October 1973, an event that shattered that unity virtually at birth.

Libya undertook integration efforts with its western neighbors when doubts about unity with Egypt and the Sudan were being raised. Thus, in December 1972, a merger scheme was declared between Tunisia and Libya, but aborted at inception, given the enormous differences in political orientation and personality existing between the francophone Habib Bourguiba and Qadhafi. Ironically, despite the man's unity efforts, and given Qadhafi's deep animosity of all Arab monarchies, it was no surprise to see Libya being implicated in the two back-to-back assassination attempts against Morocco's King Hassan II in 1971 and 1972, leading to a break in diplomatic relations—already strained by Tripoli's early support in 1972 of an independent state of what was then the Spanish Sahara. Qadhafi's frequent volte-face on failed mergers was rarely limited to vituperative exchanges or verbal onslaughts, but often involved providing financial, military, and ideological support to opposition or insurgent movements. Representative samples included pitting Takfir wal Hijra, the Islamic fundamentalist terrorist group, against Sadat, the National Front against Numeiri, the Progressive Front for the Liberation of Tunisia against Bourguiba, and the POLISARIO against Morocco.

A Turn toward the Maghreb

While ideology has motivated Qadhafi's quest for national recognition, the dual factors of personality and petroleum have been the essential tools for its implementation. Indeed, as his personal standing in the Arab world increased among ordinary people, and oil-generated wealth expanded as an incentive to influence state actors, the differences between means and ends gradually dissipated. When poorly conceived fusion plans failed to materialize in one part of the Arab world, Qadhafi was quick to turn elsewhere. Given the initial priority of the northern African region, it was consistent with his pan-Arabist vision that if the Mashriq was unenthusiastic about instant national unification, then the western Arab world could serve as a logical alternative. Yet, there, as well, Qadhafi's brash approach unnerved Maghrebi leaders.

The 1970s witnessed an array of Libyan merger efforts, each ending in failure and recrimination. The Djerba Agreement of January 1974 between Tunisia and Libya created the "Islamic Arab Republic," and illustrated Qadhafi's continuous effort to balance regional powers in order to maintain some semblance of political relevance and ideological influence for himself and his country. Given the souring of ties between Sadat and Qadhafi following the 1973 October war, it seemed logical, if not imperative, to find new partners in a region he still considered primary in his foreign policy orientation. Yet, the Djerba accord dissipated as quickly as it was formed, followed by a series of hostile provocations in which Qadhafi challenged Tunisia's claims to explore offshore oil concessions. While the International Court of Justice ultimately arbitrated this dispute in 1978 in Tunisia's favor, millions of dollars of potential revenue were lost to a country with limited natural resources and a modest economy. Additionally, foreign oil companies were unwilling to pursue such concessions in the future, fearful of Libya's aggressive behavior.

The Hassi Massoud defense pact between Algeria and Libya, concluded in December 1975, followed a familiar pattern of regional actors pursuing a merger strategy in order to promote country-specific goals at home and abroad. For one observer, this Libyan-Algerian accord "cemented the most important alliance in North Africa during the 1970s."[6] At a time of regional instability, this accord helped stabilize the Libyan regime, while serving to consolidate Algeria's position as the most determined supporter of the POLISARIO against Morocco's annexation of the Western Sahara.

Consolidation on the western "front" was intensified following Sadat's trip to Jerusalem in 1977, the signing of the Camp David Accords in 1978, and, most decisively, the conclusion of the peace treaty between Egypt and Israel in 1979, resulting in the creation, under Qadhafi's leadership, of the Steadfastness and Confrontation Front, aligning Libya, Algeria, Syria, Yemen, and the PLO against Egypt.

The pattern established in the 1970s was maintained in the 1980s, as Qadhafi continued his search for regional solidarity through a series of hastily conceived unity schemes, none of which endured more than a year or two. An aborted tripartite federation between Libya, Algeria, and Tunisia in June 1978 eventually led Qadhafi to sponsor an armed attack in Gafsa, Tunisia, in January 1980 as "punishment" for having rejected his unity offer. A Libyan-Algerian alliance in June 1980 quickly fell apart as well, when the Algerians became increasingly frustrated with Qadhafi's erratic behavior, including meddling in areas sensitive to Algerian security interests in the Saharan-Sahelian corridor. For the more instrumentalist oriented Algerians, Libya's inconstancy was found troublesome, if not dangerous, and explains, in part, the signing in March 1983 of the Treaty of Brotherhood and Concord between Algeria and Tunisia, joined later by Mauritania, but excluding Libya and Morocco.

In the balance of power strategy that has long dictated intra-Maghrebi politics, it was not long before a countervailing alliance was formed, this time bringing Morocco and Libya together. This unity effort served to promote each country's region-specific policies. Rabat was seeking support in the Western Sahara, while Tripoli looked to escape its isolation created by the Egypt-Sudan alliance in the east and the Algeria-Tunisia-Mauritania partnership in the west. To be sure, no unity scheme was more unexpected and unexplainable than that of Libya and Morocco when, on August 14, 1984, Hassan II and Qadhafi signed the Oujda Accord, creating the Arab-African Union. Yet, viewed from the personalistic and political perspectives of Qadhafi's vision of himself in the region and the world, the union was a rational act intended to advance Libyan national interests within the wider context of promoting Pan-Arabism, itself a necessary first step toward regional empowerment. Characteristically, domestic uncertainties and regional challenges occupied a prominent place in Qadhafi's calculations and contributed directly to his interest in a union with Morocco.

Indeed, given that the Libyan leader was associating himself with a monarch and a regime he had repeatedly denounced, it may plausibly be argued that the alliance was formed in spite of, rather than in response to, ideological considerations.[7] Prior to the union, Qadhafi and Hassan viewed each other with undisguised contempt. One writer attending an Arab summit in Morocco observed Qadhafi's "revulsion in Rabat at the sight of premiers, ministers, and generals bowing to kiss the hand of the monarch; to him Hassan was Idris, and in Morocco it was overdue for the Tent to confront the Palace."[8] For its part, Rabat radio replied by describing Qadhafi as the "mad clown, the imbecile tyrant."[9] Personal recriminations aside, "each leader saw the [Arab-African Union] as providing an opportunity for the manipulation of normative symbols in order to project a particular image."[10] For Qadhafi in particular, the merger was intended "to enhance his legitimacy and to reduce his international isolation,"[11] while still remaining faithful to his pan-Arabist ideological principles. Predictably and characteristically, the union collapsed after a surprisingly long two-year period.

The Arab Maghreb Union: Disillusion and Dissolution?

When the five countries of the Maghreb signed the Treaty of Marrakech, creating the Arab Maghreb Union (AMU), on February 17, 1989, "they pledged to meet every six months in order to build a North African common market that would transform the region's economic capabilities."[12] AMU's creation was intended to foster economic integration among the five North African states on the model of the European Union. There was never any serious discussion of eradicating existing political boundaries or undermining national sovereignties in the name of some larger entity. Rather, given the complementarity of economies—Morocco's agricultural surplus, Algeria's hydrocarbon reserves, Tunisia's human capital, and

Libya's absorptive labor capacity—AMU could serve as the organizational instrument to rationalize economic strategies and enhance developmental performance. Such an approach would advance local economies, while better positioning the region in its relationship with outside economic actors, especially the EU. For its part, Libya "has been the only [Maghrebi] country capable of absorbing some of the regional labor surplus. It has removed trade barriers with its neighbors while enhancing trade and allowing Libyans to go shopping in Tunisia for goods they could not find at home. Libya is [also] a major partner in the Arab Maghribi Bank for Investment and Trade and has a large number of joint projects with its neighbors . . . in the agricultural, transport, communications, industrial, and petrochemical sectors."[13]

Yet, despite these modest economic achievements, the AMU has struggled to maintain its institutional integrity in the face of chronic personal and political differences among the regional partners, with the conflict in the Western Sahara constituting the greatest source of contention, as Morocco and Algeria vie for regional hegemony. Qadhafi's flip-flop on the Saharan issue complicated the problem further, limiting the AMU's organizational efficacy. For all intents and purposes, the AMU has been moribund since 1994, stuck in a state of "prolonged hibernation."[14] Indeed, in the last decade or so, the Maghrebi countries have been intensifying bilateral, vertical relationships with the EU at the expense of horizontal, south-south ties making Maghrebi unity as elusive as ever. With Libya having "come in from the cold" by its abandonment of its WMD program in 2003, it, too, is advancing its ties to the EU and the United States at the expense of those with its North African partners. Given Qadhafi's unpredictable personality and vast petroleum power, he is increasingly viewed as a direct challenge to the political, economic, and strategic interests of Morocco, Algeria, and Tunisia, despite the fact that all the Maghrebi states need to craft common strategies to meet the challenges of socioeconomic underdevelopment and confront the threat of Islamic terrorism, uncontrolled immigration, drug trafficking, and region-wide criminality.

Qadhafi's existential, stream-of-consciousness mode of promoting unity has repeatedly offended the pragmatic sensibilities of politically savvy regional leaders. What should have been a logical historical evolution in the process of regional integration, the Arab Maghreb Union has turned into another meaningless and hollow organization devoid of serious purpose and little accomplishment. Rather than overcoming past mistakes, misperceptions, and misunderstandings, the AMU has served as an instrument to highlight differences, rather than common points of interests, among the five Maghrebi states. While issues like the conflict in the

Western Sahara have hampered the AMU, it is Qadhafi's unpredictability that has long stymied efforts at making the regional organization a truly viable entity.

At the individual level, each of the three leaders of Algeria, Morocco, and Tunisia—Bouteflika, Mohamed VI, and Ben Ali, respectively—view Qadhafi as an emerging competitor in the areas that matter most; political economy, military alliances, strategic planning, and global diplomacy. Those leaders have long ago dismissed Qadhafi's ideological excesses and rhetorical bombast as having no political weight or global impact. However, empowered by extensive hydrocarbons reserves and a small population, Qadhafi has always had the luxury of exploiting the full range of political options along any number of economic, diplomatic, and strategic issues. This is best represented by his complete turnaround on the issue of weapons of mass destruction, along with his full embrace of the United States, a country he once considered the Third World's principal enemy. For the other Maghrebi leaders, it is this very unpredictability in behavior that disrupts their efforts at stabilizing relations within the region and among key world actors at a time of domestic uncertainty created by globalization, demands for democracy, and fear of terrorist threats.

Given the volatile, erratic, and unpredictable nature of Qadhafi's foreign policy, it is no surprise that the other Maghrebi leaders view him with little-disguised derision, if not contempt. Yet, since all five North African actors face the same challenge from al-Qaida and its local offshoots, especially since the formation, in early 2007, of the region-wide "Al-Qaida in the Islamic Maghreb" (AQIM), there is an urgent need for regional and extra-regional cooperation. This is especially the case for Libya, where the Islamist challenge seemed contained, if not eliminated, until recently. There are now reports that the once ineffectual Libyan Islamic Fighting Group (LIFG) has been reinvigorated with logistical and material support from AQIM (see Chapter 3). In May 2007, Libyan security services made several arrests of suspected Islamist militants in the Benghazi region.[15]

The LIFG first appeared in the early 1990s when it was implicated in at least two assassination attempts against Qadhafi. The group's goal, like its counterparts throughout the Muslim world, is to overthrow the authoritarian state and establish an Islamic government based on Sharia law. Similar to such movements elsewhere, the core of the Libyan membership derives from veterans of the Afghan war against the USSR—a hardened group of determined fighters now further emboldened by the presence of global support for their efforts in Libya. This revived threat has led Libyan security forces to extend their intra-Maghrebi cooperation. Thus, it is has been noted that the May 2007 arrests appeared to be a "pre-emptive move against potential LIFG mobilization,"[16] with evidence provided to suggest the group was planning bombing attacks and other acts of sabotage and violence. According to the EIU report, "[t]he security services may have gleaned their information from the interrogation of three Libyans by the Algerian police, recently arrested in Algeria while allegedly attempting to link up with al-Qaida groups there, which suggests that the LIFG is set to join al-Qaida in the Islamic Maghreb. Two of the LIFG's leaders, Abu al-Layth al-Libi and Abu-Yahya al-Libi, are prominent in the core al-Qaida organization in Afghanistan."[17] The revived nature of the LIFG was also demonstrated in the riots that took place in Benghazi in early 2006, protesting the Danish cartoons that blasphemed the Prophet. It is believed that elements of the LIFG were responsible for those riots.

The first evidence of a change in policy occurred in the mid-1990s when, for example, Qadhafi assured then President Liamine Zeroual of Algeria that Tripoli would cease all aid to Algerian Islamists located in Sudanese training camps. In 1996, the Libyan leader went so far as to hand over nearly five hundred Islamist fighters to the Algerian authorities.[18] This approach marks a significant shift in Qadhafi's previous strategy of supporting Islamic opponents in neighboring countries as a way by which to gain political leverage in his quest for regional dominance. Thus, his initial support of the Islamic Salvation Front (FIS) in Algeria infuriated authorities there. The same fury was felt in Tunis when the Libyan leader provided financial assistance to the Islamic An-Nahdah Party.[19]

There now seems to be a collective effort on the part of all five AMU members to cooperate closely in America's anti-terrorist strategy in the region without, however, any single country accepting a U.S. military base on its territory or serving as the permanent headquarters for AFRICOM. To be sure, since the terrorist attacks of September 11, 2001, Qadhafi, like his neighbors, has viewed Islamic terrorism as the greatest threat to him, the region, and the world and, as such, has cooperated with North African leaders and the West to combat Islamic insurgents in the Saharan-Sahelian corridor.

The creation of the Arab Maghreb Union, which brought all five Maghrebi countries together for the first time, was intended to serve as the first step in a multi-step process leading to a more consolidated and effective integration in North Africa, which could better and more productively interact with other regional and extra regional actors, especially the European Union. Nearly two decades later, the expectations and hopes of this regional association have failed to materialize, due in great measure to Qadhafi's shifting interest away from the Arab world and toward sub-Saharan Africa. While Qadhafi's intransigence and diplomatic antics have made regional cooperation difficult, North African unity requires that Algeria and Morocco, the Maghreb's two dominant states, make a serious and prolonged commitment to cooperation. Such a commitment seems unlikely, as the ongoing political clash over the fate of the Western Sahara has rendered the "Moroccan-Algerian relationship more fratricidal than fraternal. The perennial rhetoric of fraternity has yet to overcome the enduring issues of geopolitics."[20]

Africa Redux

Qadhafi has alternated between promoting regional schemes to his east with Egypt and the Sudan, with those to his west with Algeria, Morocco, and Tunisia. In both areas, he has failed miserably, leaving behind a residue of mistrust and suspicion. By the mid-1990s, Qadhafi had completely given up on both North Africa and the Middle East as the basis for promoting his pan-Arabist schemes and turned, instead, to sub-Saharan Africa where his interests, efforts, funding, and diplomacy have been particularly active. The transformation of the Organization of African Unity (OAU) into the African Union (AU) was spearheaded by the Libyan leader, as was his so far unsuccessful effort to create a United States of Africa.

The Libyan leader's approach toward African unity mirrors that of his previous unification efforts in the Arab world. This was best reflected in the most recent summit meeting of the African Union that took place in Ghana in June 2007. Rejecting Qadhafi's call for the instant creation of the "United States of Africa" by the majority of the African leaders in attendance, Qadhafi left the conference prematurely, angry and disappointed. As he has done so frequently in the past, the Libyan leader was a polarizing figure, creating divisions and disputes over how best to promote continental unity in the context of an existing nation-state system. For Qadhafi, a United States of Africa is essential to better able to face the world's leading powers and power blocs. "If we have a United States of Africa," the Libyan leader stated, "then Africa can be on an equal footing and negotiate with [those powers]."[21] He also stated that uniting the continent would also staunch the flow of migrants to Europe, an issue of particular concern to the Maghrebi states. A united Africa, he argued, would better exploit its own resources and create jobs to keep young Africans at home. "Either we live in Africa or we die in Africa" was Qadhafi's dramatic summary of his position.

Yet, as so often is the case with the Libyan leader, rhetoric trumps reality. While the deadly flow of flimsy boats crammed with African migrants heading north across the Mediterranean to Europe had slowed substantially in the summer of 2007 compared to previous years (with Spain and Italy reporting drops of a third or more compared to 2006), the role of Libya remains problematic in this process. To be sure, Libya has recently been cooperative in stemming the flow of migrants, possibly because it is working toward a closer relationship with Europe. Yet, the country remains the launching point for many of those heading to Italy. From Rome's perspective, Libya's nondemocratic character makes it a far less reliable partner in preventing the flow of human traffic from Africa than, for example, the more open and quasi-democratic countries of Morocco and Senegal. For his part, Qadhafi has forged informal agreements with Italy to crack down on smugglers and patrol Libya's own borders to keep those fleeing the continent from heading north from its shores.[22] Yet, there are reports from human rights groups, which complain of Libyan harassment, arrest, and arbitrary deportation of migrants, even those fleeing from war zones such as Darfur and Chad. Accounts from recent migrants in Italy, for example, report how harshly Libyan security forces have come down on emigrants, with some feeling that they were being pushed into making the trip across to Italy because they might otherwise have been arrested in Libya and deported. Rather than helping Africa, like his grandiose rhetoric suggests, the Libyan leader imposes harsh policies regulating the flow of Africans within and without the continent. So much for Qadhafi's "live or die in Africa."

Conclusion and Forecast

Today, Qadhafi continues to pursue a carrot and stick foreign policy, with economic assistance, political conciliation, diplomatic mediation, and military assistance serving as incentives, and the use of assassination, sabotage, armed insurrection, military intervention, subversion, violence, and terrorism as punishments. It has been this combination of tactics in quest of some grand design utilized over decades that has made Qadhafi such a capricious figure, one deeply distrusted by his Maghrebi neighbors. Rather than serving to unite the region, as his inflated rhetoric so consistently asserts, Qadhafi's role has been that of destabilizer, a "catalyst of disunity."[23]

Libya's successive integration efforts in the Maghreb reveal one common consequence: "attempts to unite divide."[24] Despite this reality, Qadhafi's impetus to unite remained focused on the Maghreb until the last decade or so, when this effort was refocused to sub-Saharan Africa. From the narrow perspective of the country that, while rich with oil, lacked strategic centrality or geographic importance, the desire to transcend existing, colonially created borders makes sense. In the heyday of Pan-Arabism, for example, Qadhafi believed "that boundaries between any Arab states only [served] the narrow interests of the ruling elites and the imperialist dividers and conquerors."[25] From Qadhafi's revolutionary perspective, "[a]ll such states should therefore unite, to follow the progressive . . . path as Libya."[26] Seeing itself more as a "revolutionary movement" than a "territorial state," Libya has repeatedly interjected itself into the affairs of regional states. Representative examples include Libya's involvement in Tunisia, Chad, Niger, Mali, and the Sudan, among many others.

Yet, as we have seen, virtually every effort along these lines, whether violent or nonviolent, has failed, leaving a trail of bitterness, distrust, and anger that still characterizes Libya's relations with its North African neighbors to the east and west. It is no surprise, therefore, that since the mid-1980s, we have witnessed an "institutionalized stalemate" in North African relations, resulting from "[r]ivalry in the region, competition for the surrounding vacuum, the checkerboard pattern of relations, and the resulting efforts of rivalry to appropriate integration."[27] Given this pattern of "institutionalized instability" characterizing Qadhafi's foreign policy style, no Arab or African leader of any significance has followed Qadhafi's leadership. This has been the case in the past and remains so today. "Qadhafi is a lone rider."[28]

Given the recent reorientation of Libyan foreign policy since late 2003, including its most recent role as the venue for possible peace talks between the Sudanese government and rebel forces in Darfur, is Qadhafi signaling a return to previous patterns of regional interventionism, utilizing diplomacy along with coercion to advance Libyan national interests? Given the country's importance as a significant oil and natural gas producer and exporter at a time of reduced supply and increased demand worldwide, will Tripoli seek to regain its status as an influential regional actor, bridging both sides of the geographical North African divide? In other words, will Qadhafi's current regional focus and priorities in which the Maghreb is last on the foreign policy hierarchy be maintained, completely overturned, or take an altogether new direction? Given the unpredictable character of Qadhafi's past foreign policy behavior, it would be foolhardy to make any kind of accurate prediction. Yet, what is clear, however, is that the states of Algeria, Morocco, and Tunisia will remain forever cautious of the Libyan leader, given the numerous political humiliations and violent encounters they have suffered at his hands. If the Maghreb is to have any kind of political future as a viable and effective regional entity, it will have to await Qadhafi's passing from the Libyan political scene.

Notes

1. A brief portion of this chapter first appeared in "The Unchanging Politics of North Africa," *Middle East Policy* (Winter 2007). I would like to thank Kasiana McLenaghan of Stanford University for her very helpful assistance in the editing and proofreading of this chapter.

2. See Dirk Vandewalle, *Libya Since Independence: Oil and State-Building* (Ithaca, NY: Cornell University Press, 1998), and Dirk Vandewalle, *A History of Modern Libya* (Cambridge: Cambridge University Press, 2006) for full historical and analytical background.

3. See Amal Obeidi, *Political Culture in Libya* (Surrey: Curzon, 2001), 198–215, and Chapter 4 in this book for details.

4. Mansour O. El-Kikhia, *Libya's Qaddafi: The Politics of Contradiction* (Gainseville, FL: University Press of Florida, 1997), 126.

5. Mary-Jane Deeb, *Libya's Foreign Policy in North Africa* (Boulder, CO: Westview Press, 1991), 78.

6. Deeb, 1991, op. cit., 105.

7. Mark Tessler, "Libya in the Maghreb: The Union with Morocco and Related Developments," in *The Green and the Black: Qadhafi's Policies in Africa, ed.* René Lemarchand (Bloomington, IN: Indiana University Press, 1988), 73–74.

8. Ruth First, *Libya: The Elusive Revolution* (London: Penguin Books, 1974), p. 228.

9. *Ibid.*

10. Tessler, 1988, op. cit., 74.

11. *Ibid.*

12. Robert A. Mortimer, "The Arab Maghreb Union: Myth and Reality," in *North Africa in Transition: State, Society, and Economic Transformation in the 1990s,* ed. Yahia H. Zoubir (Gainseville, FL: University Press of Florida, 1999), 177.

13. Mary-Jane Deeb, "Great Socialist People's Libyan Arab Jamahiriya," in *The Government and Politics of the Middle East and North Africa*, 5th ed., ed. David Long, Bernard Reich, and Mark Gasiorowski (Boulder, CO: Westview Press, 2007), 450.

14. Mortimer, 1999, op. cit., 190.

15. See The Economist Intelligence Unit, "Libya Country Report" (July 2007), 12.

16. *Ibid.*

17. *Ibid.*

18. See Yahia Zoubir, "Libye: Islamisme radical et lutte antiterroriste," *Maghreb Machrek* 184 (Summer 2005), 62.

19. See El-Kikhia, 122–23.

20. Mortimer, 1999, op. cit., 190.

21. Reuters, "Libya's Gaddafi Tells Africa to Unite or Die," June 30, 2007.

22. See Ian Fisher, "For African Migrants, Europe Gets Further Awa," *The New York Times*, August 26, 2007.

23. I. William Zartman and A. G. Kluge, "Heroic Politics: The Foreign Policy of Libya," in *The Foreign Policies of Arab States*, ed. Bahgat Korany and Ali E. Hillal Dessouki (Boulder, CO: Westview, 1984), 191.

24. William I. Zartman, "Foreign Relations of North Africa," *The Annals* 489 (January 1987), 18.

25. Ibid.

26. *Ibid.*

27. *Ibid.*, 21.

28. *Ibid.*, 25.

8

Prodigal or Pariah?
Foreign Policy in Libya

George Joffé

The foreign policy of a state is conventionally considered to be the sum of the external actions carried out by the state as a unitary actor within the sphere of international relations.[1] In fact, the term often has a more purposive quality about it, in that the actions are designed or intended to produce outcomes that are to the advantage of the primary actor, the state, as is implied in a dictionary definition of the term "policy."[2] Conventionally, too, such actions are seen as directed primarily toward ensuring the security of a state in terms of its external relations.

There are, however, many subsidiary aims as well, some of which can, on occasion, supervene over the straightforward concern of "security."[3] One such alternative may involve the external projection of the dominant ideological preconceptions that inform the domestic structure and dynamism of the state in question—a kind of political discourse that also affects, or even determines, the nature of relations with other states or their populations. That, in turn, may raise the question of the origin of such a discourse, in that it may reflect far more the concerns of individuals or individual interests within the state, rather than the interests of the state itself as a cohesive and coherent entity.

The Policy Process in Libya

Such theoretical speculations are highly relevant to any discussion of the foreign policy of a state such as Libya, given the nature of the Libyan state and its decision-making processes. The problem is that the general trends in Libyan foreign policy—in the wake of the Great September Revolution on September 1, 1969, in which opportunist pragmatism gave way to an ideological worldview in the 1970s and early 1980s—underwent a complete reversal at the end of that decade. Thus, throughout the 1990s, Libya sought to demonstrate that its ideological commitments were nothing more than rhetoric, and that an increasing pragmatism reflected the real core of the country's foreign policy aims, particularly with respect to the United States and Europe.

Furthermore, this reversal has been achieved with no evident internal dissent or challenge, nor has the core personnel of the regime itself been adversely affected by it. Most strikingly, this transformation seems to have been accepted by those states with which Libya has to interact virtually without demur. Despite the widespread condemnation of Libya as a "pariah" or "rogue" state in the past, it has now been able to rejoin the international community with little evident compromise in its perceived interests or its ideological preconceptions, as well as its policy-making institutions or the personnel which manipulate them—the prodigal returned, in short!

The fact that this has been possible may say as much about Libyan pragmatism and opportunism, as well as about its policy-making process, as it does about Libya's interlocutors. In view of Western attitudes, in particular, toward other states identified as "pariahs," "rogues," or part of the "axis of evil"—Iraq, Cuba, Syria, North Korea, and Iran come to mind—such indulgence of Libya seems surprising and must raise questions as to why this has been the case. It is not just a question of Libya's willingness to adapt to international norms or to recognize its responsibilities. Nor is it solely a question of its natural resources in oil and gas, although both concerns must play their part. It seems, instead, to reflect Libya's potential geopolitical role within the collective policy assumptions of European states and the United States, a role that also reflects its own security interests and aspirations.

Interests

Indeed, the perceived security interests of the Libyan state have to form the background to any discussion of its detailed foreign policy, as is generally true of states in the modern world. In the case of Libya where, as we shall see, ideology has often played a predominant role in the articulation of foreign policy over the short-to-medium term, the long-term—permanent—security interests of the state often explain the opportunistic way in which such ideological concerns have been brushed aside. In many respects, in fact, Libya is the exemplar of Lord Palmerston's famous dictum: "Nations have no permanent friends or allies, only permanent interests."[4] The problem has been, perhaps, that it has taken most of the thirty-seven years since the Great September Revolution for its political elite to realize this.

Perhaps the dominating consideration for Libya is that, despite its massive geographic extent, it is a weak state with a small population. Indeed, the modern state did not exist as such until it was created as a colony by Italy after 1911. Before then, despite the attempts by the Qaramanlis to create an integrated coastal state based on corsairing,[5] Libya really consisted of three virtually separate units, which either sought independent existence or resonated to the imperatives of their neighbors. Thus, Egypt tended to be the dominant influence in Cyrenaica, and the Tunisian Beylik could influence events in Tripolitania, whilst the Fezzan depended on trans-Saharan trade and its relationship with nomadic Saharan populations and with the statelets of the Sahel. By the nineteenth century and the Second Ottoman Occupation, even the control of the coastal state was contested between the Ottomans and the Sanusi Order,[6] whilst the tribes maintained a largely independent existence from both. Foreign policy, such as it was, could reflect the interests of any one of these groups, and its articulation was localized, particularly as colonialism began to spread throughout the continent.

During the Italian occupation, of course, foreign policy was an irrelevance, nor was a proper unitary base constructed for an independent state. Even independence was fraught with difficulty as the Soviet Union claimed a protectorate over the former Italian colony and Italy, with British support, proposed to renew its presence there.[7] The independent state was so potentially fractious that a federal state seemed the only viable outcome. Even then, it was dominated by Cyrenaica and its Sanusi legacy, much to the irritation of the other two regions, especially Tripolitania. Not surprisingly, it was these tensions, combined with the corrosive effects of Arab nationalism on traditional loyalties that were to usher in the revolution in 1969.

The revolution did not alter these underlying realities, however, although it may have reversed them in order of importance within the state, even though its leaders believed that they could redefine the interests of the state. Ironically enough, the source of the ideology that first inspired them, Egypt, continued to be a permanent latent threat to the new radical state and, once President Nasser had died in 1970, the policies of his successor, Anwar Sadat, made this clear, culminating as they did in the short border war in July 1977. The Qadhafi regime seems to have realized the danger it faced, despite its rhetoric, and had formed a defense pact with Algeria—the Hassi Messaoud Treaty—in 1975.

It was Algeria that was to guarantee Libyan independence by warning Egypt not to invade two years later.[8] It has been Algeria ever since that has acted as the guarantor and mentor of the Libyan state, even when their mutual policies diverged, as over the Polisario Front in the Western Sahara, for instance, where, in the 1980s, Libyan abandoned support for the Sahrawi project of the Arab Saharan Democratic Republic on the grounds that it would "balkanise" North Africa. It was Algeria that, in 1985, warned Libya off from a war with Tunisia over issues of inward migration and longstanding differences over regional and unification policy.

In 1983, Algeria barred Libya from joining its Treaty of Concord and Fraternity with surrounding states, which was to be the first stage in an Algerian initiative for political unity within the Maghrib. The reason was that Libya would not resolve its border differences with Algeria to the latter's satisfaction. Libya allowed itself to be courted by Morocco—despite the profound ideological differences between Tripoli and Rabat—into the rival Arab-African Union, but this only lasted for two years before security imperatives reasserted themselves in the run-up to its war against Chad. And it was Algeria, with Moroccan support, which persuaded Libya to take its border dispute with Chad to the International Court of Justice after its army was defeated there in 1987.

Even today, the Algerian connection is very important and when, in June 2006, Libya irritated Algeria with a proposal for a "Greater Saharan Federation," stretching from Iraq to Mauritania, in which local populations would be the operative actors, the proposal was quickly dropped. This has not been untypical of the relationship between the two countries in the recent past, with Algeria increasingly frustrating Libyan initiatives, especially in the Sahara and the Sahel, but with the two states maintaining a wary cooperation in which Libya is the junior partner. One good example of this has been the Arab Maghreb Union (AMU), the proposed federation for the states of Libya, Tunisia, Algeria, Morocco, and Mauritania, signed in Marrakesh in 1989, but which has been virtually moribund since 1991 (see Chapter 7). It can only really be revived if Libya and Algeria agree, but, so far, neither wishes this to occur, Libya because it has other alternatives and knows that it could not dominate the organization, and Algeria because of its ongoing dispute with Morocco over the Western Sahara issue.

Border security has been the second great enduring interest for Libyan foreign policy makers after finding a state to guarantee its survival against its massive neighbor, Egypt. Associated with this has been a longstanding Libyan desire to secure the Sahara, for this is, in effect, Libya's "soft underbelly."[9] This has proved to be more important for Libya than satisfying its ideological ambitions linked to the principles of the replication of the *jamahiri* model or the achievement of political integration. It has tried to achieve this objective by creating a Saharan federation under its control. This took place initially to regional alarm but, in the late 1990s with the reluctant acquiescence of surrounding states, in the CEN-SAD community.[10]

The issue of boundary delimitation also demonstrated a degree of flexibility in securing essential interests, for Libya initially tried to achieve this through military force, combined with ideological principle, in both invading Northern Chad and in trying to force the Chadian government into a binding political relationship. Both initiatives failed, involving Libya in a major military defeat in 1987.[11] Interestingly enough, Libya then sought to ensure this key interest of the state, neither through force nor through ideological pressure, but through recourse to international arbitration. The Libyan state, in other words, recognizes the role of international law and the global commons in ensuring its security interests.[12]

This is important for the third of its basic security interests, that of energy security. Here, Libya, unlike most states which must ensure that they have untrammeled access to energy supplies, is more concerned about its access to oil services and to the international oil market, for, without this, it cannot gain the economic rent[13] on which its economy, society, and polity depend. In fact, in this respect, it shared a parallel interest with energy consumers, particularly in Europe, although American international oil companies supplied the technology. There was also an important, if unspoken, ideological dimension to this concern, in that Libya's political radicalism depended on its ability to finance the ideological experiment through its abundant oil revenues and the rent that it accrued. As Dirk Vandewalle aptly points out, *tharwa* (wealth and patrimonialism) has rendered *thawra* (revolution and radicalism) possible.[14]

The interesting aspect of this relationship is that, until 1986, Libya's ideological prejudices that played such a large part in its foreign policy did not damage these underlying commercial relationships. Even when, in 1986, the Reagan administration completed its comprehensive sanctions regime, American oil companies were reluctant to leave, and Libya made every effort to entice them back in succeeding years. European companies and states, whilst recognizing the idiosyncratic extremism of the Libyan state, were far too attached to Libyan oil to impose parallel sanctions. When they eventually did so in 1992, by joining in a United Nations sanctions regime because of alleged Libyan responsibility for the Lockerbie disaster in December 1988, they ensured that Libyan oil exports were not affected, thus betraying the shared common interest which tended to neutralize the effect of sanctions, despite Libyan claims of the damage caused.

Ideology

To a considerable extent, however, it has not been underlying security interests that have molded the foreign policy of the *jamahiriyya*. Certainly, in the early days, ideological concepts dominated the policy arena—first, Arab nationalism, and then, after 1976, the Third Universal Theory, the alternative to capitalism and communism as articulated in the *Green Book* and in Colonel Mu'ammar Qadhafi's dicta.[15] It is worth noting, in passing, that the ideology of the Libyan state is, officially, very much the personal creation of its leader, Qadhafi, a feature that will have profound implications for the way in which policy is formulated and articulated in Libya.

Formally, this is a function of both the peculiar ideology and the nature of the Libyan state, and of the decision-making processes and structures inherent in it, whether in the foreign or domestic fields. Libya defines itself as a *"jamahiriyya,"* a "state of the masses" in which the "authority of the people" is the sole source of sovereignty and decision-making through "direct democracy"[16] in a "stateless state." Thus, as will be discussed in subsequent paragraphs, policy formulation and articulation is formally the prerogative of the authority of the people, which is seen as a unified general will, parallel to that described by Rousseau in discussing the principles that should inform European society.[17] In fact, neither the parallel nor the practice is appropriate, as the inspiration for Qadhafi's ideology is rooted in his own personal, religious, and social experience.[18]

In essence, the ideological principles underlying Libyan foreign policy were originally two. First, after the revolution, Libya was conceived as an Arab nationalist state, following the principles of Nasirism, for the Libyan leader had been a very early convert to its principles, even when he was at school in Sabha. Secondly, and almost as a corollary of this, revolutionary Libya was to be a nonaligned and anti-imperialist state. These principles, in themselves, were unexceptional and brought much support to the new revolutionary state, not least because they fitted with the temper of the times. Most people in the Arab world wanted political unity. Most radical governments sought to be anti-imperialist and non-aligned, in a world where colonialism was at its last gasp, and "alignment" would have meant engagement in the Cold War alongside the United States.

When the cultural revolution in 1973 ushered the second stage of Qadhafi's ideological development, both principles were universalized and altered. Thus, in place of being primarily concerned with Arab nationalism and the vision of bringing the Arab world into a single political unit—something tried with singular lack of success between Syria and Egypt in 1958—Libya began to argue for political unity alone, primarily between Muslim peoples. This was a formulation that led to the second change, namely that the Libyan political system should be replicated, and that anti-imperialism should be an active response to the wider, Western-dominated world. Thus, whereas the early 1970s were punctuated by repeated Libyan attempts to achieve political unity with Egypt, Sudan, Syria, and even Tunisia, on the basis of Arab nationalism, by the latter part of the decade, Libya was seeking to link with Chad and to introduce the *jamahiri* system there.[19]

Of course, at root, these attempts at political mergers reflected Libya's acute sense of its weakness and potential isolation and were thus, it could be argued, merely manifestations of state interest. However, the ideological component of the process cannot be underestimated, for the Libyan leadership certainly saw them, initially, as mechanisms for expressing its conviction in Arab nationalism and the political unity of the Arab nation—feelings that were often shared by Libya's proposed political partners. Later on, they were also vehicles for the export of the political ideology that Libya had developed in the Third Universal Theory and, as such, were increasingly unattractive to Libya's potential partners, and a major reason for the failures of the initiatives themselves.[20]

Allied to this was a growing sense of a much more radical ideological commitment that arose from two concerns—Libya's commitment to Arab theses on the Arab-Israeli dispute and its vision of Islam as an active vehicle for social and political justice, and as the mobilizing principle of the anti-imperialist struggle. This led, in the early years of the revolution, to open and active support for the Palestinian movements, expressed, for instance, in Libya's campaign in Africa at the start of the 1970s to persuade African states to break their links with Israel.[21] In Africa itself, Libya became increasingly seen as a threat, both because of its allies, such as Idi Amin's Uganda and, later, Charles Taylor in Liberia or Robert Mugabe's Zimbabwe, and because of its constant attempts to undermine regimes to which it took an ideological dislike.[22]

Libya also became increasingly critical of the League of Arab States because of the role played by moderate Arab states within it, which it saw as neocolonialist. It also led to active engagement in specific Palestinian movements and to growing antagonism toward Yasir Arafat and the moderate line increasingly adopted by the Palestine Liberation Organization after 1974. Nor was the antagonism limited to the moderate Palestinians: Arab states began to look increasingly askance at Libya for its radicalism and the threat that it began to offer to the stability of states to which it was opposed in the Arab world, as well.

Tensions with Egypt rose dramatically after Sadat's dramatic dash to Jerusalem in 1977 and the subsequent Camp David Accord and the peace agreement Cairo made with the Israeli state in 1980. Saudi Arabia both disliked Libyan radicalism and its religious heterodoxy, and Jordan feared the implications of Libya's association with Palestinian radicals. Lebanon's Shi'a community could not forgive the disappearance of its leader, Imam Musa Sadr, in 1978 while on a visit to Libya. Its Christians resented Libyan support for Sunni Muslims in the civil war and for the Palestinian radicals. Sudan maintained an ambivalent relationship, even after the Ould Bashir regime came to power and only Syria seemed to be a constant friend, while revolutionary Iran, after 1980, spurned Libyan attempts at alliance.

Amongst non-state actors, Libya became associated with Abu Nidal's *Fatah Revolutionary Council* and with the *Popular Front for the Liberation of Palestine-General Command*.[23] Both groups, together with other, smaller radical Palestinian groups, and many African revolutionary groups as well, found sanctuary and support in Libya. Nor was such support passive, and, during the 1980s in particular, Libya became increasingly associated with violence and terrorism in Europe and the Middle East. In part, this was linked to the regime's anti-imperialist radicalism, but it was also linked to its internal tensions and to the role of the Revolutionary Committee Movement (*Harakat al-Lajnati ath-Thawra*) as the guardian of the Libyan revolution after 1980.[24] Thus, at the start of the 1980s, Libyan dissidents in exile in Britain, Austria, Italy, and the United States faced hostility, harassment, and even assassination.

This approach culminated with the breach in diplomatic relations with Britain in 1984, in the wake of the killing of a policewoman in front of the Libyan embassy in London. Relations with the United States had been suspended four years earlier after a mob in Tripoli destroyed the embassy there. Up to then, the idiosyncrasies and intensifying extremism of the revolutionary regime in Tripoli had been overlooked by Washington and London, despite their growing irritation about Libyan involvement in revolutionary terrorism. Although Tripoli had been at the forefront of the move by producers to push up oil prices at the start of the 1970s, it had not followed other OPEC states in taking over foreign concessions in their entirety and was thus seen to act as a stabilizing force in world oil markets.[25]

These developments in relations between Libya and the Anglo-Saxon world in the first half of the 1980s were to mark, by the end of a decade, a dramatic decline in the role of ideology within Libyan foreign policy and its replacement by an opportunist pragmatism that reflected the inevitable primacy of state interest over ideological preference. What was surprising in the Libyan case was the ability of the regime to carry out such a transformation with little apparent internal dissention, and without major changes in domestic policy where, given the advantage of oil rent, few concessions were made to popular irritation over regime policy. The transition period, was, however, to be lengthy, delayed as it was by what appears to have been a petulant last gust of ideological violence, and that was, ironically enough, to condition the structure of foreign policy thereafter.

The surprising cohesiveness of the decision-making process in Libya reflects, of course, the political institutions inside Libya, a result both of its ideological preconceptions and of the nature of the control of power within the *jamahiriyya*. It is therefore essential to consider how foreign policy, indeed all policy, in Libya is formulated and enacted, if the real nature of the country's foreign policy is to be understood. Then there remains a final irony—the fact that the transformation of Libyan foreign policy into opportunistic pragmatism reflecting underlying interests was eventually to be matched by an equally surprising willingness to accept the changes in Libya's international behavior on the part of its interlocutors, Britain and the United States, given their lengthy skepticism about the Libyan regime.

Institutions

The apparent contradiction between opportunistic pragmatism and ideological coherence, which has so marked Libya's foreign policy in the last twenty years, can be resolved once the way in which foreign policy is generated is clarified. In theory, power in Libya is expressed through the obligatory participation of the Libyan population in a series of basic popular congresses, each paralleled by a Popular Committee to handle administrative matters, in which all matters of policy (local, national, and international) are discussed, with the officers of each congress being mandated to represent the congress at regional- and national-level congresses. The regional congresses each have their associated popular committee for administrative purposes, one in each of the *sha'abiyah* or provinces.

The most senior congress is the national-level General People's Congress, which normally meets twice yearly, and which is responsible for appointing the General People's Committee—the government. The Committee, through a series of secretariats (ministries), communicates with local Popular Committees, appointed by the basic people's congresses, which handle local day-to-day administration. Thus, power and decision-making circulate upward, whilst administrative responsibility is delegated downward. In foreign policy terms, therefore, formulation and choice theoretically rests within the congress system, and the foreign affairs secretariat is merely an administrative tool in which diplomatic professionalism is an irrelevance.

This was, perhaps, most acutely demonstrated in the 1970s, when Libya's professional diplomatic corps was subordinated to a new mobilizing organization, the Revolutionary Committee Movement (*Harakat al-Lijnah al-Thawra*), as embassies around the world were transformed into "People's Bureaux." Professional diplomats were subordinated to radicals who introduced the same revolutionary attitudes to the practice of international diplomacy, as had been introduced into government in Libya itself. The Revolutionary Committee Movement was a consequence of the realities of the *jamahiri* system, although not anticipated in its founding document, the *Green Book*. It arose because, in reality, Libyans had little interest in the complex and burdensome political system that the *jamahiriyya*—in which Qadhafi has no formal role, except as "Leader of the Revolution"—turned out to be in practice.

Unlike more conventional political systems, there is no interplay between different institutions of the state so that varying views can be fed into the policy-making process. Instead, the collective views they would have represented have been either marginalized or absorbed into the unitary structure of the *jamahiriyya*. Since political parties are banned on the grounds that they are divisive within the context of the People's Authority (Law No. 71 of 1972,[26] which bans all political movements outside the then authorized Arab Socialist Union, which itself was subsequently disbanded in 1977 and absorbed into the General People's Congress), there is, in effect, no right of freedom of association or of expression. Even the normal formal independence of Islamic institutions ended in 1978 when the Qadhafi regime took over religious properties and imposed its own vision of what a state based on Islamic law should be upon the traditional religious authorities.

Inevitably, in keeping with its revolutionary traditions, and because of popular apathy to this integrated unitary political process, in 1977, Qadhafi had to organize the Revolutionary Committee Movement, which he controls directly, to reactivate the formal political process. The movement has close contacts with the security services, and has arrogated to itself authority for "revolutionary justice"—in other words, direct, uncontrolled persecution of perceived opponents to the regime. It is extralegal and is currently headed by Ahmed Ibrahim, the deputy speaker of the General People's Congress and a kinsman of the Libyan leader. This highlights another aspect of political power in Libya—the fact that it is buttressed by the tribes from whom leading members of the regime come, in a complex neo-patrimonial system[27] dominated by Qadhafi, who acts as a charismatic leader.[28] In other words, strategic power in Libya is intensely personalized around the person of the *Qa'id*, who can use the Revolutionary Committee Movement to impose his will on a government in which he has no formal role.[29]

Indeed, the Revolutionary Committee Movement is not quite what it appears to be—a radical, ideologically motivated political movement. Although it is motivated by the ideological imperatives of the Libyan revolution, its internal cohesion is also a reflection of the dominant social elements that form it. These are drawn from the tribes most closely associated with the leadership—the Qadhadhfa, the Warfalla, and the Maghraha. These tribes also play key roles in the security services, and their senior figures are drawn from them. The tribes involved, too, have a political significance, for they form part of the *marabtin* tribes, traditionally subordinate to, and dependent on, the *S'adi* tribes of Cyrenaica, on whom the Sanusi Order and, subsequently, the monarchy depended for their success.

The Libyan revolution in 1969, therefore, involved not only an ideological reformulation of the objectives of the Libyan state—it also involved a reversal of a traditional social order on which political institutions and political culture had been based. In other words, the underlying fabric of the Libyan state remains, but has been inverted, whilst the institutions and personnel have changed, as has its ideological formulation. The new institutions, despite their populist and egalitarian appearance, are thus neo-patrimonial in nature and actually provide a far more efficient mechanism for centralized control, being increasingly dependent on a charismatic leader who also legitimates the ideology, despite his lack of a formal role.

This also suggests that ideology will bear a partial cast that may well reflect the sociopolitical inversion achieved by the revolution, and integrate potential irrationalism into the decision-making process.[30] In such circumstances, it is clear that foreign policy in Libya owes its inspiration to the Guardian of the Revolution, Mu'ammar Qadhafi, and, given his highly effective control over the instruments of the Libyan stateless state, he is able to execute radical alterations, even reversals, of Libyan foreign policy without exciting resistance within its institutions. Thus, the Libyan reaction to hardening American attitudes throughout the 1980s, as opportunist pragmatism replaced ideological conviction, reflected the colonel's adjustment to new international realities, especially after the bombing of Tripoli and Benghazi in April 1986.

The Key Relationship

The change in attitude in Washington at the start of the 1980s had also coincided with the advent of the Reagan administration to power, and the emergence of a very different doctrine concerning relations in the Middle East and elsewhere. Now, affronts to the United States would be addressed by direct reaction and, over the next six years, relations steadily declined as the United States increasingly overtly opposed Libya—over the Gulf of Sirt closure to international shipping, over support for the government in Grenada, over its attempts to influence American policy, and, most particularly, over its open political and material support for terrorism.[31] There was also the question of Soviet support for the revolutionary regime in Libya from 1973 onward, particularly in the wake of Soviet expulsion from Egypt, although this waned tsoward the end of the Cold War.

Ultimately, the crisis resulted in "Operation El Dorado Canyon," the bombing of Tripoli and Benghazi in April 1986 after a bomb attributed to Libyan agents exploded in a Berlin nightclub frequented by American service personnel.[32] For the next twenty years, Libya was treated as a pariah by the United States, especially after American oil companies operating there were forced to leave by presidential fiat in June 1987. The United States actively pursued the destruction of the regime, supporting France in its interventions in Chad and indirectly contributing to Libya's humiliation there in 1987. It also saved Libyan dissidents in N'Jamena when the Habré government was forced from power there by the pro-Libyan Idriss Déby in December 1990.

In the wake of the bombings, Qadhafi and the Libyan regime seem to have come to the conclusion that it could no longer ignore the reality of American power, nor could it afford to tweak the American nose with its policies of support for international anti-imperialism and terrorism, whether merely verbal, as it claimed, or material, as the West, with reason, believed. The point was reinforced by Libya's humiliating defeat in 1987, in its war in Chad against a government buttressed with direct French and indirect American support. In fact, this change of heart reflects a very important aspect of Libya's foreign policy process, namely that—at moments of real crisis—opportunistic pragmatism over Libya's underlying national interest will supervene over issues of ideological coherence and radicalism.

This transformation in attitudes and foreign policy drivers was not immediate, but seems to have developed over a period of years in the wake of the American raids. It may well have been sparked off in 1987 by the Libyan leader's realization of regime's unpopularity, particularly in

Cyrenaica, where he spent many months, in the aftermath of the raids, rebuilding regime alliances with the influential *S'adi* tribes. Then there was the evidence from Chad, where Libya had to eventually abandon its ambitions to annex the Aouzou Strip in the face of international pressure. Even though Libya was able to place its own protégé in charge of the country in December 1990, it had to face the fact that the Habré regime had been able to assemble, with American and French help, a substantial force of dissident Libyans, designed to foment unrest inside Libya itself, as well as to guarantee international support against the Libyan regime.

Over the next few years, Libya engaged in what British diplomats, with increasing alarm, described as a successful "charm offensive," persuading European governments to reinforce their diplomatic links and their involvement in Libyan oil. Nor was there much doubt about Qadhafi's own conversion to moderation and cooperation, rather than radicalism and confrontation, even if for only tactical and pragmatic purposes. He seemed to have appreciated that the asymmetry of power between Libya and Western states, particularly the United States, predicated a different approach to international affairs. In the early 1990s, he remarked that he wanted to see Libya as the "Kuwait of the Mediterranean," by which he seems to have meant a state based on political moderation and participation, as well as economic well-being within the global community

The real target, however, of this Libyan maneuver on the diplomatic scene, was the restoration of diplomatic links with both Britain and the United States. America had suspended relations in 1980 as a result of Libyan support for the new Islamic regime in Teheran, and the sacking of the American embassy in Tripoli. Britain had angrily severed all contacts in 1984—a breach which was embarrassing, especially as Britain had become an important holiday and medical center for Libya. The rupture with the United States was far more serious because it had immediate economic implications, for the Reagan administration had imposed unilateral sanctions on the export of Libyan oil to the United States, the operations of American oil companies in Libya, and the supply of all except humanitarian goods to Libya, thus interdicting the supply of American oil field equipment on which the Libyan oil industry was based. Travel to Libya was also banned, and Libyan access to the United States was made very difficult, indeed. These were not the first American sanctions against Libya—those had begun in the 1970s under the Carter administration. They were, however, the most severe, and reinforced the point that Libya was in no position to seriously challenge American power.

Libyan hopes of achieving a rapid solution to its diplomatic problems with major Western states received a massive setback in 1991, when it was accused of responsibility for the destruction of Pan Am Flight 103 over Lockerbie in December 1988, and of a French UTA airliner over Niger in September 1989.[33] The following year, United Nations sanctions killed off any chance of a rapid change in the diplomatic scene and, four years later, in 1996, Congress passed the Iran-Libya Sanctions Act, thus reinforcing the unilateral American sanctions regime. It was only after Britain—in the wake of the arrival of New Labour and the Blair government to power in May 1997—decided to find a way of resolving the Lockerbie crisis that new opportunities emerged. The suspension of United Nations sanctions in April 1999, once the two Lockerbie suspects had been handed over for trial, provided Libya with its first real chance of ending its isolation, as far as Europe and America were concerned.

The lengthy period of gestation of this policy—some seventeen years—should not be surprising, nor should the occasional self-destructive ambiguities of Libyan policy makers, for this is inherent in the process of Libyan foreign policy.[34] It is quite possible for there to have been a coherent project of renewal and reentry into the global system, alongside the continuation of anti-Western radicalism that produced the contradictions and tragedies of Lockerbie and the UTA bombing. Indeed, the inherent opportunism of Libyan foreign policy, reflected in Qadhafi's own attitudes of truculent independence would have encouraged precisely this kind of ambiguity: with Libya seeking vengeance for Western rejection if it believed its involvement could be concealed, alongside public statements seeking a diametrically-opposed rapprochement. In addition, the lack of coherence inherent in personalized, charismatic political systems of the kind typified by Libya can easily result in the bureaucracy misinterpreting leadership objectives, especially if there had been recent radical reorientations of policy.[35]

Whatever the reason, the fact is that, in the wake of the trials of the two persons accused of responsibility for the Lockerbie affair at Kamp Zeist in The Netherlands, Libya was able to negotiate compensation agreements with the families of the victims of the crash, and to find a form of words admitting formal responsibility for the incident to appease the United States. As a result, in September 2003, United Nations sanctions were formally removed and, over the next year, remaining American objections to Libyan behavior were resolved, not least the question of Libya's weapons of mass destruction programs, which were ended in December 2003. Limited diplomatic relations with the United States began in February 2004, and, during 2004 and 2005, commercial relations did, too, with American oil companies returning to the country. Finally, on May 15, 2006, Libya was removed from the United States Department of State's state terrorism list, with the promise of full diplomatic relations to follow, despite a Saudi allegation in early 2004 of a Libyan plot to assassinate the Saudi ruler, King Abdullah.

What was surprising was that all these developments occurred with no fundamental change in the ideology or the domestic behavior of the Libyan state—or, indeed, its behavior in foreign affairs in view of the Saudi allegations—at a time when the United States and its allies had proclaimed that democracy, not stability, was the object of its policies in the Middle East and North Africa. At least as surprising has been the enthusiasm with which renewed relations have been received in Washington and London. The British case is, perhaps, easier to appreciate, for the Blair government has been increasingly desperate to point to some success from its Middle Eastern policies in recent years, and it was, after all, the government that had broken the deadlock in 1999, which, in turn, led to the end of the United Nations sanctions regime. There is also evidence that Britain wanted to rebuild its position in Europe, and saw Libya's return to the international community as a means by which it could demonstrate to its partners its influence in a region of vital importance to Europe, particularly over questions of energy supply.[36] And, of course, there were specific British interests over access to commercial opportunities in the oil sector—generally seen as the most attractive prospect for oil and gas production worldwide—and in the refurbishment of Libya's decaying infrastructure.

The spread of the change in American attitudes was far more striking, for Libya had long been held to be the archetype of a rogue state. American statesmen had long called for an end to the Qadhafi regime. Yet now, that regime, having modified only its foreign policy, was welcomed back into the international community by the Bush administration, which has been implacable in its hostility to states engaged in support for, or activities connected to, terrorism! No doubt the administration had felt under considerable pressure from commercial and industrial lobbies, such as USA Engage, which have long demanded an end to the use of sanctions as a policy that disadvantages American commercial interests abroad. There is also the well-known link between the administration and "Big Oil" —American's powerful oil sector that saw itself being shut out from the rush for new concessions in the wake of the suspension of United Nations sanctions.[37] Yet, these pressures had been resisted for the first three years of its period in office with little difficulty. The decision, in early 2004, to begin to dismantle the unilateral sanctions regime, seems, however, to have been spurred by a quite different dynamic—the sudden enthusiasm from Congress to speed an improvement in diplomatic relations.

This was particularly surprising, for Congress had been united in its hostility to Libya ever since it had passed the Iran-Libya Sanctions Act, to the dismay of the Clinton administration, in 1996. There had, however, been signs of Congressional concern over the implications of the continued sanctions regime in 2002, when news emerged of European pressure on Libya to revoke the concessions held in trust for American companies, which, in any case, would end in 2005. The turning point, however, seems to have been a Congressional visit to Libya in early 2004, with a delegation including the influential Californian congressman, Tom Lantos. The delegation returned impressed and ready to welcome a fundamental change in relations. Those relationships between Congress and Libya have been maintained ever since, and have done much to promote renewed relations. The consequent change in Congressional attitudes seems to have provided the Bush administration with the domestic consensus it required for a change in foreign policy that it may have long contemplated.

There is no doubt that Libya had concluded long ago that irritating the United States was not a viable policy option, and now its interests in engaging the international community for the sake of the rent it generates, together with Western interest in those assets, go a long way toward explaining the dramatic changes in relations in recent years. Yet, this cannot be the entire picture: no doubt the Bush administration, like the Blair government, is very anxious for evidence that its uniquely confrontational policies have generated palpable successes—and Libya did pay compensation, did renounce terrorism, and did give up its weapons of mass destruction programs. Yet, if, indeed, the reasons are based on economic interest and strategic success, it is still surprising how willing Western allies have been to abandon any demands for domestic, even regime, change. Perhaps there, Libya's geopolitical position in the Mediterranean alongside Algeria—another surprising new ally of the United States—and its commitment to the "war on terror" may have done much to render the unpalatable palatable!

Will that, then, be an end to twenty-six years of mutual irritation and misunderstanding? Well, yes and no. Were the Qadhafi regime to undergo the complete reformation at which it has hinted, with an end to its idiosyncratic and discriminatory "state of the masses," and a profound reform of its state-centered economy, the answer would, no doubt, be in the affirmative. Qadhafi, however, has shown his tenacity in the past, and is hardly likely to retire into obscurity or abandon his political vision. Nor is the regime, despite pressure for reform, necessarily about to become a shining beacon of democracy, accountability, and the rule of law in the Middle East and North Africa. The real question is whether sufficient change will occur for Washington and its allies in Europe to be able to tolerate a regime that both have disliked for many years for the sake of access to its irresistible assets in oil and gas!

Drivers of Foreign Policy in Libya

What does this, then, tell us about the foreign policy process in Libya? In view of what appears to have been a substantial spectrum of diplomatic failure up to the end of the 1980s, which was overshadowed by the catastrophe of the Lockerbie affair in the 1990s, it is worth asking the question why Libya should have engaged in such policies, and how it failed so spectacularly to achieve its objectives. A conventional neo-realist response would be to suggest that Libya's regional diplomacy is conditioned solely by its perceptions of security threats from within the region, and that its failures arise from the ideological preconceptions that were allowed to shroud these underlying realities. This, of course must be true, as the events of July 1977 involving Egypt demonstrate. The same could be said of the lengthy denouement with Britain and the United States.

It is not, however, the whole story, for, as we have seen, contemporary Libya is also a radical state in which the radicalism had not just been rhetorical in character and this, too, is reflected in its foreign policy decisions. Ideology can then supervene over perceived state interest or, as with the United States in recent years, the reverse can also be true. Yet, in reality, much of the pattern of events described above also demonstrates a significant degree of opportunism that seems to inform many Libyan diplomatic decisions, often as a result of the personalized policy process, which relies so heavily on Qadhafi himself. This opportunism, perhaps better construed as diplomatic flexibility, has been seized upon by some commentators as an explanation of the decision-making process in Tripoli. Thus, Zartman and Kluge conclude that "Libya's foreign policy is a policy of opportunity, conducted on the basis of rather constant principles."[38]

The ideological dimension of Libyan foreign policy has been incorporated by Mary-Jane Deeb in her discussion of Libyan policy in Africa. She describes Libyan foreign policy as a pyramid with the neighboring states of North Africa and the Sahel at the peak, the Arab world dominated by the Mashriq next, followed by the Islamic world overall, then the developing world and, as a substratum at the base, the industrialized countries of both the East and West. She adds that the more remote an issue has been from Libya's core interests, which are security-led in nature and dominated by North Africa, the more ideologically motivated policy will be. With respect to the role of Libyan pragmatism in foreign policy, she points to Zartman and Kluge's conclusions.[39]

For Ronald Bruce St John, Libyan foreign policy under Qadhafi has been ideologically-driven and aggressive, although it drew on the principles established for Libya's foreign relations by his monarchical predecessor, making use of a strategic constancy and a tactical flexibility, based on Arab unity and anti-imperialism, although quite prepared to exploit Western technological superiority.[40] It is a view that coincides with that of Zartman and Kluge and, given the innate pragmatism that Mary-Jane Deeb would argue, characterizes Libya's policy toward its closer neighbors, provides us with an explanation of the twists and turns of Libyan policy in the period from 1970 until the end of the 1980s, until the current practice of opportunist pragmatism asserted itself as a result of Western—primarily, American—hostility.

Yet, it is not a complete explanation, for many of the decisions that were made were to lead to Libya's discomfiture and to outcomes that were to its detriment after its early successes in the region. The main reason for this seems to have been that Libya did not preserve its pragmatic approach, but repeatedly allowed its ideological preconceptions to interfere. There appears, in short, to be a dialectic between pragmatism and ideology that undermines the neat patterns suggested above as mechanisms to explain Libya's policy choices. This, therefore, is an indication that other factors must also influence the way in which options are selected. The key to this, as described above, is the way in which in Libya, a supposedly stateless state, the attitudes, interests, and convictions of Qadhafi, its "Leader," albeit without any formal role within the state, are determinant in the policy-making process.

Indeed, it is in the intense personalization of the policy process that the answer to the conundrum of Libyan foreign policy lies, for it is here that the balance between pragmatism and ideology is struck, and where the less rational aspects of Libya's ideology can be manifested. As Mary-Jane Deeb points out, Qadhafi's regime never achieved the legitimacy of the Sanusi-based monarchy it had replaced because of its basis in the Sirtica tribes and the security services. It, therefore, has constantly been aware of its own perceptions of weakness, both internal and external, and has used ideology, particularly that of Arab nationalism and Arab unity, to buttress its pragmatic initiatives in Africa and elsewhere.[41] The personalized nature of the decision-making process increases the risk that the calculations involved can reflect more prejudice than objectivity.

Since the Qadhafi regime rejects the notion of state, its policy can extend to encompass of those non-state and trans-state actors that it perceives share its objectives. Thus, policies based on the ideological imperatives of Arab nationalism, inter-state union and anti-imperialism can easily appear to threaten the stability of states and regimes that do not share its objectives. This, in turn, would lead to the kind of policy failure and isolation that characterized Libya in the Arab world, Africa, and the West in the late 1980s and the 1990s. The reversing of this process, however, can be as abrupt and radical, given the personalized nature of the policy process. Indeed, in the late 1980s, the Qadhafi regime realized the consequences of its ideological radicalism and impulsiveness, and began a slow and often incoherent process of trying to reverse the path it had selected. Given the intervention of the Lockerbie crisis, it was not to achieve its objectives, albeit only partially, until 1997, and would only capture American acceptance in 2005.

One aspect of this was to partially abandon ideological radicalism in practice, even if the rhetoric remained. This was accompanied by an inversion of the pyramidal structure of foreign policy so that the West replaces North Africa as the target of Libyan pragmatism, whilst the Arab world is marginalized and measured against ever-stricter ideological criteria.[42] Thus, Libya has increasingly and progressively rejected the Arab League as a vehicle for regional policy on the grounds of its incompetence and because of the failure of Arab states to meet its ideological imperatives. Yet, this reversal is only partially true, for Africa has now been elevated in place of the Arab world as the ideological partner for Libya's ambitions of regional identity, whilst the Arab world retains the sympathies of Libyans at large. The real question, then, is how committed is Qadhafi to opportunist pragmatism, rather than radical ideological consistency, and to what extent the latter can serve as a rhetorical cloak to shroud the former. The pattern of policy change toward the West suggests that this will be quite acceptable to him, provided only that there is no pressure for domestic change that would endanger the stability of the regime he leads—and diplomatic cynicism seems likely to ensure that that will be the case!

Notes

1. Christopher Hill, "Foreign Policy," in *The Oxford Companion to Politics of the World*, ed. J. Krieger, *et al.* (Oxford: Oxford University Press, 2001), 290.
2. "A course of action or principle adopted or proposed by a government, party, individual, etc.; any course of action adopted as advantageous or expedient; Lesley Brown, ed., *The New Shorter Oxford English Dictionary* (Oxford: Clarendon, 1993), 2274.
3. The term "security" is also, of course, problematic, for it is to do with the perception of the absence of threat, and thus refers to subjective belief—whether on the part of leading personalities within the state or expressed through its

institutions—rather than objective reality. However, for convenience here it is taken to refer to the objective lack or successful neutralisation of threat.

4. In a speech in 1948, he remarked, "We have no eternal allies and we have no perpetual enemies. Our interests are perpetual and eternal and those interests it is our duty to follow."

5. Kola Folayan, *Tripoli During the Reign of Yusuf Pasha Qaramanli* (Ile-Ife: University of Ife Press, 1979), 26–30.

6. E. E. Evans-Pritchard, *The Sanusi of Cyrenaica* (Oxford: Clarendon, 1947), 98, refers to the "Turco-Sanusi condominium" to describe this.

7. John Wright, *Libya* (London: Ernest Benn, 1969), 201–5

8. Mary-Jane Deeb, *Libya's Foreign Policy in North Africa* (Boulder, CO: Westview Press, 1991), 104–5.

9. The term was originally coined as "The soft underbelly of Europe" by Winston Churchill in referring to the reasons for the Allied attack on Italy in 1943. The Sahara has proved to be Libya's soft underbelly, particularly with respect to Chad, ever since Libya, under the monarchy, offered support to FROLINAT in the late 1960s, and the Qadhafi regime sought to articulate Libya's claim to the Aozou Strip in 1972.

10. E. G. H. Joffé, "Libya's Saharan Destiny," *Journal of North African Studies* 10, no. 3–4 (September–December 2005), 613.

11. E. G. H. Joffé, "Chad: Power Vacuum or Geo-political Focus?" in *The Geography of the Landlocked States of Africa and Asia*, ed. I. Griffiths, B. W. Hodder, K. S. McLachlan, and R. N. Schofield, (London: UCL Press, 1996).

12. Libyan had had recourse to the International Court of Justice on at least three occasions—its maritime border disputes with Tunisia (1982) and Malta (1985), cases that it won, and in its land boundary dispute with Chad in 1988, where it lost because of the innate conservatism of the court. It also pursued a case against the United States, under the Montreal Convention, over the Lockerbie affair, but this was overtaken by events. It has also engaged in an arbitration with Mobil Oil over the latter's desire to withdraw from Libya, and its claims against the Jamahiriya, where, in place of paying a demand for $312 million in damages, it won $96 million in unpaid taxes!

13. Oil revenues are rent in that they are the result of the exploitation of an asset for which no prior investment has been made because they are a "gift of nature." The Libyan state is utterly dependent on them and must, therefore, ensure that the appropriate conditions exist for their regular and continued generation.

14. Dirk Vandewalle, *Libya Since Independence: Oil and State-building* (Ithaca, NY: Cornell University Press, 1998), 82.

15. These have been collected in annual volumes as *al-Sijil al-Qawmi*, and specifically religious discourses are available as *Khutab wa-Ahadith al-Qa'id al-Dinyah*.

16. Mu'ammar Al-Qadhafi, *Green Book*, vol. 1 (Tripoli: Global Centre for Study and Research on the *Green Book*, 1979), 23.

17. The first and most important deduction from the principles we have so far laid down is that the general will alone can direct the State according to the object for which it was instituted, i.e., the common good: for if the clashing of particular interests made the establishment of societies necessary, the agreement of these very interests made it possible. The common element in these different interests is what forms the social tie; and, were there no point of agreement between them all, no society could exist. It is solely on the basis of this common interest that every society should be governed. Jean-Jacques Rousseau, *The social contract or principles of political right*, J. D. Cole, trans., *1762*, Book 2; Section 1: "That sovereignty is inalienable." Available at http://www.constitution.org/jjr/socon_02.htm.

18. Mahmoud M. Ayoub, *Islam and the Third Universal Theory: the religious thought of Mu'ammar al-Qadhdhafi* (London: Kegan-Paul International, 1987), 104–8.

19. Political union between Libya, Egypt, Syria, and Sudan was proposed in 1971, and politely rejected by Egypt's president, Anwar Sadat, whilst the Numayri government in Sudan ignored Libyan initiatives, eventually exciting Libyan hostility. In Tunisia, President Bourguiba was initially seduced into accepting Colonel Qadhafi's proposals, until his prime minister, Hedi Nouira, drew his attention to the disadvantages. There were also short-lived plans for similar links with Algeria. See Mary-Jane Deeb, *Libya's Foreign Policy in North Africa* (Boulder, CO: Westview, 1991), 71–135.

20. An interesting counterview is contained in an early study of the Qadhafi regime: H. P. Habib *Libya past and present* (Valetta and Tripoli: Aadam, 1979), 285. This argues that unity is essential for Arab survival, and Libya, in promoting such initiatives, was misunderstood by politicians who did not appreciate the underlying realities facing the Arab world.

21. George Joffé, "Libya's Saharan destiny," *Journal of North African Studies* 10, no. 3–4 (September–December 2005), 608.

22. René Lemarchand counted fourteen different Libyan attempts at destabilization in Africa, including four direct military interventions up to 1987. René Lemarchand, ed., *The Green and the Black: Qadhafi's policies in Africa* (Bloomington and Indianapolis: University of Indiana Press, 1998), 9–10.

23. See Patrick Seale, *Abu Nidal: a gun for hire* (London: Hutchinson, 1992).

24. Lorna Hahn, *Historical dictionary of Libya* (Metuchen and London: Scarecrow, 1981), 63.

25. At the end of 1979, 40 percent of Libya's oil exports went to the United States! See F. Wadhams, *The Libyan oil industry* (London: Croom Helm, 1980), 324–30.

26. The law actually condemns any form of group activity based on a political ideology that challenges the principles of the "al-Fateh revolution," and Article 3 of the law provides the death sentence for joining or supporting any group prohibited by law. This law is backed up by a series of provisions in the Penal Code: Article 206 (Law 48 of 1976) provides for the death penalty for membership of a proscribed organization; Article 208 bans forming or joining an

international organisation; Article 178 provides life imprisonment for disseminating information that "tarnishes" Libya's reputation abroad; and Article 207 provides for the death sentence for any challenge to the basic principles of the Libyan state or for any attempt to overthrow it.

27. The term combines Weber's "patrimonial" and "legal-rational" concepts of bureaucracy and aptly describes the crucial feature of access to the authority of the leader as the path for decision-making and articulation of power.

28. "The term "charisma" will be applied to a certain quality of an individual personality by virtue of which he is set apart from ordinary men and treated as endowed with supernatural, superhuman, or at least specifically exceptional powers or qualities. These are such as are not accessible to the ordinary person, but are regarded as of divine origin or as exemplary, and on the basis of them the individual concerned is treated as a leader." Max Weber, *Theory of social and economic organisation*, Talcott Parsons and A. M. Henderson, trans. (New York: Free, 1947), 358.

29. Colonel Qadhafi has no formal position within the Libyan state structure, being merely the "Guide of the Revolution." In reality, he dominates and controls the whole system. Now his former henchmen in the Revolutionary Command Council have been marginalized: Major Jalloud is in enforced retirement, and the others are largely ceremonial figures. In their place, members of Colonel Qadhafi's family—his sons, Mohamed, Sa'di, Saif al-Islam, Mua'tasim, and Khamis—are beginning to take a more prominent role in political life and may well come to dominate the political system. The colonel's personal security, incidentally, is handled by the *Haras as-Sauri*, the Revolutionary Guard.

30. It is this that explains the truculence and resentment that often colours the foreign policy statements and actions of the Libyan state and of Colonel Qadhafi himself.

31. Martin Sicker, *The Making of a Pariah State: The Adventurist Politics of Muammar Qaddafi* (New York: Praeger, 1987), 112–20.

32. This is discussed in great detail in Joseph T. Stanik, *El Dorado Canyon: Reagan's undeclared war with Qaddafi* (Annapolis: Naval Institute Press, 2003).

33. Indeed, some commentators (*viz* Guy Arnold, *The maverick state: Gaddafi and the New World Order* (London: Cassell, 1996), 151–52) have suggested that the sudden and, at the time surprising, designation of Libya as being responsible for the Lockerbie incident had a lot to do with Libya's diplomatic successes in Europe. The UTA incident was far less ambiguous because there was evidence of a Libyan diplomat handing a passenger a booby-trapped briefcase before he boarded the flight. It was assumed to be linked to Libyan resentment at the role played by France in Libya's defeat in Chad.

34. The issue of Lockerbie, where PanAm Flight No: 103 was destroyed by a bomb over the Scottish town of Lockerbie on December 18, 1988, has never been satisfactorily explained. Although one of those directly accused of the incident was eventually found guilty by a Scottish court sitting in the Netherlands at Kamp Zeist, his co-accused was found not guilty and there were serious questions about

the quality of the evidence produced. In Libya, his guilt has never been accepted, either officially or unofficially and, even in its formal acceptance of responsibility for the incident, Libya did not go beyond accepting formal responsibility for the actions of its representatives—an obligation it has under international law. It should also be remembered that, until 1990, the main weight of the enquiry into the incident, in Britain, was directed toward Iran, because of the 1988 Iran Airbus incident over the Persian Gulf, where the USS Vincennes shot down a civilian airliner. Scottish police had begun to enquire into the Libyan dimension of the affair in that year, partly because of the evidence of timers, of the type used in the Lockerbie bomb, having been supplied to East Germany and Libya by a Swiss company.

35. Hannah Arendt points out that such charismatic authoritarian systems often generate large areas of political autonomy within the bureaucratic structures in which the leading elements anticipate leadership decisions and orientations in making autonomous decisions of their own. The conventional superficial pyramidal system of authority is, in effect, a cover for bureaucratic confusion and autonomy, which can lead to self-defeating policies in both the domestic and external spheres. See Hannah Arendt, *Eichmann in Jerusalem: a report on the banality of evil* (New York: Viking, 1965). It is precisely such views that are now adduced to explain the 1932–33 famine in the Soviet Union, rather than solely the malevolence of the Soviet leader, Joseph Stalin. See S. G. Wheatcroft and R. W. Davies, "The Soviet famine of 1932–1933 and the crisis in agriculture," in *Challenging traditional views of Russian history*, ed. S.G. Wheatcroft (London: Palgrave-Macmillan, 2002).

36. The trade statistics demonstrate clearly Libya's dependence on access to the industrialised world, particularly the European Union, where three countries—Germany, Italy and Spain—alone absorb 80 percent of Libya's exports, and where the European Union absorbs 85 percent of all exports and generates 75 percent of Libya's imports. See E.G.H. Joffé, "Libya and Europe," *Journal of North African Studies* 6, no. 4 (Winter 2001).

37. There was the specific problem of oil companies forced to abandon their interests in Libya when the Reagan administration introduced its own presidential sanctions in 1986. The five American oil companies that were forced to leave— Marathon, Occidental, Oasis, Amerada Hess and Hunt—left behind assets worth $2 billion and generating an income flow of $2.3 billion a year, but these have been worked in trust for them by companies linked to and created by NOC for this specific purpose. The companies concerned have now returned to Libya, spearheading what is expected to be an enthusiastic commercial invasion.

38. W. I. Zartman and A. C. Kluge, "Qaddafi's foreign policy," *American-Arab Affairs* 6 (Fall 1983), 183.

39. Mary-Jane Deeb, op.cit., 8–9.

40. Ronald Bruce St John, *Qaddafi's world design: Libyan foreign policy 1969–1987* (London: Saqi Books, 1987), 143–50.

41. Mary-Jane Deeb, op.cit., 188–91.

42. Michael Nowlis; personal communication 2005.

9

From International Reconciliation to Civil War, 2003–2011*

Dirk Vandewalle

While many Libyans still viewed Qadhafi with some grudging admiration at the beginning of the twenty-first century, there were clear indications that the energy of his revolution had dissipated beyond the possibility of rejuvenating it as an active force in the country's political life. Almost two generations of Libyans had grown up since the 1969 coup, many of them well educated, often in the West, and impatient with a political and economic experiment that promised few opportunities for employment beyond some of the country's enormous and enormously inefficient bureaucracies that promised no real chance for personal advancement. Qadhafi's exhortations for internal political activism continued, but, as described in this book, the disappointments of his grander plans for regional unity (see Chapters 7 and 8), the difficulties within the country's oil sector, the lingering effects of the earlier economic boycotts (Chapter 5), the unresolved debacle over Lockerbie, and the seeming indifference that remained among the population all contributed to a subtle shifting of the leader's rhetoric (Chapters 3 and 4). Unbeknown to virtually anyone beyond a handful of confidantes, the regime had started a round of quiet diplomacy with the British government in 1999, roughly at the same time that the multilateral economic sanctions had been suspended. Telling

* Material in this chapter originally appeared in Dirk Vandewalle, *A History of Modern Libya*, New York: Cambridge University Press, 2006.

for what was unfolding in Libya, the talks with the British had been held not only by the usual assembly of a handful of trusted Qadhafi confidants, but included his son, Saif al-Islam al-Qadhafi. That this young new player, who seemed to symbolize the shifting dynamics of political life in Libya, had no official role or standing in the country's political system only reinforced the strength of the informal structure of politics in Libya discussed by Mattes in Chapter 2.

It was clear to Saif al-Islam, and some of the others involved in the negotiations, that there existed at least a possibility that Libya had a chance to further emerge from its diplomatic and economic isolation. European and other foreign investors were slowly making their way back to Tripoli. It was also clear, however, that only a complete lifting of the U.S. sanctions could deliver the kind of economic resurgence and the necessary international diplomatic *imprimatur* that the regime sought. This could only be accomplished if the *jamahiriyya* was taken off the State Department's list of sponsors of state terrorism and, eventually, diplomatic relations were restored.[1] There were several other conundrums those pushing for greater reforms faced. The country's economy, beyond the oil sector, remained unproductive and actively involved few of the country's citizens. The infrastructure of the oil sector itself was aging, and Libya needed substantial investment to update it—conservatively estimated from $10–$30 billion in the medium to long term in order to increase its oil production to three million barrels per day within a decade. Although the Libyan National Oil Company (LNOC) had attempted to establish itself as a capable manager of the oilfields it had taken over, its officials were the first to admit that the country required international technology and know-how that would enable it to expand production, in part by drilling for oil beyond the Sirte basin, and offshore. Libya needed the kind of expertise and capital investment that could only be provided by some of the Western—including U.S.—companies that had left the country as a result of the sanctions or because of the uncertainty of the investment climate in Libya.[2]

The regime's agreement to allow the Lockerbie suspects to be tried, its willingness to settle the UTA issue, and the diplomatic attempt to salvage its international reputation, were all indications that the Qadhafi regime was seemingly willing to settle for a more pragmatic and responsible set of policies that would reintegrate the country politically, diplomatically, and economically within the international community. There were, however, still enormous hurdles to be crossed. These included a monetary settlement for the Lockerbie victims, whose families had come to constitute a determined lobbying group in Washington; a clear disavowal of terrorism as a foreign policy tool; and, most importantly, transparency on the issue of weapons of mass destruction. Although there was some evidence emerging that a new generation of technocrats and young intellectuals was able to assert some internal pressure on the regime, the lack of institutionalization within the country's political system still left much of the process, as it lurched forward, subject to the vicissitudes of Qadhafi's own decisions. This could be explained, in part, because, against these trends that seemingly pushed Libya forward on a path to reconciliation with the West, stood the ever-present imperatives of regime survival. Every decision made needed to be weighed against its impact on the fate of the coalitions of supporters— and possible opponents—within the country. How powerful and painful those trade-offs could be had already been attested to by the two waves of *infitah* in 1987 and after 1990 (see Chapter 1) that, in effect, constituted a subterfuge, comprising a selective economic liberalization that relieved some of the internal pressures in light of the hardships Libyan citizens had faced, combined with a curtailing of some of the revolution's excesses, without, however, affecting the basic power structure of the regime.

As always, and despite the reluctance the sanctions had engendered among international firms, Libya remained an extremely attractive target for the international oil companies. In 2000, 2001, and 2002, executives from international oil and gas companies continued to rank the *jamahiriyya* as the top exploration spot anywhere in the world.[3] Part of this enthusiasm was the fact that three-fourths of the country's territory remained unexplored, and that its natural gas reserves were known to be enormous and also largely untapped. Few international oil executives, therefore, doubted that substantial discoveries and profits could be made in the future—but the general uncertainties and unpredictability of working in Libya, and the effects of the boycott and sanctions, had created an environment where investments, despite the continuing professionalism of the LNOC staff and the fact that the oil sector remained isolated from internal political developments, were held in abeyance. Rumors had circulated throughout the 1990s that Libya would open up new concessions under EPSA IV—conditions that would make it attractive for companies to invest or to return to Libya (see Chapter 5). None of this could take place, however, until the larger political issues surrounding Libya's interaction with the international community had been solved.

In December 2003, the regime made a spectacular announcement that captured attention worldwide, indicating its willingness to give up its weapons of mass destruction (WMD). After decades of confrontation with the West, the Libyan decision to cooperate on the WMD issue marked the apotheosis of a process of reappraisal the country's leadership had embarked upon. The agreement came at the end of a period of protracted negotiations and back-channel diplomacy on WMD and other issues that had started—almost exclusively at first at the behest of the British government—between Libya, Great Britain, and the United States. In the end, it was a process of careful and sustained diplomatic negotiations, holding out a set of both carrots and sticks to the Libyan side that produced the agreements.

For western policymakers and academic observers alike, the agreement raised a large number of questions. If the Libyan government appeared increasingly pragmatic in the years leading up to the WMD announcement, much of that pragmatism was seen as having been forced upon the country's leadership by the impact of the sanctions and by the general isolation Libya found itself in during most of the 1990s. How genuine, therefore, was Libya's newfound willingness to play by internationally accepted norms of state behavior? Was the pragmatism part of a process of adjustments to a number of economic and political realities that could in the future be reversed? Or was it simply a means to ensure a return of international investment, and of United States technology, to the country's decaying oil infrastructure?

But, as discussed in this book, beyond these immediate policy concerns were also a number of pressing questions fundamental to the future of Libya as a political community. The first set of questions concerns oil revenues. They initially made Qadhafi's radical internal experiments and foreign adventures possible. As the lifting of the economic sanctions promised to bring back international oil companies—likely to increase Libya's oil revenues in the years ahead, even beyond those of the 1970s—how would the country's leadership put this latest influx of wealth to use? What mechanisms, if any, would be put into place to ensure that the revenues will not be used, once more, for their previous purposes of fostering inefficiency, of pursuing ideological adventures, and of keeping Libyan citizens beholden not to the state, but to its leader?

The second set of questions focuses on the institutional nature of the Libya state. How far could these reforms take place in a political system where extensive patronage had been part and parcel of political survival for so long? How does a state where charismatic leadership had been such a dominant feature of politics respond and adapt to a slow process of bureaucratization that would accompany economic liberalization and that would inexorably reshape the interaction between the Libyan state and its citizens? To what extent could the groups of would-be reformers freely articulate and push through their agenda in a system where the ultimate authority resided with Qadhafi?

The ultimate question, then, regarding the *jamahiriyya*, was to what extent the shadow of the country's past—its hollowing out of state institutions for the sake of personal survival of Qadhafi and his supporters—would be the shadow of its future?

Answers to these questions are inextricably bound, as well, to Libya's reintegration into the international community. As intractable as the impasse between the *jamahiriyya* and the West still appeared in the first two years of the new millennium, relations between the two sides had—albeit it at a glacial pace—started to change by that time. A number of pinprick indicators—after Libya had turned over the Lockerbie suspects in April 1999, and once the UN sanctions were lifted—hinted at the possibility of a rapprochement between Libya and the West. Back-channel conferences and talks, initially between Great Britain and the *jamahiriyya*, were slowly laying out the differing talking points that would form the background to the reconciliation and to the December 2003 agreement. In June 1999, Libyan and U.S. officials met for the first time in eighteen years in an official capacity in order to discuss the UN sanctions. In March 2000, U.S. State Department officials visited Libya to assess lifting the existing travel restrictions to the *jamahiriyya*. As a sign of changing times, perhaps none was as symbolically indicative of the unfolding changes as the appearance of an article in May 2001 in *Foreign Affairs*, the United States' most important establishment journal, arguing that a rogue regime had come in from the cold.[4]

Domestic constituencies within the United States—particularly the Pan Am 103 families—continued to press for the marginalization and punishment of Libya, however. As a result, U.S. policymakers saw little urgency in restoring any type of relationship with Libya. In April 2000, the U.S. Congress, in a Sense of the Senate resolution, advised the president not to lift travel restrictions and to consult with the Senate on U.S. policy toward Libya. In November 2000, the State Department renewed the travel ban, and the president reauthorized the Iranian-Libyan Sanctions Act (ILSA) in August 2001. After Libya turned over the Lockerbie suspects, and after the United Sanctions were lifted, however, it became more difficult for the United States to contain Libya by enlisting international cooperation in pursuit of justice for the Lockerbie victims. While the United States retained its unilateral sanctions in the wake of the Lockerbie verdict, and insisted that Libya meet all United Nations demands before the suspension of the multilateral sanctions could be extended formally into lifting them, it was clear that the dynamics and the interaction between Libya and the international community was caught in a maelstrom of change—and that the United States, willy-nilly perhaps, needed to reexamine its previous policies as well. For, viewed from a United States perspective, how much sense did unilateral sanctions make when the international community was welcoming Libya back into the fold? Could a sanctions-led policy still retain the purpose it had during the 1990s when multilateral cooperation was assured and when the threats emanating from Libya were tangible? The answers to these questions had seemingly changed in the wake of the Lockerbie settlement. Washington could encourage the positive changes in Libyan behavior, knowing that retaining the country's isolation looked increasingly problematic and impractical, or insist on keeping the regime isolated and find itself on the margins of the gradual reintegration of the *jamahiriyya* into the international community.

Libya's support for U.S. efforts in its campaign against international terrorism, in the wake of the September 11, 2001 attacks on the World Trade Center, added to Washington's dilemma. Qadhafi quickly condemned the attacks and described the invasion of Afghanistan as a justified act of self-defense by the United States, labeling the Taliban regime "Godless promoters of political Islam."[5] While the United States kept insisting on the need for Libya to fulfill all its obligations under the UN resolutions, and continued to highlight the country's pursuit of weapons of mass destruction, a number of trilateral talks between Britain, the United States, and Libya, as well as negotiations between American and Libyan lawyers over the details of compensation for the Lockerbie victims, quietly took place.

At the same time, Libya's earlier activist policies had started to change. In early 2000, U.S. officials acknowledged that the *jamahiriyya* had distanced itself from further involvement in terrorism and from supporting groups involved in terrorism.[6] The Abu Nidal Organization and several other groups had been asked to leave the *jamahiriyya*. Ronald Neumann, at the time Deputy Assistant Secretary of State for Near Eastern Affairs, argued that Libya's actions in regard to the Abu Nidal Organization were "not window dressing but a serious, credible step."[7]

Slowly, also, Qadhafi's rhetoric regarding a solution to the Arab-Israeli conflict had been altered, in effect questioning both the tactics and the rationale of what had once been one of the *jamahiriyya*'s ideological cornerstones. His earlier dismissal of the Camp David agreement and of the 1993 Israeli-PLO Oslo Accords had gradually yielded to a previously unknown pragmatism—one admittedly met by some skepticism among those who argued that, here, as elsewhere, it represented nothing but a cynical ploy to attract investment to the country and to reshape the country's image internationally.[8] But, whereas in February 1996—following a number of suicide bombings in Israel—the leader had still praised the attacks and hectored Arab states to help against "Israeli terrorism," within three years, in 1999, he announced to Palestinian militants that Libya would only deal with President Arafat's Palestinian Authority in addressing the lingering crisis in the occupied territories. Although his rhetoric, at times, remained fiery and seemingly uncompromising, Qadhafi cautiously endorsed Saudi Arabia's two-state solution at the Beirut 2002 Arab league summit.

At the same time, many of Libya's foreign policy initiatives—particularly in sub-Saharan Africa—changed considerably in scope and nature (see Chapter 7 and 9). From its earlier destabilizing or confrontational ventures in Uganda, Chad, Tunisia, and Egypt, the regime gradually distanced itself from direct or indirect involvement in most of the regional insurgencies it had, in the past, supported. After the humiliating military defeat in Chad in 1987, the dispute over the Aouzou strip had been referred to the International Court of Justice. When the court ruled in favor of Chad, Libya acquiesced in the ruling, and has abided by the decision ever since. Relations with Egypt turned cordial after years of open hostility. Both countries embarked upon on collaborative effort to find a solution for neighboring Sudan's longstanding civil war. The effort resulted in Sudan's acceptance of an Egyptian-Libya peace plan that nevertheless left the conflict festering. In April 1999, Qadhafi brokered a peace accord between Uganda and the Congo, sending Libyan troops to Uganda to help implement it.

The following month, Libya embarked on a quiet round of negotiations with Great Britain in an attempt to break its diplomatic and economic isolation. The talks had been urged upon Qadhafi by a bevy of long-time senior advisors. That year, the country's per capita GDP had fallen to its lowest level in over a decade—despite the adoption of Law No. 5 of 1997 that had created a formal legal framework for direct foreign investment. Under the circumstances at the time, Law No. 5 had very few chances of attracting investment beyond the oil sector. At the same time, however, the regime, without officially approving it, allowed small retailers and investors to reopen stores and to reinvigorate the country's small-scale commercial life that had been absent since the revolutionary decade. Almost overnight—and despite periodic efforts by municipal committees to restrict commercial activities—Libya's main streets were filled, once more, with small restaurants, cafes, and shops selling household goods, groceries, and electronics.

The round of negotiations, informal meetings, and off-the-record conferences initiated by Britain steadily grew in scope to eventually include Libyan activities in sub-Saharan Africa, issues surrounding the 1984 London shooting of Yvonne Fletcher, Lockerbie, Libyan cooperation in illegal migration toward Europe, and a number of smaller issues. When Libya agreed to settle the Lockerbie issue by promising to adhere to a tiered process of compensation for the victims' families that would eventually, in return, lead to the suspension of U.S. sanctions against Libya and to the removal of the *jamahiriyya* from the State Department's list of sponsors of terrorism, most outstanding issues between Libya and the West had been addressed.

The only major issue left that remained of great concern to the United States in particular concerned Libya's attempt to produce unconventional weapons and weapons of mass destruction. Throughout the 1980s, Washington had watched Libyan efforts to acquire such weapons with increasing concern, devoting considerable attention to gathering intelligence on the country's progress. The ongoing controversy in the 1980s and 1990s over an underground facility at Rabta, and an industrial complex in Tarhuna—where the administration accused Libya of gearing up for chemical weapons production—accelerated U.S. efforts to deny the Libyan government any technology or imports that could be used for such purposes.

In 1997, the CIA had concluded that the *jamahiriyya*'s efforts to acquire unconventional weapons had started to slow down—a conclusion that was later proven to be true for chemical weapons, but not for Libya's attempts at obtaining further missile and nuclear technology.[9] When the UN sanctions were suspended, however, Washington's concern focused on the fact that Libya would now be able to purchase the technology and components necessary to resume its quest for nonconventional weapons. This concern increased when Chinese Scud missile parts were discovered en route to Libya, as well as by the interception of a ship in Malaysia, with parts used for nuclear technology, that was also bound for Libya. Although most analysts were skeptical that Libya had the capacity and knowledge to produce nuclear weapons, in 2001, the CIA warned of a renewal of a Soviet-Libyan civilian nuclear program that could lead to weapons-related research.[10]

Once Libya had signed the agreement on the WMD issue, a flurry of diplomatic and economic activities followed, seemingly indicating the eagerness of both the West and the *jamahiriyya* to settle whatever issues were left outstanding. In February 2004, the United States lifted its travel ban to Libya. The following month, the first U.S. Congressional delegation visited Tripoli. In April, British Prime Minister Blair paid an official visit to the country while the United States lifted most of its economic sanctions against the *jamahiriyya*. Later that month, the Libyan leader flew to Brussels for an official visit to the European Union. In June, the United States and Libya formalized the emerging new relationship by officially reestablishing diplomatic relations. By that time, the United States had removed all of the country's nuclear weapons' program equipment and had started to get rid of the country's chemical weapons.[11] The diplomatic and political initiatives were matched by a flurry of commercial activities that intensified throughout 2004, and beyond, as oil companies, oil support firms, tourist agencies, and other service businesses vied for what was considered an undeveloped and potentially highly lucrative market.

Libya's willingness to consider and adopt reforms resonated in London and Washington. For the West, there were a number of overlapping interests in rehabilitating Libya: to convince its leadership to abandon, once and for always, its support of terrorism that had marked much of the country's revolutionary decade, but which the government had all but abandoned since the late 1990s. Second, both London and Washington were interested in putting a halt to the country's weapons proliferation, particularly WMD. Clearly, the United States administration viewed an agreement on WMD with Libya as an important gesture that would send the right signals to other proliferating countries. Finally, Great Britain and the Clinton and Bush administrations viewed the *jamahiriyya*'s policies in sub-Saharan Africa with considerable skepticism, and hoped to circumscribe its actions there.

There was, as well, a realization and understanding in Washington that its policy of isolating Libya was increasingly turning counterproductive, as Britain and other European countries were willing to reengage with the country in the wake of the Lockerbie trial and the Libyan government's willingness to settle victims' claims. In April 2003, the Atlantic Council—an organization hardly friendly to Libya—had issued a report entitled "U.S.-Libyan Relations: Toward Cautious Reengagement." The report advocated a "A New Strategy for a New Context," and aptly summarized in its pages the new realities the U.S.-Libyan relationship faced "at the end of the millennium."[12]

Although the WMD announcement therefore captured a dramatic moment in Libya's political life, its underlying pragmatism was based on a number of developments that had started to worry Qadhafi over a much longer period of time—developments that prompted the *jamahiriyya* to come to terms with the progressively worsening state of its economy. By the time of the publication of the Atlantic Council study, Libya had already taken a number of corrective measures to break the isolation due to the sanctions and had started to reform its economy. The country's economic liberalization and its attempt to settle all outstanding issues with the West, not surprisingly, coincided. By the time the WMD agreement was formally announced, Libya had already embarked, for almost two years, on economic reforms.

In January 2002, the country announced its intention to further open up its economy and to attract foreign capital to the country. For that purpose, it unified its exchange rate, pegging the Libyan dinar to the IMF's Special Drawing Rights, in effect devaluing the country's official exchange rate more than half as part of a strategy toward unification of the country's multi-tiered (official, commercial, black-market) foreign exchange system. The devaluation was also meant to increase the competitiveness of Libyan firms, and to help attract foreign investment into the country. The same month, Libya cut its customs duty rate by 50 percent on most imports, hoping to offset the effects of its currency devaluation.

In March 2003, a few months before the WMD agreement, the General People's Congress adopted legislation meant to augur in the country's third attempt at *infitah*. The legislation included an authorization to privatize a large number of the country's state-owned economic enterprises. In June, Qadhafi admitted that the country's public sector had failed and should be abolished, and called, in addition, for privatization of the country's oil sector. Libya's Parliament, during the same month, selected former Trade and Economy Minister Shukri Muhammad Ghanem, a proponent of liberalization and privatization, as Prime Minister. Ghanem, a technocrat who had been brought back to Libya after a period working at OPEC, clearly saw his task as removing as much as possible the inefficiencies the state-controlled economy had created in the previous decades. Determined to implement his reforms, but aware of the enormous resistance this would entail within the country's patronage-driven system, he slowly set about trying to build up a technocratic team around him.[13] The Energy Ministry was restored, and Abdallah Badri—a technocrat with long experience in the oil sector— was appointed to head the NOC in order, in part, to negotiate the return of the Oasis Group (Marathon Oil, ConocoPhillips, and Amerada Hess) to their Waha and Zuetina concessions, a move that was meant to send reassuring signals to other U.S. oil companies.

After decades of avoiding the advice of international financial institutions, the country also accepted its obligations under Article VIII of the IMF's Articles of Agreement, and, in October 2003, released the details of the IMF's first Article IV consultations, which called, among other issues, for wide structural reforms, improved macroeconomic management, and the removal of trade barriers and price subsidies. The IMF report, in part, informed the deliberations and adoption of a number of the economic directives adopted by the General People's Congress in March 2004.

As the new millennium dawned, the *jamahiriyya* found itself burdened by an accumulation of economic problems the country's leadership found impossible to ignore. In contrast to 1975, when a technocratically-inclined faction (centered around Muhayshi) had lost out to the revolutionaries inside Libya, conditions in early 2003 proved infinitely more difficult. For Libya, the reasons for settling the outstanding issues with the West were very clear: after roughly two decades of sanctions, the combination of the country's economic legacy of an inefficiently state-run economy, the economic and political hardships engendered by those sanctions, as well as the internal pressures from a burgeoning younger population with scant possibilities of meaningful employment—Libya's unemployment in 2003 was estimated at 30 percent—had made the continuation of the previous three decades' economic experiments impossible. The *jamahiriyya* needed outside investment and expertise for new oil and natural gas exploration, and for restoring or updating some of the oil industry's industrial and oil infrastructure, which the NOC readily admitted was outdated.[14] The country was also determined to break out of the physical (until the lifting of the United Nations' travel ban) and diplomatic isolation it found itself in.

In addition, for reasons that had been noted only by careful Libya observers during the last decade, a process of generational turnover was slowly taking place inside the country that brought a number of reform-minded, younger intellectuals and technocrats slowly to the fore, including the leader's own son, Saif al-Islam al-Qadhafi. Their hand was strengthened by the dire condition of the country's economy, and by the fact that the lifting of the sanctions acted as a catalyst to push their ideas forward. In contrast to 1975, when revolutionary fervor and ample resources made a disregard for economic efficiency possible, the new millennium offered the Libyan regime no longer such options.

Many of the country's elite—including the leader himself—had seemingly reached the conclusion that the Al Fatih revolution, as a mobilizational tool, had run its course inside Libya. In private conversations and public speeches, Qadhafi, and those around him, now distinguished between the revolutionary period, when the confrontation with the West had made the strategy of isolation and confrontation necessary, and the changed international context that now made those earlier policies obsolete. Ever attuned to portraying the new changes as the result of Libya's steadfastness in the face of adversity, the Libyan leader noted, at the March 2004 General People's Congress, that they were an indication of a battle Libya had won. Clearly, although the country's leadership was determined to break the diplomatic isolation it found itself in, the breakthrough was to be portrayed as a Libyan victory.

The practical measures in support of the new strategy were adopted by the General People's Congress at its March 2004 annual meeting. The government envisioned the privatization of 360 of the country's state companies—privatization now euphemistically referred, in light of the *Green Book*'s original directives against private ownership, as "the extension of popular ownership." In addition, the reforms included extensive banking sector reform and the introduction of private banks. The proposals also encompassed tax reform, the creation of a stock exchange, newly relaxed rules for foreign companies investing in the *jamahiriyya*, and a plan to promote the country's almost nonexistent tourist sector. The measures, in effect, amounted to the dismantling of what until now had been a semi-socialist economy, hoping to reduce in the process the stagnation and stranglehold the country's bureaucracy had come to exert over the economy.

The dry technical language of the IMF report summarized the challenges Libya would face as it embarked upon Ghanem's reforms:

> The key challenge facing the authorities in the medium and long-term is to achieve sustainable high rates of economic growth to generate employment opportunities for a rapidly growing labour force. The authorities agreed that this goal would not be achievable without a drastic reduction in the dominant role of the public sector. . . . Unemployment, which may be as high as 30 percent, remains one of Libya's greatest problems, with the bloated state sector unable to accommodate the many new job-seekers produced by the fast growing population. Until private sector reform starts delivering tangible results, the problem—compounded by Muammar Qaddafi's 1997 move to open Libya's border to 2 million African immigrants—is only likely to worsen.

The IMF urged the Libyan authorities to move toward greater budget transparency and to cast the country's budget within a coordinated medium-term framework that would take into account the nonrenewable nature of Libya's hydrocarbon resources. From a purely technical economic viewpoint, Libya's economic situation, and its attempts to transit toward a market-led development strategy, shows many similarities to those of centrally controlled economies that have liberalized in the past two decades. Libya is, perhaps, more favorably located, since it has ample financial reserves to cushion temporary imbalances, and can look forward to a high sustained income as more oil comes on line.

Although the new reforms asked for greater diversification of Libya's economy, the hydrocarbon sector would once more be called upon to provide the necessary revenues. By 2003, only one-quarter of the country's territory had been seriously explored for oil and, except for one patch along Libya's western coastal area, only one area for offshore drilling. Both the Libyan government and international oil companies expected that the country's proven reserves of 30 billion barrels could easily be raised to 130 billion barrels, clearly making Libya one of the top three investment destinations worldwide for oil companies.

In 2003, Libya was exporting roughly 1.5 million barrels per day, significantly less than its 1970 production. LNOC now wanted to increase production to 3 million barrels per day—the equivalent of its 1970 production—but admitted that Libya needs roughly $30 billion in foreign investment to do so, $10 billion alone by 2010. In addition, plans were developed to extensively exploit the country's enormous natural gas deposits—increasing production for export to 40–50 billion cubic meters per year within ten years—and to update the country's LNG infrastructure, which is limited to one liquefaction plant at Marsa al-Burayqa. In order to encourage investment in the hydrocarbon sector, Libya carefully designed a new Exploration and Production Sharing Agreements (EPSA IV) that, judging by the enthusiasm with which international oil companies flocked to Tripoli, once more proved the attractiveness of Libyan oil.

In August 2004, for the first time in almost two decades, Libya formally announced its intention to open up fifteen new offshore and onshore blocks for exploration and production agreements. Among the more than 120 companies who registered bids or expressed interest for further exploration of oil and natural gas in the country were Occidental, Amerada Hess, ChevronTexaco, ConocoPhilips, Marathon Oil, and Anadarko, as well as a number of European and international companies. The announcement of the winners at the end of January 2005 by the National Oil Corporation's exploration department, and the terms of the contracts, clearly revealed Libya's priorities. Beside awarding contracts to Brazil's oil giant Petrobras, Algeria's Sonatrach, the Indian Oil Corporation—all state-owned—and an array of other international companies, eleven of the fifteen oil exploration licenses went to U.S. companies, including Occidental, Amerada Hess, and ChevronTexaco. Clearly, one of Libya's priorities was to have U.S. firms closely involved, once more, in the country's oil industry, even if doing so seemingly came at the expense of the European companies—particularly French-owned Total—that had supported the country during the sanctions period.[15] The conditions of the contracts were stringent, with the successful companies required to pay a total of $132.9 million upon the signing of the contracts, and with obligations to spend a further $300 million for exploration. Successful companies would take shares ranging from 10.8 percent to 38.9 percent of production, with the remainder accruing to the government.

At the January 2005 Davos economic summit, Saif al-Islam al-Qadhafi announced a vast reform program for the Libyan economy, announcing that "the old times are finished and Libya is ready to move onto a new stage of modernization ... [which] will be conducted in a well organized manner that ensures new ownership and ownership by the people of Libya, not just a small class of oligarchs like Russia or Egypt." With Abd al-Hafid Zlitni, the chairman of Libya's National Planning Council beside him, Saif al-Islam al-Qadhafi added that Libya had recruited some world experts to help in the effort, and conceded that "[t]here may be some reaction against them in Libya, but they are the best."[16] His statement clearly pinpointed some of the challenges ahead for Libya, but what he left—understandably—

unconsidered, however, were precisely those aspects of Libya's three decades of, at best, erratic economic management that will be instrumental in determining how far the country can or will successfully reform beyond the oil sector and some carefully controlled private sector initiatives.

By the summer of 2007, two-and-a-half years after Saif al-Islam's announcement, the Libyan government had announced further major initiatives to reform the country's economy (see also Ronald Bruce St John's analysis in Chapter 5). Salaries for government employees and those working in state-owned companies, after being frozen for decades, were raised substantially. Several major companies, including banks and the country's mobile phone sector, had been selected for privatization. Many of the onerous requirements for business visitors were eased, and custom tariffs on a whole range of goods and commodities reduced or abolished. Local technocrats investigated the possibilities for increasing the efficiency and attractiveness of free economic zones along the coast. Domestic fuel prices were allowed to rise, and traditional subsidies for water and electricity reduced. Under the aegis of the country's National Economic Strategy Project, the National Council of Economic Development was established in early 2007, meant to coordinate, speed up, and oversee the different privatization and liberalization initiatives. As always, in the past, the oil and gas sector had been the recipient of the most prudent, independent advice, further indicating the privileged position it enjoyed in the country's economy.

But while the debate at the Spring 2005 GPC meeting had seemingly indicated a willingness of the country's reformers to publicly tackle a number of economic and political issues crucial to expand and solidify the liberalization and reform measures at the expense of regime stalwarts, subsequent developments provided indications of how sensitive the reforms were once more viewed by the regime itself. A cabinet reshuffle in March 2006 removed the reform-minded Prime Minister Ghanem, further slowing down what was already problematic progress in the non-hydrocarbon sector. The Libyan leader's own pronouncements on the country's economic strategy proved, as always, more in tune with political and security considerations than economic ones. As recalled in St John's chapter, his speeches throughout 2006 and into 2007 continued to show his personal suspicion of the new country's economic strategy. While they were unlikely to unilaterally derail the larger initiatives the country had embarked upon, they sustained the uncertainty that had long prevailed in Libya: an uncertainty that made individuals suspicious of becoming entrepreneurs and slowed down needed changes in the five clusters identified in the National Economic Strategy plan.

In many ways, the differing pronouncements of the Libyan leader and of his son, Saif al-Islam, on Libyan economic reforms were good indicators of the larger, more structural issues at hand. While Saif al-Islam's speeches are laced with all the buzzwords of the powerful international vocabulary officials of transition economies now routinely use—deregulation, transparency, rule of law, property rights, efficiency, markets—these expressions of modern capitalist language do not reveal the history of institutional development they conceal. As the plethora of reports and consultancy agreements from companies and agencies now engaged in Libya reiterate, their acceptance in principle does not always translate into a practical reality. The fact that Saif al-Islam is seemingly emerging as a young oligarch himself, the fact that the major reform statement was made by someone who has no official standing within Libyan political life, and did so without consulting the General People's Congress—those facts alone attest to the lingering personal politics and lack of institutionalization that still surrounds policy formulation in the *jamahiriyya*.

There is also a deeper and lingering structural problem in reforming the *jamahiriyya*'s economy. In most Western economies, institutional development in support of economic development took place over relatively long periods of time. Above all, what most efforts at sustained economic reform throughout the world have shown is that moving toward markets, under conditions where there is no real history of them, requires careful and greater regulation by the state—not simply handing over everything to the market but, at least initially, a greater willingness to involve itself in sustained regulation. However, for reasons that closely link economic strategy to regime survival, Libya, at several junctures during its revolutionary phase, deliberately stepped back from regulation and from creating or maintaining state institutions that could have established such regulation. It is, therefore, worth asking how well will Libya deal with what amounts to developing the state's ability to more carefully fine-tune its ability to regulate? A second question necessarily follows: Cui bono? Who would benefit from the reforms? If Libya's transition, as the reformers argue, is for the benefit of all Libyans, and is about restructuring social entitlements, are they willing to allow what is almost inevitably linked to deep economic reform: the changing of a peculiar social contract—the way the state and its citizens interact—that has become part and parcel of how the regime operates and survives since 1969?

It was, in part, this more essential question that informed the—by Libyan standards—remarkable debates during the January 2005 GPC meeting in Sirte. The debate within the GPC over the economic reforms pitted then Prime Minister Ghanem and his supporters against a coalition of opponents headed by Ahmed Ibrahim, the Assistant Secretary of the GPC and by Abd al-Qadr al-Baghdadi. It proved both uncommonly vigorous and acrimonious.[17] Above all, the debate, perhaps for the first time, also showed how clearly both sides perceived that what was at stake was not simply economic reform, but also a number of surrounding political and institutional reforms that would be needed if the former was to succeed—issues that had been considered off-limits until then.

Ghanem, at the time, argued for the right of the Prime Minister to make his own cabinet appointments, and for substantially increased power to push the reforms through. He also insisted on a clear separation of power between the legislature and the executive to ensure that proposed legislation would not be hostage to what he described as "invisible" forces, and for greater power for the judiciary. In words unimaginable a few years ago, Ghanem asked, in effect, for a constitution for the country. To those requests, Ahmad Ibrahim and al-Baghdadi responded that there was no need for separation of power or for a constitution since Law No. 1 and Qadhafi constitute the only political references in Libya. When Qadhafi attended the meeting toward its conclusion, he cautiously supported Ghanem in his reform efforts, but left the larger questions the Prime Minister had raised untouched.

Much of that initial wave of enthusiasm seemed to have waned by the summer of 2007. Although the times are now certainly more auspicious for the country's latest wave of reforms, and the Libyan leadership realized that the international threat environment in the wake of the Lockerbie settlement, the lifting of United Nations sanctions, and the reestablishment of diplomatic relations with the United States in 2006 had changed substantially, a number of major obstacles to systematic, more structural reform remain: the impact of a long history of statelessness and often deliberately induced chaos that economically left the country with weak institutions, depoliticized its citizens, and reduced economic life largely to distributive measures.

As it embarked upon its process of reintegration into the international community, Libya faced an unprecedented opportunity in its history to chart a new economic future, and to rebuild its economy for long-term growth and development in ways that can benefit all Libyan citizens. Certainly, the actions of the Libyan government have shown, these last few years, that it can make pragmatic choices—even if those new choices necessitate adjusting the ideological (economic) underpinnings of the regime. Part of this new pragmatism is, of course, that even so-called revolutionary states—and particularly those like Libya so intricately tied into the international economy—are not immune from some forms of rationalization and institutionalization that, slowly but inexorably, induce them to adopt to norms and behavior that were previously unacceptable. Willy-nilly, social differentiation, and the clamor for greater participation among a new, educated generation, and for more efficient use of local wealth, has taken place in Libya.

But while there was a slowly emerging class of technocrats and intellectuals who had become both emboldened and empowered by the growing challenges the country faces that were pressing for reform, the obstacles they faced remain considerable. With its vast potential for further exploration, high quality oil, and easy access to European markets, Libya continued to be sought out eagerly for economic ventures that promised to deliver revenues on a scale not witnessed since the oil crises of the 1970s. When considering the new economic direction the country had embarked on within the interwoven structures of Libya's political economy and of its weak institutional architecture, it was clear that thorough economic reform would have a number of ripple effects far beyond the economic sphere, and that the reforms, to be successful, would need changes beyond that economic sphere. The proposed strategy also meant that the Libyan state would have no choice but to substantially upgrade its ability to regulate what would in effect become, down the road, a more deregulated economy. How it could do so without instinctively holding on to its ability to control that process and the economic riches that flow from it remained much less clear. In addition to the practical difficulties of moving a highly centralized, minimally diversified, state-dominated economy toward more openness, nothing in Libya's history since 1969 has suggested a willingness to let the country's citizens be involved in such choices.

It remained therefore particularly worrisome that the country's political structures—the pretensions of People's Power notwithstanding—were not subject to the same kind of liberalization measures to match and facilitate the economic transition. It was equally worrisome that much of the current impetus for economic reform came about and remained—as most other political or economic initiatives in Libya's modern history—to a large extent noninstitutionalized. Its major public supporter, Saif al-Islam al-Qadhafi, had no official standing in the country's political or economic hierarchy, and his plans and announcements did not carry the imprimatur of the General People's Congress—in principle, the country's legislative body—nor the consultation of those nominally in charge of managing the country's economic and political affairs. They also contained a lingering Libyan conviction that heaping international expertise on Libya's economic problems, without seriously considering an internal political restructuring and a more open governance structure, will bring about the hoped-for results—a conviction often eagerly endorsed by the international consultants the country relied on.[18]

Libya's historical dilemmas thus put it at a particularly important fork in the road. It could pursue a type of state-led market reform—as in neighboring Tunisia or Egypt—that would lead to a highly authoritarian state, relying on cooperation between the state and a number of business coalitions, guarded by the country's own security organizations and fueled once more by oil in the Libyan case that kept the current structures in place while maintaining circumscribed social contracts that deliver political quiescence. Alternatively, the *jamahiriyya* could pursue economic liberalization in earnest, giving increasing and real voice to the country's reformers—realizing that such a pursuit would inevitably lead to further demands for accountability, transparency, and political voice—while moving away from the patronage-driven and patrimonial system of the past. The latter is more difficult for it would ultimately mean reshaping the social contract, recalibrating the entitlements of different groups, and overcoming the objections that will be raised on a number of social, cultural, and ideological grounds by groups that had deliberately been fostered by the regime during its revolutionary phase.

As several contributors have argued in this book, Libya, for a combination of interlocking reasons that are both historical and institutional, faced a set of peculiar problems in addressing this latest wave of economic and political reform measures. The development of good state institutions that would allow for sustained reform—those that provide incentives for generating market-promoting public goods while minimizing rent-seeking into the hands of the government—had often, until now, been abandoned in favor of a social contract that carefully subscribed the role of the individual vis-à-vis the revolution. It was also important, again, to consider that reforming social contracts by creating finely tuned regulatory and legal institutions in effect opens up the creation and pursuit of such social contracts to real public discussion and debate—something the Qadhafi government has not addressed until now.

The presence of security sector and informal institutions without real accountability except to the leader himself, much like the wholesale state management of the economy until the recent reforms, had often been a shortcut, indicative of an inability to construct over time complex layers of regulatory, stabilizing, and legitimating state institutions. Fundamentally then, the two essential issues Libya faced in its latest attempt to reform—neither of which is inherently easier than the other—were either to create viable institutions beyond the coercive and distributive ones or to reform and adapt existing institutions to reduce powerful coalitional and patronage systems.

In gauging the nature and thoroughness of sustained economic reform—and ultimately of how Libya continues to construct itself as a state—a number of aspects need to be considered: the use of oil revenues, the country's lingering institutional weaknesses, the bifurcation between revolutionary power versus real popular control, and the use of patronage that traditionally kept the Qadhafi regime in power. Questions remained in early 2011 as to whether the economic reforms would substantially move beyond a refurbishing of the oil sector, private investment in the lucrative tourism sector, and further opening up the retail trade. It remained unclear to what extent the country's weak institutional frame-work would prevent thorough economic reform, or whether, in lieu, the reforms would simply create new oligopolies that left the patronage-driven system largely intact.

The structural legacies of the past—centralized control of virtually all economic resources and political energy—continued to cast a heavy shadow over the ongoing reform efforts that threatened to upset patron-age networks that were deliberately created and maintained since the beginning of the revolution to ensure regime survival. Ever since 1969—or perhaps more precisely since the publication of the *Green Book*—Libya had pursued a policy of statelessness that, at least in theory, put all power in the hands of the people. Ironically, as statelessness was pursued, virtu-ally all economic activity within the country came under state control. As opposed to nonoil economies where, over time, the state develops and fine-tunes a set of regulatory, extractive, and distributive mechanisms to calibrate the interactions between the state and local societies, in Libya this evolutionary process of state- and institution-building was curtailed. Anticolonial and nationalist sentiments, the subsequent rapid inflows of capital, but in most cases simply lack of alternatives prompted the local government to take a firm hand in guiding the local economies—particu-larly in Libya where the political imagination was simply a tabula rasa as state-building started. In Libya, the panoply of social, economic, and polit-ical challenges that faced the *jamahiriyya* far outstripped the capabilities of the state to deal with them. The result has been a number of institutional shortcuts, of which wholesale state management and emerging social con-tracts became a glaring example. In the *jamahiriyya*, the appearance of a social contract reflected the truncated process of state building under which it took place.

If "the revenues of the state are the state," as Burke reminds us, Libya grew in a peculiar fashion as a result of the provenance of its revenues.[19] The questions that are at the heart of every political system were histori-cally less pressing to the Qadhafi government: how revenues are gathered, what compromises the ruler must make with his subjects to obtain them, which institutional capabilities the state needed to develop this task, and how those institutional arrangements reflected the interests of both ruled and ruler. The result, in Libya, was the emergence of a state that was seemingly highly autonomous, but without much regulatory capacity, exacerbated by an official ideology that celebrated this hollowing out of state power and regulatory capabilities.

Throughout the 1960s and 1970s, the challenge was not to extract wealth, but to spend it. In Libya, economic growth could, during prolonged periods, simply be "bought" by increasing the sale of the revenue-gathering resource. Distributive policies become the most common method to meet social contracts or to stimulate domestic economic sectors.

State institutions became intricate channels for economic largesse and distributive purposes, while their regulatory and legal capacities—already weak by the initial state-building processes described above—tended to remain inefficient and underdeveloped. The lack of economic data in Libya, the occasional physical destruction of state bureaucratic offices and records, and the state's sporadic direct intervention in issues ranging from employment to price setting to property rights issues, were all signs of regulatory weakness. In effect, the country's relative stability into the first decade of the twenty-first century was, more than anything, due to the fact that Libya had not yet been forced to flex its institutional capacity for economic activity beyond distribution. The country had become a prime example of the by now familiar litany of the "too much state, too little state" phenomenon: pervasiveness and lingering control by those in charge of the state that has not translated into efficiency, capability, or capacity.

Under such circumstances, social stratification in Libya resulted overwhelmingly from the distributive and spending patterns of the state—forcing the Qadhafi government to assiduously promote its clients. Much of this maneuvering is concealed by the way in which the country's revenues are shielded from public scrutiny. Decisions concerning economic policies, distribution, and investments are kept to the purview of small coalitions, rather than assigned to the market. Not surprisingly, distributive largesse is augmented with reliance on informal mechanisms linked to history, religion, or culture.

Why is it that a seemingly omnipresent state like Libya, capable of regulating the minutiae of its citizens' lives, did not have the capacity to successfully implement reforms at the end of the 1980s and early 1990s? The answer lies within the broader social and political structures within which its political economy is embedded. The country's institutions, often created as a direct response to international economic forces during the oil booms, appeared inflexible and undifferentiated to deal with fiscal crises that threatened previous distributive policies. Economic crises thus threatened to become profound political crises. Why, then, was Libya immune from the kind of upheaval it finally witnessed fullblown in February 2011?

Undoubtedly, as described by Mattes in Chapter 2, one major answer lies in the presence of an extensive security sector. The combination of state-building and easy access to revenues created in Libya a powerful and narrow political system that relied on this security sector which, in addition to the military itself, remains barnacled by layers of attendant security organizations. The continued access to revenues proved a key factor in the persistence of the security sector. In contrast to sub-Saharan Africa, for example, where successful transitions to reform were often less the work of strong societies than the "hollowing out" of the coercive organizations due to fiscal crises, in Libya, they have not suffered for lack of financial resources. As in most oil states, Libya's security sector remains governed, in large part, by the logic of patrimonialism; is not subject to civilian control; and remains the most privileged of any group inside Libya.

These enduring legacies of the revolutionary period continued to cast long shadows over the economic reforms and the timid attempts at altering the political system. By 2011, it had become clear that the voices for reform and effective state consolidation had lost their impact. The earlier signs of pragmatism showed no indications that the country's system of governance was changing or that a process of greater accountability was being implemented. With new windfalls from an expanded oil sector flowing into the country, this lack of institutional checks and balances remained highly problematic. At the eve of the uprising in 2011, Libya had institutionally changed little. While the pressure to economically perform more efficiently and to use the country's riches for the greater benefit of all Libyans had undoubtedly grown since 2003, there were no institutional guarantees that the government could be forced to do so. The remaining bifurcation between the formal and the informal in the country's political life, the amorphous status of Qadhafi within its political system, the inability to oppose the revolution, the lack of accountability by the country's security sector apparatuses and the lack of clear succession rules: these challenges were left unresolved on the eve of the civil war.

Libya's Civil War

In many ways Qadhafi's self-styled revolution had, as the Libyan leader repeatedly argued, been completed by 2011. It had successfully suppressed all opposition for over four decades and had been able to at least rhetorically to maintain the fiction of popular participation while its political system made any real participation impossible. With its recent economic fortunes dramatically enhanced, and its traditional coercive mechanisms solidly in place, the regime looked as invincible and unassailable as it had ever been. Many argued that political change would not come to Libya as long as Qadhafi remained in power. But at the same time, Qadhafi's revolution had become totally irrelevant to most Libyans beyond the patronage it provided. It certainly had not created a sense of identification or of nationhood. It had provided neither mobilization nor a measurable level of support. People lived with the revolution and could not escape it, but they ignored it whenever possible. As so much in Arab society, what was private and what was public were kept perfectly separated.

It was not surprising therefore that the uprising that started on February 17 very quickly revealed the depth of lingering resentment against the regime. The conflict started in Benghazi and then quickly spread throughout the eastern part of the country—an area Qadhafi had to some degree economically neglected. Initially it looked as if the rebels would have little chance of succeeding in the long term against the onslaught of the regime that could bring loyal brigades, its air force, and bands of mercenaries to bear down on rebel-held territory. Loyalist troops steadily advanced toward Benghazi and were about to start encircling the capital of Cyrenaica on March 16 when NATO forces intervened—based on United Nations Security Council Resolution 1973. Already by that time several of the country's top diplomats had started to defect, a process that would continue over the next few months. At the same time both the United Nations and Europe had implemented a number of sanctions that targeted Qadhafi and his family, and once more imposed arms embargoes and travel bans reminiscent of the 1980s and 1990s.

The Transitional National Council that emerged in Cyrenaica declared itself the sole representative of the Libya people and was soon recognized by France and then by a number of other countries. Forced to take a position by the actions of the African Union, by the growing consensus within the United Nations, by growing internal pressures, and by the dire situation of the rebels in Cyrenaica and particularly in Benghazi, the United States administration agreed to take a leading initial role in enforcing the no-fly zone over Libya once the United Nations Security Council adopted Resolution 1973 on March 17, 2011.

However, the resolution proved problematic: it had authorized not only the no-fly zone but also additional measures to protect civilian lives. This somewhat vague clause would leave room to expand NATO's mission if judged necessary—something that indeed took place as it increasingly became clear that the West wanted to bring about regime change in Libya. In effect, although particularly the United States made it clear that it did not want to commit ground forces to the conflict, the rhetoric of many of the western leaders suggested as well from the beginning that anything less than the removal of the regime was unacceptable. And "no boots on the ground" also did not mean that western military advisors did not find their way into eastern Libya. The situation on the ground worsened when it became clear that only NATO's help would enable the rebels to regain the initiative in the fighting. Thus the international coalition had effectively become the arbiter of whether Libya would remain in a sustained civil war.

As the war of attrition between the two sides became a stalemated civil war, a number of plausible scenarios emerged.[20] The first involved more intense NATO support for the rebels who could then steadily move westward and unify the country by overpowering the western province of Tripolitania. A second scenario was to simply allow Libya to separate into two smaller states, focused around Tripolitania in the west, and around Cyrenaica in the east. This would have necessitated a longstanding commitment from the international coalition to protect Cyrenaica—certainly not a prospect either the United States or the European Union were enamored of, and not a scenario any of the warring parties were considering either.

A third scenario involved the somewhat patient process of gradually undermining the credibility and prospects of the Qadhafi government over time. This meant systematically undercutting the regime's traditional methods of using patronage for its survival as the international sanctions took hold and the regime's financial resources were depleted, hoping that eventually internal desertions and perhaps a palace coup or more general revolt would take place within the inner circles of the regime.

The final scenario was one that could prove the least attractive for many Libyans, but one that could well have proved most feasible to the many parties now involved in the conflict. It was perhaps also the most promising for the future of the country and certainly would have minimized the dislocations and potential infighting some of the other scenarios entailed. It consisted essentially of a diplomatic compromise whereby Qadhafi (and perhaps his family and his closest confidants) would depart into exile. The range of countries willing to accept Qadhafi would be tiny and would be made even smaller by the fact that the Libyan leader would undoubtedly try to find asylum in a country that does not recognize the authority of the International Criminal Court after it decided to indict him for a string of human rights violations.

By the middle of June 2011 several attempts at a diplomatic solution—including those by President Zuma of South Africa—were giving way to the realization that, as Qadhafi himself repeatedly emphasized, the Libyan leader refused to leave the country. Also, it had become clear that a division of the country would be the most unlikely scenario considering the emerging realities on the ground—and in light of the stiff opposition by the warring sides and NATO alike to the idea. The resources and options of the Qadhafi government were steadily diminishing, even though the regime still possessed power and strength in Tripolitania. The ultimate reality, however, was that the international community—in the form of NATO—had become the indispensable element to bring about the creation of a new Libya. In many ways this proved to be a repeat of the process whereby the new Libya will be created in large part as a result of the intervention of the international community—this time through NATO rather than through the United Nations as in 1951 when the country became independent. Undoubtedly this is not an ideal scenario—and one likely to cause considerable chaos in its wake. In the end, this unfortunate outcome may well prove the ultimate legacy of Qadhafi in Libya: that by destroying all local institutions the hope for a new Libya ultimately depended in part on the West he had so desperately struggled against ever since coming to power in 1969.

Notes

1. Libya remained on the list in 2005, in part because of an alleged attempt by the regime to assassinate the Crown Prince Abdullah of Saudi Arabia in 2004.
2. Interview with Abu Zayed Dorda, Tripoli, January 17, 2005.
3. Economist Intelligence Unit, *Country Report: Libya*, April 2002, 17–18. The poll was conducted by the British firm Robertson International.
4. Ray Takeyh, "The Rogue Who Came in From the Cold," *Foreign Affair* 80, no. 3 (May–June 2001), 62–72.
5. Economist Intelligence Unit, *Country Report: Libya*, January 2002, 12.
6. See United States of America, Department of State, *Patterns of Global Terrorism*, 2001, 67.
7. See Ronald E. Neumann, Testimony on U.S. policy toward Libya before the Subcommittee on near Eastern and South Asian Affairs, Senate Foreign Relations Committee, 106th Congress, second session, May 4, 2000 (GPO 2002), and his "Libya: A U.S. Policy Perspective," *Middle East Policy* 7 (February 2000), 142–45.
8. See, for example, Howard Schneider, "Libya, Seeking Investors, Moves from Fringe toward Mainstream," *Washington Post*, July 20, 1999, A13.
9. See "Libya Hampered by Decade-Old U.N. Ban, Says CIA," *Jane's Defence Weekly*, August 12, 1998, p. 1. Also cited by O'Sullivan 382–83, 115n.
10. United States of America, Central Intelligence Agency, *Unclassified Report to Congress on the Acquisition of Technology Relating to Weapons of Mass Destruction and Advanced Conventional Munitions, 1 January through June 2000*, February 2001.

11. See the testimony of Paula A. DeSutter, Assistant Secretary of State for Verification and Compliance before the subcommittee on International Terrorism, Nonproliferation and Human Rights (Washington: Federal Document Clearing House Media), September 22, 2004.

12. Atlantic Council of the United States, *U.S.-Libyan Relations: Toward Cautious Reengagement* (Washington, DC: The Atlantic Council, 2003), vii.

13. Interview with Shukri Ghanem, Tripoli, January 16, 2005.

14. Presentation by Dr. Abo Rima Belgassem, Chairman, the Petroleum Research Centre, at "Libya's Future: Domestic, Regional and Global Contexts," a conference organized by the London Middle East Institute and the Academy for Graduate Studies (Tripoli), London, July 26–27, 2004.

15. A strategy in line with Chorin's observations that Libya has remained interested in a special relationship with the United States (see Chapter 8 in this book).

16. Saif al-Islam al-Qadhafi, quoted in *The Daily Star*, January 29, 2005.

17. Ibrahim was the author of a book specifically endorsing violence during the revolutionary decade. See his *Revolutionary Organization* (Tripoli: Green Book Center, 1983).

18. Tom Crampton, "Libya Plans to Shed Old and Begin a New Era," *International Herald Tribune*, January 28, 2005.

19. Edmund Burke, *Reflections on the Revolution in France* (New York: Liberal Arts, 1955), 26.

20. An earlier version of this more speculative appraisal of the Qadhafi regime's future appeared as "Libya's Divisions" in *Newsweek*, April 17, 2011. See also my "After Gaddafi," *Newsweek*, March 7, 2011; Dirk Vandewalle, "The Reconstruction of Libya: Local and International Constraints and Opportunities," testimony before the Senate Foreign Relations Committee, April 6, 2011; Dirk Vandewalle, "To the Shores of Tripoli," *Foreign Affairs*, March 2011. Republished in Council on Foreign Relations, *The New Arab Revolt* (Council on Foreign Relations, New York): May 2011); and Dirk Vandewalle, "How Not To Intervene In Libya," *Foreign Policy*, March 2011.

Bibliography

Manuscripts

Allan, J. A. *Libya: The Experience of Oil*. London: Croom Helm, 1981.

al-Jamal, Misa. *Political Elite in Egypt: A Case Study of Executive Elite* [in Arabic]. Beirut: Center for Arab Unity Studies, 1998.

Al-Lijan ath-thawriya [in Arabic] n.a. Tripoli: al-Markaz al-'alami li-dirasat wa-abhath al-kitab al-akhdar, 1985.

Arendt, Hannah. *Eichmann in Jerusalem: A Report on the Banality of Evil*. New York: Viking, 1965.

Arnold, Guy. *The Maverick State: Gaddafi and the New World Order*. London: Cassell, 1996.

Atlantic Council of the United States. *US-Libyan Relations: Toward Cautious Reengagement*. Washington, DC: The Atlantic Council, 2003.

Ayoub, Mahmoud M. *Islam and the Third Universal Theory: The Religious Thought of Mu'ammar al-Qadhdhafi*. London: Kegan-Paul International, 1987.

Ayub, Nazih. *Political Islam: Religion and Politics in the Arab World*. London: Routledge, 1991.

Ben-Halim, Mustafa. *Forgotten Pages From Libya's Political History: The Memoirs of Mustafa Ahmad Ben-Halim* [Arabic Version]. London: Alhani International Books, 1992.

Bleuchot, Hervé. *Chroniques et documents libyens, 1969–1980*. Paris: Editions du Centre National de la Recherche Scientifique, 1983.

Brown, Lesley, ed. *The New Shorter Oxford English Dictionary*. Oxford: Clarendon, 1993.

Burke, Edmund. *Reflections on the Revolution in France*. New York: Liberal Arts, 1955.

Bukheit, Ramadan. *Hikayat Al Madi Al Qarib: Qisas Qasira*. Benghazi: Dar Al-Kutub Al-Wataniyya, 1996.

CNRS Edition. *Annuaire de l'Afrique du Nord 1981*. Paris: CNRS Edition, 1981.

Davis, John. *Libyan Politics: Tribe and Revolution*. London: I. B. Tauris, 1987.

Deeb, Mary-Jane. *Libya's Foreign Policy in North Africa*. Boulder, CO: Westview, 1991.

Desfosses, Helen, and Jacques Levesque, eds. *Socialism in the Third World*. New York: Praeger, 1975.

El-Fathaly, Omar I., and Monte Palmer. *Political Development and Social Change in Libya*. Lexington, MA: Lexington, 1980.

El-Fathaly, Omar I., Monte Palmer, and Richard Chackerian. *Political Development and Bureaucracy in Libya.* Lexington, MA: Lexington, 1977.

El-Hesnawi, Habib. *The Revolutionary Committees and Their Role in the Confirmation and Consolidation of the People's Authority.* Tripoli: Green Book Center, 1987.

El-Kikhia, Mansour O. *Libya's Qaddafi: The Politics of Contradiction.* Gainseville, FL: University Press of Florida, 1997.

El-Qathafi, Mu'Ammar. *Discourses.* Valetta, Malta: Adam, 1975.

Evans-Pritchard, E. E. *The Sanusi of Cyrenaica.* Oxford: Clarendon, 1947.

Faqih, Ibrahim. *The Libyan Short Story: The Realistic Approach, in Majmu'a al-A'maal Al Kamila.* CD, 2004.

First, Ruth. *Libya: The Elusive Revolution.* London: Penguin, 1974.

Folayan, Kola. *Tripoli During the Reign of Yusuf Pasha Qaramanli.* Ile-Ife, Nigeria: University of Ife Press, 1979.

Gidney, Dennis. *Esso Standard Libya Inc (ESL) Training and Development Program pre-1982,* unpublished.

Graeff-Wassink, Maria. *La Femme en armes. Khadafi féministe?* Paris: Colin, 1990.

Griffiths, I., B. W. Hodder, K. S. McLachlan, and R. N. Schofield, eds. *The Geography of the Landlocked States of Africa and Asia.* London: UCL Press, 1996.

Gurney, Judith. *Libya. The Political Economy of Oil.* Oxford: Oxford University Press, 1996.

Hinnebusch, Raymond, and Anooushiravan Ehteshami, eds. *The Foreign Policies of Middle East States.* Boulder, CO: Lynne Rienner, 2002.

Ibrahim, Ahmad. *Revolutionary Organization.* Tripoli: Green Book Center, 1983.

Joffé, E. G. H., and K. S. Mclachlan, eds. *Social & Economic Development of Libya.* Kent: Menas, 1982.

Kamoche, Ken, ed. *Managing Human Resources in Africa.* London: Routledge, 2004.

Keith, Agnes Newton. *Children of Allah Between the Sea and Sahara.* London: Michael Joseph, 1966.

Kepel, Gilles. *Jihad: The Trial of Political Islam, rev. ed.* London: I. B Taurus, 2004.

Khader, Bichara, and Bashir El-Wifati, eds. *The Economic Development of Libya.* London: Croom Helm, 1987.

Khoury, Philip S., and Joseph Kostiner, eds. *Tribes and State Formation in the Middle East.* London: I. B. Taurus, 1990.

Khutab wa-Ahadith al-Qa'id al-Dinyah. Tripoli: Green Book Center, different years.

Korany, Bahgat, and Ali E. Hillal Dessouki, eds. *The Foreign Policies of Arab States.* Boulder, CO: Westview, 1984.

Kousa, Musa M. *"The Political Leader and his Social Background: Muammar Qadafi, the Libyan Leader"* MA thesis, Michigan State University, 1978.

Krieger, J., ed. *The Oxford Companion to Politics of the World.* Oxford: Oxford University Press, 2001.

Habib, H. P. *Libya Past and Present.* Valetta and Tripoli: Aadam, 1979.

Legum, Colin, ed. *Africa Contemporary Record, Vol. 27 (1998-2000).* New York: Africana, 2004.

————. *Africa Contemporary Record, Vol. 28 (2001-2002)*. New York: Africana, 2006.

Lemarchand, René, ed. *The Green and the Black: Qadhafi's Policies in Africa*. Bloomington: University of Indiana Press, 1998.

Long, David, Bernard Reich, and Mark Gasiorowski, eds. *The Government and Politics of the Middle East and North Africa*, 5th ed. Boulder, CO: Westview, 2007.

Matar, Hisham. *In the Country of Men*. New York: Dial, 2007.

Matar, Khalil I., and Robert W. Thabit. *Lockerbie and Libya: A Study in International Relations*. Jefferson, NC: McFarland, 2004.

Mattes, Hanspeter. *Die Volksrevolution in der Sozialistischen Libyschen Arabischen Volksgamahiriyya*. Heidelberg, Germany: Kivouvou Verlag, 1982.

Mayer, Elizabeth. "In Search of sacred Law: The Meandering Course of Qadhafi's Legal Policy," in *Qadhafi's Libya, 1969 to 1994*, 114–15 Edited by Dirk Vandewalle. New York: St. Martin's, 1995.

National Front for the Salvation of Libya. *Libya Under Gaddafi And The NFSL Challenge*. National Front for the Salvation of Libya, 1992.

Nayhoum, Sadiq. *Al-Awdat Al-Mahzan Ila Al-Bahr*. Reprint, Tala, 2004.

Niblock, Tim. *Pariah States and Sanctions in the Middle East: Iraq, Libya, Sudan*. Boulder, CO: Lynne Rienner, Inc., 2001.

Obeidi, Amal. *Political Culture in Libya*. Surrey: Curzon, 2001.

Qadhafi, Mu'ammar al-. *The Green Book*. Tripoli: Global Centre for Study and Research on the Green Book, 1979.

————. *As-Sijil al-qawmi bayanat wa ahadith al-aqid Mu'ammar al-Qadhdhafi*. Tripoli: Marakiz ath-thaqafiya al-qawmiya, 1969–70.

————. "Legislation and the Crisis of Power," *Commentary on the Green Book*. Tripoli: Global Centre for Study and Research on the Green Book, 1984.

————. *"Je suis un opposant à l'échelon mondial." Entretiens avec Hamid Barrada*. Lausanne/Paris: Favre/ABY, 1984.

————. *The Village . . . The Village . . . The Earth . . . The Earth And the Suicide of the Astronaut*. Sirte: Ad-Dar Jamahiriya, 1996.

————. *al-Sijil al-Qawmi (Tripoli: The Green Book Center, different years)*.

Qanwus, Subhi. *Libya al-Thawra fi Thalathwon Amman: al-Tahwulat al-Siyasiyya wa al-Iqtisadiya wa al-Ijtima'iyah 1969-1999 [Revolutionary Libya in Thirty Years: Political-Economic-Social Transformational 1969-1999]*. Misrata: A-Dar al-Jamahiriyya lil-Nashir wa al-Tawuz' wa al-I'alan, 1999.

Pliez, Olivier, ed. *La Nouvelle Libye: Societes, espaces et geopolitique au lendemain de l'embargo*. Paris: Karthala-Iremam, 2004.

Salem, Hasan Salaheddin. "*The Genesis of the Political Leadership of Libya 1952–1969*." PhD diss., The George Washington University, 1973.

Seale, Patrick. *Abu Nidal: A Gun for Hire*. London: Hutchinson, 1992.

Shembesh, Ali Mohammed. "*The Analysis of Libya's Foreign Policy, 1969–1973*." PhD diss., Emory University, 1975.

Sicker, Martin. *The Making of a Pariah State: The Adventurist Politics of Muammar Qaddafi*. New York: Praeger, 1987.

St John, Ronald Bruce. *Qaddafi's World Design: Libyan Foreign Policy 1969–1987*. London: Saqi, 1987.

———. *Historical Dictionary of Libya*. London: Scarecrow, 1991.

———. *Libya and the United States: Two Centuries of Strife*. Philadelphia: University of Pennsylvania, 2002.

Stanik, Joseph T. *El Dorado Canyon: Reagan's Undeclared War with Qaddafi*. Annapolis: Naval Institute, 2003.

Vandewalle, Dirk, ed. *Qadhafi's Libya 1969 to 1994*. New York: St. Martin's, 1995.

Vandewalle, Dirk. *Libya Since Independence: Oil and State-Building*. Ithaca, NY: Cornell University Press, 1998.

———. *A History of Modern Libya*. Cambridge: Cambridge University Press, 2006.

Wadhams, F. *The Libyan Oil Industry*. London: Croom Helm, 1980.

Weber, Max. *Theory of Social and Economic Organisation*. Translated by Parsons, Talcott, and Henderson, A. M. New York: Free, 1947.

Wheatcroft, S. G., ed. *Challenging Traditional Views of Russian History*. London: Palgrave-Macmillan, 2002.

Williams, Gwyn. *Green Mountain*, Dar Al-Fergiani. Reprint, London: Faber & Faber, 1963.

Wright, John. *Libya*. London: Ernest Benn, 1969.

———. *Libya: A Modern History*. Washington, DC: Johns Hopkins University Press, 1981.

Zartman, William I., ed. *Political Elites in Arab North Africa: Morocco, Algeria, Tunisia, Libya, and Egypt*. New York: Longman, 1982.

Zahi El-Mogherbi, Mohamed. "The Structure of the Libyan Executive Political Elite 1969–2000," in *Les Elites au Maghreb Congres*. Zaghouan: Temimi Foundation & Konrad Adenauer Stiftung, 2002.

Zoubir, Yahia H., ed. *North Africa in Transition: State, Society, and Economic Transformation in the 1990s*. Gainseville, FL: University Press of Florida, 1999.

Zubaida, Sami. *Islam, the People and the State*. London: Routledge, 1989.

Academic Journals

Abedin, Mahan. "From *Mujahid* to Activist: An Interview with a Libyan Veteran of the Afghan Jihad," *Jamestown Foundation* 3, issue 2 (March 22, 2005).

———. "Libya, Radical Islam and the War on Terror: A Libyan Oppositionist's View," *Jamestown Foundation* 3, issue 3 (March 25, 2005).

Alexander, Nathan [Ronald Bruce St John]. "Libya: The Continuous Revolution," *Middle Eastern Studies* 17, no. 2 (April 1981).

Al-Qadhafi, Saif Al-Islam. "Libyan-American Relations," *Middle East Policy* x, no. 1 (Spring 2003).

Deeb, Mary-Jane. "New Thinking in Libya," *Current History* 89, no. 546 (April 1990).

———. "Qadhafi's Changed Policy: Causes and Consequences," *Middle East Policy* 7, no. 2 (February 2000).

Joffé, E. G. H. "Libya and Europe," *Journal of North African Studies* 6, no. 4 (Winter 2001).

———. "Libya's Saharan Destiny," *Journal of North African Studies* 10, no. 3–4 (September–December 2005).

Gambill, Gary. "The Libyan Islamic Fighting Group," *Jamestown Foundation* 3, issue 6, March 24, 2005).

Harding, Jeremy. "The Great Unleashing," *London Review of Books* 24, no. 14 (July 25, 2002).

Mahmud, Mustafa Bakar, and Alex Russell. "An Analysis of Libya's Revenue per Barrel from Crude Oil Upstream Activities, 1961–93," *OPEC Review* 23, no. 3 (September 1999).

Martinez, Luis. "L'apres-embargo en Libya," *Maghreb-Machrek*, no. 170 (October–December 2000).

Sarkis, Nicolas. "Les Perspectives Pétrolières Libyennes," *Maghreb-Machrek*, no. 181 (Autumn 2004).

Schumacher, Edward. "The United States and Libya," *Foreign Affairs* 65, no. 2 (Winter 1986–87).

Soudan, François. "Le Kaddafi nouveau arrive," *Jeune Afrique*, no. 1355–56 (December 24–31, 1986).

St John, Ronald Bruce. "The Determinants of Libyan Foreign Policy, 1969–1983," *The Maghreb Review* 8, no. 3–4 (May–August 1983).

———. "The Ideology of Muammar al Qadhdhafi: Theory and Practice," *International Journal of Middle East Studies* 15, no. 4 (November 1983).

———. "Libya in Africa: Looking Back, Moving Forward," *The Journal of Libyan Studies* 1, no. 1 (Summer 2000).

———. "Libyan Foreign Policy: Newfound Flexibility," *Orbis* 47, no. 3 (Summer 2003).

———. "Libya Is Not Iraq: Preemptive Strikes, WMD, and Diplomacy," *The Middle East Journal* 58, no. 3 (Summer 2004).

———. "Libya and the United States: The Next Steps," *Atlantic Council Issue Brief* (March 2006).

———. "Libya's Oil & Gas Industry: Blending Old and New," *The Journal of North African Studies* 12, no. 2 (June 2007).

Takeyh, Ray. "Qadhafi and the Challenge of Militant Islam," *Washington Quarterly* 21, no. 3 (Summer 1998).

———. "The Rogue Who Came in From the Cold," *Foreign Affairs* 80, no. 3, (May–June 2001).

Vandewalle, Dirk. "Qadhafi's 'Perestroika': Economic and Political Liberalization in Libya," *The Middle East Journal* 45, no. 2 (Spring 1991).

———. "Libya: Prospects for Change," *Middle East Institute Policy Brief* 18 (September 2006).

Zartman, William I. "Foreign Relations of North Africa," *The Annals*, no. 489 (January 1987).

Zartman, William I., and A. C. Kluge. "Qaddafi's foreign policy," *American-Arab Affairs*, no. 6 (Fall 1983).

Zoubir, Yahia. "Libye: Islamisme radical et lutte antiterroriste," *Maghreb Machrek*, no 184 (Summer 2005).

Government Publications

India. *Economic and Commercial Report January 2006* (Tripoli: Embassy of India, 2006).

Libyan Arab Republic, Ministry of Justice. "Constitutional Proclamation," *al-Jarida al-Rasmiyya*—Libyan Official Gazaite, N.3, 15. 12. 1969.

Libyan Arab Republic. *The Third International Theory: The Divine Concept of Islam and the Popular Revolution in Libya* (Tripoli: Ministry of Information and Culture, 1973).

Libyan Arab Republic. *The Revolution of 1st September: The Fourth Anniversary* (Benghazi: Ministry of Information and Culture, 1973).

United States of America. *Public Papers of Presidents: Ronald Reagan, 1986, vol. 1, 18* (Washington, DC: Government Printing Office, 1988).

United States of America, Central Intelligence Agency. *Unclassified Report to Congress on the Acquisition of Technology Relating to Weapons of Mass Destruction and Advanced Conventional Munitions, 1 January through June 2000*, February 2001.

United States of America, Department of State. *Patterns of Global Terrorism* (Washington, DC: Department of State, 2001).

United States of America, *Public Papers of Presidents: Ronald Reagan, 1986, vol. 1, 18* (Washington, DC: Government Printing Office, 1988).

United States of America, Senate Foreign Relations Committee, 106th Congress, second session, May 4, 2000, *Ronald E. Neumann, Testimony on US policy toward Libya before the Subcommittee on near Eastern and South Asian Affairs* (Washington, DC: Government Printing Office, 2002).

United States of America, *The Subcommittee on International Terrorism, Nonproliferation and Human Rights*, September 22, 2004., *Paula A. DeSutter, Assistant Secretary of State for Verification and Compliance* (Washington, DC: Federal Document Clearing House Media: 2005).

Other Publications

Economist Intelligence Unit. *Country Report: Libya* (different years).

International Monetary Fund. "Socialist People's Libyan Arab Jamahiriya 2004 Article IV Consultation–Staff Report," *IMF Country Report*, no. 05/83 (March 2005).

International Monetary Fund. "The Socialist People's Libyan Arab Jamahiriya: Staff Report for the 2005 Article IV Consultation," *IMF Country Report*, no. 06/136 (April 2006).

International Monetary Fund. "The Socialist People's Libyan Arab Jamahiriya: 2006 Article IV Consultation–Staff Report; Staff Statement; Public Information

Notice on the Executive Board Discussion; and Statement by the Executive Director for The Socialist People's Libyan Arab Jamahiriya," *IMF Country Report*, no. 07/149 (May 2007).

National Democratic Institute for International Affairs. *The Libyan Political System and Prospects for Reform: A Report from NDI's 2006 Delegation* (April 17–25, 2006).

The World Bank. *World Development Indicators, 2000* (Washington, DC: The World Bank, 2000).

The World Bank. "Socialist People's Libyan Arab Jamahiriya Country Economic Report," Report, no. 30295-LY (Washington, DC: The World Bank, July 2006).

The World Bank. "Socialist People's Libyan Arab Jamahiriya: Country Economic Report"; *Monitor Group and Cambridge Economic Research Associates, "National Economic Strategy: An Assessment of the Competitiveness of the Libyan Arab Jamahiriya"* (Washington, DC: The World Bank, 2006).

Newspapers and Magazines

Agence France Press
Al-Fajr Al-Jadid
Al-Hayat
All Headline News
Al-Jarida Al-Rasmiyya
Al-Manara
Al-Zahf Al-Akhdar
Asia Times
Bloomberg
Business Africa
Business Report
Daily Star
FBIS-MEA
Financial Times
Foreign Affairs
Foreign Policy
Houston Chronicle
International Herald Tribune
Jana
Jeune Afrique
Jidda
The Jordan Times
JR
Khaleej Times
Le Monde
Los Angeles Times
MEES

Menas Associates
Middle East Economic Digest
Middle East Online
Middle East Policy
Newsweek
The New York Times
Nida'ul Islam Magazine
Petroleum Intelligence Weekly
Platts Commodity News
Reuters
Rigzone
SQ
Washington Post

Websites

http://www.algathafi.org/terrorism/terrorism.htm.
http://www.allheadlinenews.com.
http://www.almuqatila.com.
http://www.atimes.com.
http://www.bbc.co.uk.
http://www.busrep.co.za.
http://www.chron.com.
http://www.colonyinc.com.
http://www.constitution.org/jjr/socon_02.htm.
http://www.eiu.com.
http://www.en.noclibya.com.ly.
http://www.fas.org/irp/world/para/docs/fig-interview.htm.
http://www.fpif.org.
http://www.fsboa.com/vw/index.php?subject=7&rec=25.
http://www.gaddaficharity.org.
http://www.gdf.org.ly.
http://www.gulf-news.com.
http://http://icms.iac.iafrica.com.
http://www.ikhwanonline.com.
http://www.iol.co.za.
http://www.imf.org.
http://www.jamahiriyanews.com.
http://www.jamestown.org.
http://www.khaleejtimes.com.
http://www.latimes.com.
http://www.libya-almostakbal.com/letters/drFathiF030105P1.htm.
http://www.libya-watch.org/lw_paper_hl_eng.html.
http://www.libyanet.com/feb1987.htm.

http://www.menas.co.uk.
http://www.middle-east-online.com.
http://www.mideasti.org.
http://news.bbc.co.uk/1/hi/programmes/hardtalk/6927651.stm.
http://www.ndi.org.
http://www.oxan.com.
http://www.platts.com.
http://www.reuters.com.
http://www.rigzone.com.
http://southmovement.alphalink.com.au/countries/Libya/Qadhafi-ATV.htm.
http://www.theglobeandmail.com.
http://www.upstreamonline.com.
http://www.worldbank.org.

Index